Southern Biography Series

LOUIS T. WIGFALL

Titles in the
SOUTHERN BIOGRAPHY SERIES
Edited by
FRED C. COLE *and*
WENDELL H. STEPHENSON

FELIX GRUNDY, *by Joseph Howard Parks*

THOMAS SPAULDING OF SAPELO, *by Merton Coulter*

EDWARD LIVINGSTON, *by William B. Hatcher*

FIGHTIN' JOE WHEELER, *by John P. Dyer*

JOHN SHARP WILLIAMS, *by George Coleman Osborn*

GEORGE FITZHUGH, *by Harvey Wish*

PITCHFORK BEN TILLMAN, *by Francis Butler Simkins*

SEARGENT S. PRENTISS, *by Dallas C. Dickey*

ZACHARY TAYLOR, *by Brainerd Dyer*

Edited by
T. HARRY WILLIAMS

JOHN BELL OF TENNESSEE, *by Joseph Howard Parks*

JAMES HARROD OF KENTUCKY, *by Kathryn Harrod Mason*

ARTHUR PUE GORMAN, *by John R. Lambert*

GENERAL EDMUND KIRBY SMITH, *by Joseph Howard Parks*

WILLIAM BLOUNT, *by William H. Masterson*

P. G. T. BEAUREGARD, *by T. Harry Williams*

HOKE SMITH AND THE POLITICS OF THE NEW SOUTH,
     by Dewey W. Grantham, Jr.

GENERAL LEONIDAS POLK, C.S.A., *by Joseph Howard Parks*

MR. CRUMP OF MEMPHIS, *by William D. Miller*

GENERAL WILLIAM J. HARDEE, *by Nathaniel Cheairs Hughes, Jr.*

MONTAGUE OF VIRGINIA, *by William E. Larsen*

THOMAS MANN RANDOLPH, *by William H. Gaines, Jr.*

JAMES LUSK ALCORN, *by Lillian A. Pereyra*

ROBERT TOOMBS OF GEORGIA, *by William Y. Thompson*

THE WHITE CHIEF: JAMES KIMBALL VARDAMAN,
     by William F. Holmes

LOUIS T. WIGFALL: SOUTHERN FIRE-EATER, *by Alvy L. King*

LOUIS TREZEVANT WIGFALL: Senator in
United States and Confederate congresses,
CSA brigadier general, and southern fire-eater

LOUIS T. WIGFALL

Southern Fire-eater

by ALVY L. KING

LOUISIANA STATE UNIVERSITY PRESS / Baton Rouge

To my wife
and to Twyla, Lowell,
Nancy, and Lori

Preface

SECESSION AND CIVIL WAR marked the failure of the American political order in the 1860's. The system was based upon majority rule, and it failed because majority rule became meaningless when a minority chose rebellion to acceptance of political defeat. Why, after seventy years of union, did the South prefer rebellion to majority rule? Politics has been described as "the art of compromise," and the political, economic, and moral issues which divided the people of the North and the people of the South were so great that the leaders of the two sections could not resolve their differences.

Not all leaders in that generation were blunderers, but each section had too many politicians, editors, and others who were unable or unwilling to understand the peculiar problems of the other section or to foresee where their self-righteous emotionalism was leading them. These leaders cannot be excused on the grounds that their actions were unpremeditated, that secession and war were impulsive deeds. Some southerners, such as Louis Trezevant Wigfall, had been trying to bring about secession twenty-five years before it came. Perhaps by focusing upon these individuals and trying to understand their actions, fears, and desires, we can better understand the forces of change and resistance that led the nation into a civil war.

Louis T. Wigfall is particularly suited for a case study of the radical brand of southern proslavery leaders often referred to as "fire-eaters." As the perceptive correspondent for the London *Times*, William H. Russell, said, Wigfall was an ideal type of the fire-eating secessionist.[1] Furthermore, he was often in a position to influence the course of events. Both Wigfall's wife Charlotte and Mary B. Chesnut, the observant diarist of the Old South, referred to Wigfall as a "stormy petrel," [2] and the image was an apt one. He was usually on the scene of a crisis when it occurred. He entered the United States Senate in December of 1859, in time to become involved in the sectional storm as it peaked. When the eyes of the world were drawn to Fort Sumter by the opening shots of war in April of 1861, he was already there, making his presence felt in a dramatic and, as usual, controversial action. Throughout the war he was continually in a military or political maelstrom either as a Confederate general or senator—and for a brief period as both.

Other members of the Wigfall family were well situated to record different aspects of the conflict. Charlotte Wigfall, noted for her feud with Mrs. Jefferson Davis, the first lady of the Confederacy, became something of a storm center herself. The Wigfall's precocious daughter "Louly" was often more incisive than the adults in her observations and comments as she viewed events in Boston and Providence as well as in various southern cities. Halsey, the Wigfall's hot-blooded sixteen-year-old son, joined the Confederate army and saw service with Jeb Stuart in the East, with Joseph E. Johnston in the Atlanta Campaign, and with John B. Hood in Tennessee before returning to Virginia for the last stand of the Confederacy. Throughout the war and most of the Reconstruction period, the Wigfalls were separated and in writing to one another left valuable accounts from their respective vantage points. Thus, not only the Senator, but the entire family offers opportunities for worthwhile study.

[1] William H. Russell, *My Diary North and South: The Civil War in America* (New York, 1954), 62.

[2] Mary Boykin Chesnut, *A Diary From Dixie*, ed. by Ben Ames Williams (Boston, 1961), 33–34.

Louis T. Wigfall has been honored and condemned by his contemporaries and by later generations, usually with little understanding of why he acted as he did. Because he was a defender of a social order based on white supremacy, there are many people today who continue to look upon him as a hero. On the other hand, it is easy, perhaps too easy, for others to condemn Wigfall by measuring him with today's standards of human rights and equality for all men, standards not so widely accepted in the nineteenth century. It would have been difficult, if not impossible, for Wigfall to accept the abolition of slavery, with the concommitant destruction of the influence of the planter class. While this study is, in its final analysis, critical of Wigfall, its primary objective is to attempt to understand why he acted as he did.

I wish to express my appreciation to the many people who have been helpful in the preparation of this study. I am especially indebted to Professors Lawrence L. Graves, Lowell H. Harrison, James V. Reese, Merton L. Dillon, Ima C. Barlow, Paul J. Woods, George S. Robbert, and J. William Davis for their interest, criticism, and inspiration. Grateful acknowledgment is made to my family for their aid and interest and particularly to my wife for her unfailing and patient encouragement. There are others who gave freely of aid and encouragement but whose names cannot be mentioned here; to them also, thank you.

A. L. KING
1970

Contents

LOUIS T.
WIGFALL

Chapter I

A Well of Fire

WHEN LOUIS T. WIGFALL, the newly elected senator from Texas, strode down the halls of the United States Congress in 1860, he brought with him convictions molded by his forty-three years of life in the South. Epitomized in him were the southern beliefs in white supremacy, slavery, the low tariff, and states' rights. Thus, he joined the strengthening phalanx of "fire-eaters" sent to assert southern rights in the national legislature.

The Thirty-sixth Congress, the last "united" legislature to convene before the American Civil War, was filled with strong personalities adamant in defense of their respective sectional interests. But even in this charged atmosphere Lou Wigfall's unmistakable air of aggressive determination set him apart from his peers. William H. Russell, the correspondent for the London *Times*, described Wigfall as "a tall, powerful looking man" with a muscular neck and a face that

> was not one to be forgotten, a straight, broad brow, from which the hair rose up like the vegetation on a riverbank, beetling black eyebrows—a mouth coarse and firm, yet full of power, a square jaw— a thick, argumentative nose . . . , these were relieved by eyes of wonderful depth and light, such as I never saw before but in the head of a wild beast. If you look . . . into the eye of the Bengal tiger, in the Regent's Park . . . , you will form some notion of the expression I mean. It was flashing, fierce, yet calm—with a well of fire burning behind and spouting through it, an eye pitiless in anger, which now and then sought to conceal its expression beneath half-closed

lid, and then burst out with an angry glare, as if disdaining concealment.[1]

Such was the appearance of the man whom the Texas Legislature had selected in 1859 to represent the state in the nation's highest council. His election had been opposed by many moderate Texans who thought that he was a dangerous man and that his disunionist tendencies were too pronounced and inflexible. Wigfall, a proslavery fanatic, probably would not have been elected to the Senate had it not been for the abolitionist fanatic John Brown. Brown's raid on Harper's Ferry had taken place far from Texas, but in the six-week interval between that event on October 16 and December 5, 1859, the date of Texas' senatorial election, the shock rings of fear and reaction had shaken the South severely.

If Brown intended to achieve the immediate end of slavery by this direct assault, he failed. It is highly possible, however, that he had in mind a more indirect plan. Perhaps he hoped to become a martyr around whom antislavery zeal would crystalize and against whom proslavery zealots would react so strongly that they would endanger their own cause. Whether he had that indirect objective in mind or not, he achieved it. Never far beneath the surface of the conscious southern mind was the unspeakable fear of a slave insurrection. And many southerners were convinced by John Brown's raid that the Republicans, who were growing in strength, meant to inflict such an atrocity upon the South. Thus, a majority in the Texas Legislature decided that an inflexible fire-eater like Louis Wigfall was the type of man to deal with the likes of John Brown and the growing number of antislavery senators from the North.

Wigfall was typical of the emotional, inflexible southern leadership during the 1850's and the early 1860's. He was, as correspondent Russell observed, "a good type of the man whom the institutions of the [South] produce . . . a remarkable man, noted for his ready, natural eloquence; his exceeding ability as a quick,

1 Russell, *Diary*, 62.

bitter debater; the acerbity of his taunts; and his readiness for personal encounter." [2]

What were the institutions and forces that shaped this man? One of the most conservative societies of the civilized world, antebellum South Carolina, had conditioned Wigfall's attitudes.[3] He was born at a time when a new, vibrant nationalism was surging through the young republic of the United States. Even tradition-bound South Carolina was not immune to the nationalistic fervor. Indeed, the Palmetto State's frontier districts, where Wigfall was reared, had spawned one of the most nationalistic of the "War Hawks," John C. Calhoun.

Americans from the territory of Maine to the new southwestern state of Louisiana, from the Great Lakes to Georgia, took a soul-satisfying pride in their "triumph" over Great Britain in the War of 1812. Even to those who might admit that the war had been inconclusive, Andrew Jackson's victory at New Orleans had proved "American superiority." Francis Scott Key's recently penned words of the "Star Spangled Banner" were on the lips of Americans everywhere. Uncle Sam, the national symbol of the United States, was born about the same time as Louis Wigfall.

This burst of nationalism proved premature. During the Missouri controversy, a hairline sectional fracture was disclosed in the conflict of interests between the slave and free states in the dispute centering upon the admission of Missouri into the Union. After vitriolic debates Missouri was finally admitted as a slave state, but it was agreed that there would be no more such states carved from any of the remaining Louisiana Territory north of the line of 36°30'. The aged Thomas Jefferson expressed his prophetic fear that such a sectional line, coinciding with a moral and political principle, "once conceived and held up to the angry passions of men, will never be obliterated; and every new irritation will mark it deeper and deeper." [4]

2 *Ibid.*

3 Clement Eaton, *The Mind of the Old South* (Baton Rouge, 1964), 22–23.

4 Jefferson to John Holmes, April 22, 1820, in Paul L. Ford (ed.), *The Works of Thomas Jefferson* (10 vols.; New Orleans, 1892–99), X, 158.

By 1828, however, South Carolina and Calhoun had become disenchanted with centralism. They were the leaders of a South which was coming to espouse slavery as a "positive good," which was claiming the right to carry their "property" (slaves) into any territory of the Union, and which was bitterly opposing any tariff that protected northern industry. Thus, southern spokesmen turned to the doctrine of states' rights to protect their section. The all-important function of deciding when the national government had transcended those powers expressly delegated in the Constitution was not to be left to the Supreme Court, which was, after all, a part of the national government. Rather it was a function of the sovereign states to decide when the Congress had acted unconstitutionally. If a state so decided, then it could declare the offensive congressional act null and void in that state.

Calhoun refined this theory put forth by Thomas Jefferson and James Madison in their Kentucky and Virginia Resolutions of 1798–1799, and he carried it still further, spelling out the mechanics of how the states were to exercise their sovereign power. His was the basic states' rights doctrine that Louis Wigfall and most other southerners of his generation preached and acted upon. Significantly, part of Calhoun's theories were first penned in letters to Wigfall's cousin, James Hamilton, Jr., who was governor of South Carolina (1830–32).[5]

South Carolina, going even further than the formula laid down by Calhoun, declared the Tariff of 1832 null in that state. President Jackson immediately issued a proclamation denouncing nullification as a false doctrine and began military and naval preparations to collect the tax by force if necessary. South Carolina raised an army to resist. An armed conflict was averted by the Compromise Tariff of 1833, which provided for a gradual reduction of tariff rates over the next nine years.

This crisis made a deep and abiding impression on sixteen-year-old Louis Wigfall. Undoubtedly, he felt personally involved

[5] John Timothee Trezevant, *The Trezevant Family in the United States . . .* (Columbia, South Carolina, 1914), 60, 108–109.

in it.[6] His older brother Arthur was proprietor and editor of the *Carolinian*, the only significant newspaper in Edgefield at this time. The *Carolinian* was, like Edgefield itself, unequivocally nullificationist. Further, Governor Hamilton was in personal command of the South Carolina militia which was drawn up around Edgefield to ward off an expected invasion by United States troops poised just across the Savannah River at Augusta, Georgia.

Wigfall could well have said, as Milledge Bonham, another Edgefield native of the same generation, did: "Though but a boy at the time of that . . . struggle for the constitutional rights of a whole Section, I learned my first political lesson in that school." [7] It is not unnatural that Wigfall absorbed the lessons of that school, or that he took careful note of the virtual reverence with which many southerners spoke of John Calhoun and how they accepted the gospel of states' rights according to John.

Wigfall, like other budding politicians of his time in South Carolina, could not remember anything good about his state's relations with the federal government. He was of that generation which had heard the vocabulary of states' rights and southern patriotism since youth. All the appeals that Wigfall and other fire-eaters used to stir the southern people in the 1850's, all the denunciations of the "tyranny of the numerical majority," all the cries for "constitutional rights," had been heard by Wigfall for twenty years from Calhoun, James Hamilton, and other nullifiers in South Carolina.[8]

Wigfall's natal state was conservative not only in such major areas as states' rights, "the preservation of slavery, orthodox religion, and aristocratic government," but also in such lesser matters as "a preference for the old writers of English literature, . . .

6 Louis Wigfall, "Answer to the Letter of Many Officers of the Seventh Regiment [of South Carolina Militia]," Edgefield *Advertiser*, September 25, 1844, Thompkins Library, Edgefield, South Carolina, microfilm at University of Texas Library, typescript University of Texas Archives, Austin, Texas. Unless otherwise designated, all citations of newspapers are from the University of Texas collection.

7 *Congressional Globe*, 36th Cong., 1st Sess., 166.

8 Harold S. Schultz, *Nationalism and Sectionalism in South Carolina, 1852–1860* (Durham, North Carolina, 1950), 9.

an archaic sense of honor, and an absurd emphasis on genealogy."
In South Carolina Louis Trezevant Wigfall's genealogy was a
definite asset.[9] The Wigfalls and especially the Trezevants were
among the first families of South Carolina from the standpoints
of arrival and social prominence. The founder of the Trezevant
family of South Carolina was Daniel Trezevant, the great-great-
great grandfather of Louis Wigfall. Daniel, a wealthy merchant
of Bordeaux, was one of the French Huguenots who left France
in 1685, shortly before the revocation of the Edict of Nantes.
After fleeing with his family to England he made his way to
Charleston and settled there some time before the end of 1695.[10]

The Trezevants were soon established among the Tidewater
aristocracy and were well represented in the professions with
a number of medical doctors, civil engineers, successful merchants, plantation and slave owners, soldiers, civil officials and
politicians, and, most numerous of all, lawyers and judges. Many
of the Trezevant women married well-known men. Elizabeth
Martha Trezevant, Louis Wigfall's grandmother, was the wife
of James Hamden Thomson, A.M., once a tutor in the College
of New Jersey and then a respected schoolmaster in Charleston.
One of their three daughters, Eliza, married Levi Durand Wigfall, a well-to-do Charleston merchant. Levi was a descendant of
two prominent Charleston families; many of the Durand and
Wigfall men were successful merchants and ministers as well as
landholders. To Levi and Eliza were born four children. The
third was Louis Trezevant Wigfall.[11]

Louis Wigfall married another member of the Trezevant family, his lovely second cousin Charlotte Maria Cross. Her grandmother, Charlotte Trezevant, was the younger sister of Louis'

9 Eaton, *Mind of the Old South*, 41.
10 Trezevant, *Family*, 11–12.
11 *Ibid.*, 18, 19ff., 58, 103–104; Robert F. Clute (ed.), *The Annals and Parish
Register of St. Thomas and St. Denis Parish from 1680 to 1884* (Charleston, 1884),
110–11; J. B. O'Neall, *Biographical Sketches of Bench and Bar of South Carolina*
(2 vols.; Charleston, 1859); *South Carolina Historical and Genealogical Magazine*,
II (October, 1901), 276, XL (October, 1939), 115–16; Anne King Gregorie, *Christ
Church, 1706–1959: A Plantation Parish of the South Carolina Establishment*
(Charleston, 1961), 16ff.

grandmother, Elizabeth Martha Trezevant. It was not at all unusual in antebellum Tidewater society for cousins to marry, and
the Wigfall and Trezevant families were closely interrelated.

Wigfall was at once the product of the aristocratic traditions
of the Tidewater and of the frontier influence of western South
Carolina. His father, with money made as a merchant in Charleston, bought a plantation in Edgefield District, western South
Carolina, and moved his family there in 1814. Two years later
Louis was born in the plantation home. The Edgefield area where
Louis was reared was more the farming South than the plantation
South, but a few distinguished families owned sizable planta-
tions there. Nevertheless, an air of Charleston, "the great cultural
center of southernism, . . . the most elegant pattern of southern
civilization," permeated the Wigfall home.[12]

Charleston and Edgefield contributed most of the famous
leaders of the Palmetto State. Indeed, Edgefield became so infamous for its trouble-making sons that one state historian has
called it the breeding ground for the species.[13] By 1841, when
Wigfall was twenty-five years old, the notoriety of the district had
spread. After suffering the effects of some young Edgefield war-
riors in his command, one army major said that he knew "the
devil must have his headquarters there." [14]

The population of Edgefield District was essentially Anglo-
Saxon and Negro, with the blacks having a slight numerical majority. Many of the Negroes were of the Gullah tribe who made
the most obstreperous slaves. These factors undoubtedly help explain why there were avid feelings of white supremacy among
the Anglo-Saxons there. Further, the upper class entertained definite aristocratic attitudes, although just two generations before
Wigfall's birth this area had been unexplored wilderness. The
morals of the lower class, however, reflected the cruder aspects of

12 Trezevant, *Family*, 103–104; see also Roy Franklin Nichols, *The Disruption of
American Democracy* (New York, 1962), 288.
13 William Francis Guess, *South Carolina, Annals of Pride and Protest* (New
York, 1957), 229; see also Schultz, *Nationalism and Sectionalism*, 21.
14 Major David E. Twiggs, quoted in John A. Chapman, *A History of Edgefield
County* (Newberry, South Carolina, 1897), 195.

frontier influence. To both classes in western South Carolina the essential test to a law was "Will it leave us alone? Will it leave us free?" [15]

Most Edgefieldians were fundamentalist Baptists and Methodists, but Wigfall's religious background was Episcopalian, the church of most of the upper class of the Old South. Free-Thinking and Deism had once affected the southern country gentlemen, but by Wigfall's generation these had, like other liberal tendencies, been inundated by a rising tide of conservatism. A stringent religious orthodoxy helped to smother any liberal ideas in South Carolina.[16] It is understandable how the liberal Francis Lieber would brood over his "exile" while teaching there: "Everything is arid here; arid soil; arid life; arid society; not a breath of scientific air nor a spark of intellectual electricity." [17]

Nevertheless, the well-furnished Wigfall plantation home included a sizable library. Like most southern libraries it had an accessible niche for Sir Walter Scott's *Waverly Novels,* highly romanticized tales of English chivalry which reflected, and helped to form, the ideals of southern society.[18] Wigfall probably gained his enduring affinity for history and the classics in this library during his youth.

At an early age Wigfall lost the guidance of his parents. His father died when Louis was but two and his mother when he was thirteen.[19] His inheritance of $13,000 was a comfortable one,

15 Ben Robertson, *Red Hills and Cotton: An Upcountry Memory* (Columbia, South Carolina, 1960), 128–29, 9, 59, 60, 64–65, 71, 90, 135–37, 178, 223.
16 Clement Eaton, *Freedom of Thought in the Old South* (New York, 1951), Chap. 11; Gregorie, *Christ Church,* 16ff.
17 Lieber is quoted in Daniel Walker Hollis, *South Carolina College* (Columbia, South Carolina, 1951), 181.
18 Edgefield District Records, May 8, 1832, Book E, 305–306, Edgefield District Court House, Edgefield, South Carolina, microfilm in author's possession; *The Waverly Novels,* published in England, 1814–31, were read avidly by Wigfall and his generation of southerners, as well as by his children and their generation; Louly Wigfall to Mrs. Wigfall, March 28, April 1, 1861, in Wigfall Family Papers, Library of Congress, microfilm in author's possession; Clement Eaton, *A History of the Southern Confederacy* (New York, 1958), 225–26; Eaton, *Mind of the Old South,* Chap. 12.
19 Clyde W. Lord, "Young Louis Wigfall: South Carolina Politician and Duelist," *South Carolina Historical Magazine,* LIX (April, 1958), 96; Edgefield District

however, and his guardian and tutor, Allen B. Addison, apparently took seriously his charge from Eliza Wigfall to bring her son up "carefully and handsomely . . . according to his degree." Itemized expenses by Addison included "cash for concert" and "book money" as well as generous amounts of "pocket money." [20]

There were also liberal allotments for Wigfall's education at exclusive schools. At age eighteen he enrolled at the private military academy Rice Creek Springs School. Situated in the Sand Hills near Camden and Columbia, the new elite school catered to the young men of the well-to-do families who made their summer homes in the area. The proprietors of the school boasted that it was modeled after the gymnasia of Europe and that it remedied many of the defects of the common schools of America. The student body was restricted to one hundred, and classes were limited to twelve.

Wigfall's curriculum consisted of classical languages, belles lettres (including rhetoric and history), and military science. Along with the other students he served in a military corps of cadets because school officials believed that "Every American should have a knowledge of military science." Uniforms were worn to classes and to the required sessions of daily prayer and to Sunday worship.[21] Judging from his later career, Wigfall was more deeply impressed by the military aspects of his education than by the academic or religious.

After a year at Rice Creek School, Wigfall spent one year at the University of Virginia where he distinguished himself in Latin as well as in less desirable activities. His quick temper and sensitive honor caused trouble at a dance given by one of the professors, when the following incident ensued:

> Louis Wigfall . . . felt insulted by the refusal of a Southern Belle, a Miss Leiper, to dance with him. Believing that he was "elevated by wine," to use her expression, she took the arm of another student and hastened precipitously away. Wigfall was a youth of high

Records: Judgements and Decrees, Roll 2688, Book XX, 139–41, Office of the Probate Judge.

20 Edgefield District Records, Apartment 47, Package 2023.

21 Columbia *Telescope*, January 9, 1829.

mettle and fiery spirit and accordingly sent a challenge to Miss
Leiper's escort for uttering language during the altercation "that
I could suffer from no one."

College authorities prevented the duel, and students convened
a court of honor to decide whether Wigfall had been insulted. In
a court scrupulously conducted, Miss Leiper testified that she had
been mistaken in assuming that Wigfall was under the influence
of alcohol when he insisted upon dancing with her. The court
then reported its conclusion that the affair had arisen out of a
misconception and "a delicate sensibility" displayed by both
parties. There was no point of honor involved, and Wigfall's conduct was not rude nor due to alcohol, but rather due to a "natural impetuosity." [22]

For the last and most important phase of his formal education, Wigfall returned to his native state to attend South Carolina College. Were it not for the degree he received and the
friends and acquaintances he made at the college, Wigfall's career could not have been as significant as it was. The school was
a powerful force in shaping the minds of antebellum South Carolina leaders.[23]

One of the main reasons that the college assumed prodigious
influence was Thomas Cooper, the second president of the school
(1821–34), who was among the first "to invoke the demon of disunion." As early as July 2, 1827, this testy Englishman had exhorted South Carolina to leave the Union. He had warned: "We
shall before long be forced to calculate the value of the Union." [24]
The states' rights principles with which he indoctrinated the
minds of his students were to have great impact. By the time
Wigfall arrived at South Carolina College in 1836, theoretical
justification of nullification and secession was an overriding in-

22 Eaton, in *Mind of the Old South*, 223, uses this incident to depict the typical
sense of honor and values of the upper class of the Old South.
23 Hollis, *South Carolina College*, 259. One of the trustees who helped establish
the college in 1801 was Judge Lewis C. Wigfall, Louis' uncle; *ibid.*, 24; E. L.
Green, *A History of the University of South Carolina* (Columbia, South Carolina,
1916), 264–65; Schultz, *Nationalism and Sectionalism*, 8–10.
24 Dumas Malone, *The Public Life of Thomas Cooper, 1783–1839* (Columbia,
South Carolina, 1961), 3, 309.

fluence at the school, and the school oratorical societies had been debating the issue of secession for seven or eight years. The major difference of opinion was when and how secession should take place. [25]

A confirmed Nullifier, Robert Woodward Barnwell, succeeded Cooper as president of the college. Under Barnwell's administration "objectionable" (liberal and nationalistic) faculty members were gradually removed and other reforms were instituted.[26] Wigfall enrolled during the second year of Barnwell's presidency, in time to catch the flow of the nullificationist tide at the school. Entrance requirements for Wigfall and the other candidates for admission after the reorganization of 1835 were stricter than ever before. Thus, in oral examinations he had to convince the faculty that he had "an accurate knowledge of the English, Latin, and Greek grammars," that he had studied Morse's or Worcester's geography, that he was "well acquainted with arithmetic," and that he had read the whole of Sallust, Virgil, and Cicero's *Select Orations*, as well as other Latin compositions, Jacob's *Greek Reader*, and one book of Homer. Wigfall qualified and was admitted to the college and its junior class. He started his career at South Carolina College with 113 schoolmates, including 11 graduate students. His curriculum, a newly revised one for juniors and seniors, maintained its core of classical studies and still provided for no electives. It included Latin, Greek, mathematics, English, history, philosophy, metaphysics, sacred literature, geology, and physiology.[27]

Wigfall's attire and activities, the same as for students for thirty years before him, were prescribed by the puritanical regulations provided by the founders of the school. College law carefully described his uniform, from the round black hat to the black trim that edged his dark gray suit. His day was as regimented as his

25 Hollis, *South Carolina College*, 70–74.

26 Francis Lieber, a nationalistic German, was kept because he was a powerful exponent of free trade. *Ibid.*, 74ff., 110, 126ff.; see also Malone, *Thomas Cooper*, 309ff.

27 *South Carolina College Catalog, 1836*, quoted in Green, *University of South Carolina*, 173–76, 181–84, 229, 437; see also Hollis, *South Carolina College*, 30.

uniform. He and his fellow scholars began their college day by convening at sunrise to attend prayers. From there they went to recitations, lectures, or to pursue their studies until they were summoned to breakfast. At nine they returned to study in their rooms until noon unless summoned to more recitations or lectures. Between twelve and two they dined, and then they returned to their rooms at two to study until five. At that hour they attended prayers at the chapel. Presumably Wigfall then dined. At the ringing of a bell at seven he went to his room to study until nine-thirty and remained there the rest of the night. On Saturdays students were dismissed after morning recitations and were free until nine o'clock at night. Even when they had an opportunity, Wigfall and his colleagues were forbidden to visit taverns, hotels, or places of public amusement unless they had prior permission from the president of the school. Violation of this rule could bring expulsion.[28]

Other prohibitions included not only such crimes as blasphemy, dueling, robbery, and fornication, but also drinking and playing cards. Further, students were not to play on any musical instrument in study hours, nor could they smoke in any part of the college except in their own rooms. Smoking on the streets of Columbia was considered ungentlemanly and was forbidden. College trustees in 1835 determined that the necessary expenses, including pocket money, of a student for a collegiate year to be $350. This limit was called for, the trustees explained to the parents, because "Young gentlemen are sent to the College for the purpose of study, and not for pleasure." [29]

Since he did not have relatives residing in Columbia, Wigfall roomed in the campus dormitories and boarded at the commons. The commons system was the most chronic source of friction on the campus. Typically, presidential reports included some statement such as Dr. Cooper's lament: "The College is in yearly

---

28 *South Carolina College Catalog, 1836*, quoted in Green, *University of South Carolina*, 224–25, 228–29; see also Hollis, *South Carolina College*, 30.
29 Green, *University of South Carolina*, 218–22, 225, 229–300.

jeopardy of being destroyed by the disputes about eating." [30]
Once President Barnwell tried a voluntary commons, letting the
students eat in town. But Wigfall and others took advantage of
this to frequent taverns where liquor as well as food was served.
Typical of the student hangout was Billy Maybin's Congaree
Hotel, which a later alumnus memorialized in verse:

> Come, doff your gowns, good fellows, don't
>   put your coats on slow,
> For a drinking at old Billy's we are ready
>   for to go;
> Above he serves good suppers, good liquors
>   down below,
> And many a time we've had a spree at Billy
>   Maybin's, O!
> . . . .
> Next Monday morning surely old sheriff comes
>   around,
> And you're up before the faculty for going
>   up the town,
> "Did you go into an eating house?" "Did you
>   take a drink or no?"
> Oh, yes sirs; took a drink or two at Billy
>   Maybin's, O! [31]

The college presidents and faculty often deplored the southern youths' lack of discipline, saying the students were very neg-
ligently managed, and their parents were too indulgent of their
whims. Louis Wigfall was in particular a "nightmare to faculty
slumbers," and it did not take him long to establish a reputation
for insurgency.[32] He was notable for being careless about attending class, absent for days at a time, and was adept at throwing
bread in commons. Soon he was looked upon as one of the all-
time great campus lawyers. He was the "writer of endless student
petitions and expositions regarding student rights and was very
fond of visiting taverns up town, particularly during the evening

[30] Presidential Report of Dr. Thomas Cooper, quoted in Green, *University of South Carolina*, 290.
[31] Quoted in Hollis, *South Carolina College*, 136–37, 158; also in Green, *University of South Carolina*, 343–44.
[32] Hollis, *South Carolina College*, 92, 110; Guess, *South Carolina*, 229.

hours." [33] One unauthorized but popular activity especially favored by Wigfall's class was the "wine supper." Friendly Columbia tavernkeepers provided, for a price, accommodations and provisions, so that drinking was frequent and drunkenness not uncommon.[34]

College officials doubtless enjoyed the brief respite afforded them when Wigfall and other of the most high-spirited students answered the call in 1836 for South Carolina men to war against the Seminole Indians in Florida. During the campaigns Wigfall rose to the rank of lieutenant of volunteers. But within three months he and his fellow scholars were back at the college continuing their studies and making life unpleasant for the faculty.[35]

Maximilian LaBorde's history of the college gives the impression that the students were almost constantly in active rebellion. LaBorde spoke with authority for he was a contemporary of Wigfall and was associated with South Carolina College for about fifty years, most of that time as a professor. There were a number of infamous uprisings, some of which included attacks upon professors' homes and even upon the professors themselves. Perhaps there would have been less mischief by the students had there been other outlets for their exuberance. But there were no organized athletics, so the students devised all of their own recreation.[36]

The fact that the professors sometimes took seriously their charge to keep a tight rein on students usually made their pranks only that much more fun. Francis Lieber, one of Wigfall's teachers, once fell over a pile of bricks during a futile chase after a young wrongdoer. As he sat upon the ground, nursing his bruised

33 South Carolina College Faculty Minutes for February, October, and November, 1836; January, February, June, and November, 1837, quoted in Hollis, *South Carolina College*, 138.

34 Green, *University of South Carolina*, 242–43, 247.

35 Chapman, *Edgefield*, 77; see also *Appleton's Cyclopedia of American Biography*, VI, 499; and Lord, "Young Louis Wigfall," 97.

36 Maximilian LaBorde, *A History of the South Carolina College* . . . (Charleston, 1874), 63–70, 218–19, 266–69; Green, *University of South Carolina*, 242–53.

shins, the native of Germany was heard to mutter, "Mein Gott. All dis for two tousant tollar." [37]

The honor system was a more effective check on student behavior. The practice was simple. A faculty member who suspected a student of any breach of the rules could have him called before a faculty board and questioned about his activities. If he denied that he was guilty of the offense, his denial alone was to be considered *prima facie* proof of his innocence.[38] On the subject of student honor, Lieber acknowledged in his diary, during the last year that Wigfall was at the college: "Not once have I yet appealed to their honor and found myself disappointed. If you treat them *en gens d'arme*, of course they not only try to kick, but you give a zest to their resistance." [39] Another professor at South Carolina College, Joseph LeConte, said in his autobiography that while the students were high-spirited and turbulent, he never saw so high a sense of honor among students in their relations to one another and to the faculty. No form of untruthfulness among themselves nor toward the faculty, such as cheating at examinations, was tolerated. Any student suspected of such practices was cut by his fellow students and compelled to leave.[40]

This high sense of honor helps explain the prevalence of dueling. Young Wigfall lived in an era when duels were not uncommon. Even Andrew Jackson, who was President of the United States while Wigfall was at college, was a celebrated duelist. The incidence of dueling was especially high in South Carolina where the aristocracy clung so firmly to chivalric ideals. As Dr. Marion Sims, one of Wigfall's contemporaries, put it, he was educated to believe that duels inspired the proprieties of society and protected the honor of women. He had scarcely a doubt that if anything had happened while he was a student in South Carolina College

[37] Green, *University of South Carolina,* 242–43.
[38] *South Carolina College Catalog, 1836,* quoted in Green, *University of South Carolina,* 258.
[39] Francis Lieber, Diary, entry of May 15, 1837, quoted in Green, *University of South Carolina,* 241, 258–59.
[40] Green, *University of South Carolina,* 259.

to make it necessary for him to fight a duel, he would have gone out with the utmost coolness and allowed himself to be shot down. But, Sims added, his views on that subject changed soon after leaving college.[41] So far as is known, Wigfall's involvement in duels during his college years extended no further than the challenge he sent while at the University of Virginia. Later, however, he established a reputation as a duelist and one of the best marksmen in the state. Duels among South Carolina College students were certainly not unknown. The most famous duel in the history of the college grew out of a contest between two good friends who argued over a piece of trout at commons. One of the duelists was killed and the other seriously wounded.[42]

Not all South Carolina College friendships culminated in such violent fashion. Years later, when Wigfall had occasion to discourse publicly on the benefits of college, he said that one of the great advantages is the personal contacts one forms. There were, he said, no friendships as lasting, no ties so binding, as those of college life.[43] The closest friends that Wigfall had in college were David Johnson and John L. Manning, both of whom were sons of governors, and one of whom, Manning, later became governor himself.

Manning and Wigfall served on a committee to establish a college literary journal. Wigfall went so far as to devise a subscription plan which would defray the estimated costs, but for some reason the plan lapsed, and the college did not have a journal in the antebellum period. The literary committee was a creation of the Euphradians ("those dedicated to eloquence and correct speaking"), one of the two oratorical societies at the college and the one in which Wigfall was a member. One probable reason for the failure of the literary committee was the great success of the parent organization in its primary purpose—oratory. This was by far the more important vehicle of expression in South

41 Dr. Marion Simms, quoted in *ibid.*, 224.

42 Green, *University of South Carolina*, 244–46.

43 "Chairman's Report for the Committee on State Affairs . . ." in the *Texas Republican*, July 30, 1859. Wigfall was serving as chairman of the committee which was looking into the propriety of establishing a state university.

Carolina. About this time, Wigfall himself wrote to Manning, "after all the pen is but a poor substitute for the tongue." During the antebellum period other parts of the country, especially other southern states, placed great emphasis upon the spoken word, but the enthusiasm of South Carolinians for oratory amounted nearly to a singular preoccupation.[44]

It was not difficult for Wigfall to cultivate a glib tongue. Already possessing a flair for verbal pyrotechnics, he learned to put his knowledge of history, Latin, and classical literature to work in order to sway rural southerners. John Quincy Adams had a classification for the Wigfall-type speaker: "the South Carolina school of orator states[men]—pompous, flashy, and shallow." [45] Nevertheless, the addiction of the southern people to emotional and florid oratory was one of the conditions that gave Wigfall the opportunity to rise in southern politics.

While he was enhancing his distinction as a campus trouble-maker and orator, Wigfall also demonstrated a keen intellect; he was awarded the B. A. degree. It is doubtless true, however, that the faculty and administration of his college gave a sigh of relief as he was graduated in 1837.[46] Now he was a problem for the community of Edgefield.

[44] Hollis, *South Carolina College*, 230, 253–54; Wigfall to Manning, November 11, 1839, in Williams-Chestnut-Manning Collection, the South Caroliniana Library, University of South Carolina, Columbia; typed transcription in University of Texas Archives, Austin, Texas; microfilm in Southwest Collection, Texas Tech University. The Euphradians and their sister oratorical society the Clariosophics served as combination political, social, fraternal, and intellectual clubs, according to Hollis, *South Carolina College*, 230, 253; see also Green, *University of South Carolina*, 267, 272.
[45] Hollis, *South Carolina College*, 261.
[46] *Ibid.*, 138; LaBorde, *History of South Carolina College*, 538.

Chapter II

With Pen and Pistol

LOU WIGFALL was a fire-eater socially before becoming one politically. Despite sporadic efforts to reform in effort to become a respected lawyer and political leader during his twenties in the decade of 1836–46, Wigfall earned a reputation for social and financial irresponsibility which culminated in the ruination of his law practice in Edgefield and his being charged with murder. Even marriage and a family failed to sober him. A decade and a half ahead of most Carolinians in advocating secession, Wigfall also became unpopular for his radicalism in politics. Thus, his bankruptcy was social and political as well as financial, and so complete was it that he felt the necessity of leaving his beloved South Carolina to seek a new life in the turbulent new state of Texas.

Wigfall chose the law for his profession, as did one out of four of the graduates of antebellum South Carolina College and many members of the Trezevant family.[1] After graduation from college, Louis returned to Edgefield where his elder brother Arthur already had a well-established and lucrative law practice. As Arthur planned to retire soon to enter the ministry, Louis would have a ready-made clientele if he could be admitted to the bar in time.

A major obstacle between Wigfall and admission to the bar

1 Hollis, *South Carolina College*, 80, 255.

was the bar examination—no inconsequential barrier. It required study, and as Wigfall assessed himself on this matter: "I have I believe always been on the extreme in everything I ever attempted *except study*." [2] Indeed, his extreme recklessness in social and financial affairs had earned him a reputation as an irresponsible, self-assured hedonist. The ability for which he was best known was his marksmanship with a pistol. This, combined with his fearlessness, at least made him a good friend to have in certain situations. He acted as a second for Sam Bacon in 1839 when he dueled another Edgefieldian, Joseph Glover. Bacon explained that pistols would be used, and said he was afraid that he would be murdered unless he had someone on the field who was a good shot and not afraid of the Glover clan. His fears were well-founded. In the exchange of fire, Glover was slightly wounded. When he drew a second pistol to fire on the then unarmed Bacon, Wigfall passed a pistol to Bacon with the advice to blow the "damned scondrel's [*sic*] brains out." But Glover grappled with Bacon, their pistols dropped, and Wigfall separated them. According to Wigfall, the Glovers swore to kill him but were afraid to try because they knew he was always armed with two pistols.[3] Unfortunately, Wigfall's faith in pistols, his courage, and his touchy sense of honor were to bring him a great deal of trouble and subvert his determination to be a useful member of society in good standing with his fellow citizens.

Two years out of college and approaching his middle twenties, Wigfall determined to change his way of living and dedicate himself to his chosen profession. In one of several personal resolutions made in the late 1830's, he wrote with enthusiasm to Manning, "wine and women have lost their charms for me. Ambition shall be my mistress and Law my Liquor." He had, he confessed, often thought that he and dissipation "had shaken hands," but this time he was sure of it.[4]

2 Wigfall to Manning, undated, but early 1839; March 4, [1839], Williams-Chesnut-Manning Collection. All of Wigfall's letters to Manning are to be found in this collection unless otherwise stated.

3 *Ibid.*, February 22, [1839].

4 *Ibid.*, undated, but early 1839.

He backslid often, even though with each failure he seemed more concerned about the life he was leading. At one point he expressed hope that after a while he would not be such a "damned fool" and confessed that his fatuousness had lost him the respect of many. He classified himself with most men who "act foolishly from want of judgment or in other words because they do not know how to value things." Some men knew these things by instinct, he continued, some never learned, but he and others like him could be taught by experience. As Wigfall analyzed his "very foolish course," he ascribed it to John Bulwer's novels, to gentlemen-blackleg [gambler] friends, and to his own entire lack of common sense. These, he admitted, had "damned nearly ruined me." But, he resolved (again), "Wine, *women* & cards & your humble servant have however *finally shaken hands*." As proof that he was serious about his efforts, Wigfall proudly related that on a recent trip he had been in Augusta with some of his Georgia friends, and he had not attended the racecourse or "houses of a certain description or got *even tipsy* at dinner. 'Pro-d-i-g-i-o-u-s!!' you will say—very well—I say 'it was for me.' " [5]

At times Wigfall seemed so confident of reforming himself that he was able to devote some time to instructing Manning. Wigfall urged him not to be so lazy, that lack of ambition was ruining a promising career. "Remember . . . that you can do nothing without burning the midnight oil." Wigfall was fearful, he said, that his rich married friend's domestic and pecuniary affairs would engross all of his time. [6]

More often Wigfall filled his lengthy letters with his own dreams and problems. During the particularly troubled periods in his life, he seemed to need one close friend in whom to confide. In the late 1830's and early 1840's, it was Manning. Often he received epistles from Wigfall with instructions to burn his letters because he did not want anyone else to see them. But they remain, and they reveal Wigfall as a troubled man, hungry for security and love, as well as for respect. For several months he

5 *Ibid.*, February 22, [1839].
6 *Ibid.*, and Wigfall to Manning, undated, but early 1839.

wrote repeatedly to Manning, asking why he and David Johnson, another South Carolina College friend, did not write to him. Once he asked for a portrait of Manning.[7]

Wigfall's quest for respectability was sufficient to settle him down at least enough to study law and to improve his reputation somewhat. Relating his progress to Manning, Wigfall said that his appreciation of "moral character" had increased. Capitalizing upon his rising reputation, as well as his experience in military school and the Seminole War, and the influence of friends, Wigfall obtained an appointment as a colonel in command of the Seventh Regiment of South Carolina Militia. Proudly Colonel Wigfall told Manning of Governor McDuffie's comment that "with such officers as the commander of the gallant 7th he could make regulars out of *North* Carolina Militia in less than a month." Wigfall found great satisfaction in militia training and parades. After one bivouac, he reported that he had had a merry week of it and was sorry when it was over.[8]

The honor of making public speeches also swelled Wigfall's ego. With lighthearted vanity, he told Manning of his success: "the dish of 4th of July froth . . . which I had the honor of serving up—proved to be more agreeable to the palates of 'my friends & fellow citizens' than I had ever *hoped*. I am told that it has done me some credit." [9] No doubt his prestige was enhanced when he was admitted to the bar in the fall of 1839. The judge complimented him on his maiden speech in court, but Wigfall said that he was more pleased with the $300 it was worth. However, his profession and his concern for his community standing did not yet occupy him totally. Even after he was admitted to the bar, Wigfall had to refuse a trip to Columbia unless he came on business, having already spent too much money and time in pursuing pleasure.[10]

Despite his own pleasures and his newly acquired social stand-

7 *Ibid.*, July 27, September 24, November 11, December 19, 1839.
8 *Ibid.*, February 22, [1839], September 17, 24, 1839.
9 *Ibid.*, July 27, 1839.
10 O'Neall, *Bench and Bar*, II, 614; Wigfall to Manning, November 11, 1839.

ing, Wigfall almost certainly envied Manning's security, wealth, family, and possible political future. On several occasions Wigfall contrasted their financial and social positions, as when he said that his friends would tell him nothing agreeable, but Manning's would tell him nothing disagreeable; "that is the difference between a rich man & a poor man." In the same letter he blamed Manning for not writing more often, lamenting: "I have no 'blooming wife' nor 'child to cheer my hope.' " [11]

Sometimes arguing vigorously (with himself?), he stoutly maintained that he would never marry. At age twenty-three he vowed that he was a predestined old bachelor. He would not have his mind distressed by the cares of a family. Women, he observed, "ruined the first man—the wisest—the best man—the strongest man—(Adam, Solomon, David, Sampson) & I expect she will ruin the last man. They have come damned near ruining me." From then on he would devote his time to law. "Tell me not of women when I can get a jury to hang upon my lips!" He had to make a lawyer of himself and get five hundred dollar fees. But shortly afterward, Wigfall added money to the category of items he would gladly forsake. With exaggerated professionalism he swore that if he possessed the wealth of a Croesus, he would give it all to see a tear start in the eye of a juryman. [12]

At other times Wigfall was more honest with himself in expressing his unhappiness to Manning, as when he wrote that the want of money or the want of love was the cause of the unhappiness of ninety-nine of every hundred unhappy men in existence and admitted he was "damnably in need of both." Nor could he find solace in religion. He said he believed that religion might be a fiction, but it was nevertheless a comfort to all those who possessed it. He did not. If he had any prospects for a happy life after death, he would not prolong his existence a moment longer, he mourned. [13]

In the same manner he had expressed his views on a wife and

11 Wigfall to Manning, March 4, [1839].
12 *Ibid.*, undated, but early 1839, and February 22, [1839].
13 *Ibid.*, January, [1839], and September 24, 1839.

riches, Wigfall stated his distaste for politics and ambition too strongly and too erratically to be convincing. He would have nothing to do with politics, he vowed to Manning. Necessity forced him to stay with the law profession, though it did not suit his "taste & inclinations." In his words, he wanted a life which would everyday give "promise of a pleasure or peril of a grave." It was extremely difficult, he said, for a man of his education, notions, and habits to be content with practicing law. He could rouse himself at any time without difficulty to one great effort, suffering in order to accomplish some noble goal which would afford pleasure to a man with a soul. But sitting in an office from morning till night, being cut off from society, that "damned practical—unpoetical—utilitarian—common place . . . sort of life" would be the death of him.[14]

This craving for excitement and a tangible goal helped steer Wigfall into a political career. He first became involved in political affairs during the South Carolina gubernatorial campaign of 1840. In this power struggle between aristocratic cliques, Wigfall cast his support for Manning's uncle John P. Richardson. His friendship for Manning alone would probably have been sufficient cause for him to support Richardson. Also, Wigfall liked a good fight and he disliked the influential Brooks family, which supported James H. Hammond, Richardson's principal opponent. The Brooks clan, which was headed by Colonel Whitfield Brooks, Sr., and which included Wigfall's college classmate Preston Brooks (who later caned Senator Charles Sumner), was not averse to fighting either.[15]

Behind the scene, Manning had already started to coordinate his uncle's campaign, but he was slow to take advantage of Wigfall's offer. Probably he thought that Wigfall would be more of a liability than an asset. By Wigfall's own admission, it was well

14 *Ibid.*, January, and July 18, [1839].
15 David Duncan Wallace, *A History of South Carolina* (4 vols.; New York, 1934), II, 477, 478; Eaton *Mind of the Old South,* 40; Wigfall to Manning, July 27, 1839, February 20, [1840]; James P. Carroll to James H. Hammond, April 14, 1840, Hammond Papers, Manuscript Division, Library of Congress; typed transcriptions of selected Hammond papers are in the University of Texas Archives.

known in Edgefield that he would have nothing to do with Calhoun, or Congressman Francis W. Pickens, or any of their group. Why this situation arose is not certain. It seems to have started with Wigfall's mistrust of Pickens, a trusted confidant of Calhoun and Hammond. Calhoun's support for Richardson was essential. Could Manning afford to enlist the aid of a man who was not favored by Calhoun? [16]

To get the support of Edgefield for Richardson would be a formidable task. His opponent Hammond hoped that Congressman Pickens' support would give the impression that he (Hammond) was backed by Calhoun. (In reality, though he kept a politically discreet silence, Calhoun wanted Richardson to win.) Furthermore, the editor of the only significant newspaper of that day in the district, the Edgefield *Advertiser*, was allied by marriage with the Brookses, and he had pledged the *Advertiser*'s support to Hammond.

But Wigfall had a plan. He would simply convince the *Advertiser*'s owner, W. F. Durisoe, that Calhoun supported Richardson, though Wigfall himself did not know whether this was true. Wigfall worked covertly because he was afraid people would not believe that he and Calhoun were for the same candidate and because he was not ready for the Brookses to know what he was doing. Thus he enlisted the aid of Dr. John H. Burt of Edgefield, a cousin of Abbeville's Dr. Armistead Burt who was generally thought to be an intimate of Calhoun. John Burt was partially successful in convincing Durisoe that Calhoun was extremely anxious to have South Carolinians united behind Richardson. The *Advertiser* carried a mild editorial endorsement which amounted to its nomination of Richardson.[17]

---

16 Wigfall to Manning, undated, but mid-1839, undated, but January, 1840, March 19, [1840]; Pickens to Hammond, March 8, April 4, 1840, Hammond Papers. See also A. L. King, "The Emergence of a Fire-Eater: Louis T. Wigfall," *Louisiana Studies*, VII (Spring, 1968), 73–82; and Lord, "Young Louis Wigfall," 101.

17 Wigfall to Manning, July 18, [1839], September 24, 1839; January 17, [1840]; February 11, 1840. Edgefield *Advertiser*, January 16, 1840. South Carolina was still under its 1790 constitution which allowed nominations for major offices to be made by newspapers, and election of the governor was to be accomplished by the legislature.

But Hammond did not give up, however. He brought his influence to bear upon the *Advertiser*'s editor and proprietor, and in two weeks they retracted the endorsement of Richardson. Hammond and his advisors were sure then that they had control of the paper. Wigfall intensified his efforts, resorting to money to win the *Advertiser*. He told Manning that they had to have a number of pro-Richardson subscribers for the paper immediately. When Manning was slow to answer, Wigfall jogged him, "If you don't answer this *fully* & *at once* . . . Brooks & the paper may all go to Hell together." In a few days pro-Richardson subscription requests began to pour in to the *Advertiser* office.[18]

Aided by the subscription money and by the fact that his opposition did not yet know who their enemy was, Wigfall brought his talent for persuasion directly to bear upon Durisoe. Reinforcing his case with the astute use of the magic name "Calhoun" and with well-written pro-Richardson letters to the editor (most of them written by Wigfall himself), Wigfall won Durisoe and his *Advertiser* for Richardson. The pro-Hammond editor resigned in humiliation. By default Wigfall became the editor of the *Advertiser*. Rhapsodically the new editor gloated over his influence upon Durisoe: "I can now say to him 'go' and he goeth—'come' and he cometh." Wigfall was astounded at the ease and totality to his coup: " 'With these bars against me & I *no friends to back my suit withal*. And yet to win her . . . .' Don't I write elegantly when I have a pen?" Of one of his editorials, he asked Manning if there was bluff enough in it. Wigfall had learned the value of a device he would use frequently in the future, having found that a "command of countenance & a high brag will make most people 'take water.' "[19]

18 Wigfall to Manning, undated, but *ca*. January 18, 1840; and *ibid.*, undated, but *ca*. January 25, 1840. In the antebellum period newspapers had more political influence than they do now, but most were dependent upon the sale of subscriptions for income. The subscription rate for the *Advertiser* was probably about ten dollars a year in an advance lump-sum payment (putting it beyond the means of most working men). Thus, the newspaper proprietor might well be influenced by a sizable group of subscribers who insisted that the paper support Richardson.

19 *Ibid.*, [early February], February 13, [20], 27, 1840; Edgefield *Advertiser*, January 30, 1840.

Because he was busy preparing for court part of the time, Wigfall could not devote as much time to his editorial responsibilities as he would have liked. His greatest concern was that he had no time to write carefully. He was sure that by publishing so hurriedly he was doing credit to his heart at the expense of his head. Even though he wrote anonymously, Wigfall was sure that people would find out the identity of the author, and he wanted to be proud of everything he wrote. But he was willing to make these and even greater sacrifices for Manning, even at the risk of losing some friends and making some enemies. Wigfall's philosophical view of this was that sacrifices had to be made and he who feared for his personal safety or his popularity in the discharge of his duty either to his friends or country was a poor-spirited creature. As for caution, Wigfall said that he had never been accused of possessing it, and that he did not want anyone to accuse him of it then.[20]

Wigfall's lack of caution and tact ("diplomacy was never my forte") had helped increase the animosity between himself and the Brookses during the campaign. But Wigfall did not consider everyone in the opposite political camp to be his personal enemy, and he demonstrated a morality in politics that was on a considerably higher plane than that of some of the Brookses. Scrupulously, he refused to use information which he said was significant and which had been given to him by Hammond before he knew that Wigfall was supporting Richardson. Wigfall could show compassion also. He asked Richardson for mercy for Dr. Maximilian LaBorde, a brother-in-law of Colonel Brooks, who complied with a request to write an article endorsing Hammond. Probably it was LaBorde's politically vulnerable trusteeship at South Carolina College that Wigfall was trying to protect. Whatever the case, Wigfall asked for mercy for him: "LaBorde is a good creature—he has no sense & a large family & nothing to feed them on." Neither was Wigfall hostile toward his cousin Thomas Player, who supported Hammond. Perhaps such scruples, along with his writing and speaking ability, were the reasons why Wig-

20 Wigfall to Manning, February 17, 1840, and [February or March, 1840].

fall was considered a young man of promise even by some of the political opposition, including Pierce Butler, a relative of the Brookses. Many of the Brooks family, however, harbored an acute hatred for Wigfall, who reciprocated with a vengeance. Indeed, it appears that Wigfall's primary objective was to defeat the Brookses—hating them as he did—with "a perfect appetite." [21]

The Wigfall-Brooks hostility extended beyond mere political fronts by March of 1840. Wigfall was sure that the Brooks clan had kept his brother Arthur, who would soon be ordained as an Episcopalian minister, from obtaining a church in Edgefield. Jealousy over a woman may also have stood between Wigfall and Preston Brooks. In a letter to Manning, Wigfall summed up his animosity against the Brookses and fancied how it might be redressed: "We must not be cut out of *our* Governor—if we have been out of our church & I'll try not [to] be out of [a] wife either. If I go to Augusta, . . . make love to la belle Anna—shoot two [Brookses] in the morning—return to Edgefield & gain all my cases[,] do you think she could say No? Would that not be brilliant? Damn me!" [22]

Wigfall soon had a chance to shoot a Brooks—Preston—on the field of honor. As a matter of fact, over a period of five months Wigfall was involved in a fistfight, three near-duels, two duels, and one shooting—all of which left one dead and two, including Wigfall, wounded.

As the political campaign of 1840 became heated, the published charges about Wigfall, made by Preston Brooks and his father Colonel Whitfield Brooks, grew more vicious and personal. Wigfall's publications in the meantime were critical but impersonal, concerned only with political issues. The trigger for violence was Preston Brooks's assertion that Wigfall had called Joseph Glover a coward. Wigfall had had trouble with Glover during the Bacon-Glover duel but had since then come to be on good terms with

21 *Ibid.*, February 11, [1840], March 10, 19, 1840; Maximilian LaBorde to Hammond, July 8, 1840, and Pierce Butler to Hammond, July 2, 6, 8, 1840, both in Hammond Papers; LaBorde, *History of South Carolina College*, v, x, xi.
22 Wigfall to Manning, February 17, March 4, 19, 1840.

him. Wigfall denied saying anything derogatory about Glover since their dispute was settled, and he sent word by Glover back to Brooks that he was a liar. This led to a public confrontation in which Wigfall, according to a friend of his, kept his temper, argued coolly, and gave Brooks a severe tongue-lashing. Then, though Wigfall tried to avoid a fistfight, Brooks assailed him and a scuffle ensued. They parted with the understanding that Brooks was to send a challenge. Wigfall was so anxious to get Brooks onto the field of honor that Thomas Player, Wigfall's cousin, concluded that he had a monomania on dueling. Many southerners considered the practice of dueling to be "wholesome and meritorious," but Wigfall's extreme faith in the *Code Duello* as a governor of morals and manners of a society was at the least fanatical.[23]

Since his brother Arthur, who by that time had been ordained to the Episcopal ministry, opposed dueling, Louis kept news of the coming duel from him as much as possible. Perhaps Arthur was interested in expunging the *Code Duello* as a result of the death of another brother, Hamden. There is a disputed story that Hamden was killed in a duel while a student at South Carolina College. According to histories of the school, however, he simply withdrew in his sophomore year. Perhaps he was killed dueling after he left there.[24]

23 Edgefield *Advertiser*, October 22, 1840; Maxey Gregg to Manning, August 4, 1840; Williams-Chesnut-Manning Collection; J. P. Carroll to Hammond, June 30, 1840, and T. Player to Hammond, July 6, 26, 1840, both in Hammond Papers; Russell, *Diary*, 38; Louise Wigfall Wright (Mrs. D. Giraud Wright, Wigfall's daughter), *A Southern Girl in '61* (New York, 1905), 33. For interpretations of how dueling reflected the romantic spirit of the Old South and how this romanticism could impell southerners to actions in negation of realism, see Clement Eaton, *The Growth of Southern Civilization* (New York, 1961), 2, 275–77; Rollin Osterweiss, *Romanticism and Nationalism in the Old South* (New Haven, 1949); and Charles S. Sydnor, "Southerners and the Laws," *Journal of Southern History*, VI (February, 1940), 1–23.

24 Wigfall to Manning, March 19, 1840; Arthur Wigfall, *Sermon Upon Duelling, Together with the Constitution of the Grahamville Asso. for the Suppression of Duelling* (Charleston, 1856), quoted in Jack Kenny Williams, "The Code of Honor in Ante-Bellum South Carolina," *South Carolina Historical Magazine*, LIV (July, 1953), 122–23; Lord, "Young Louis Wigfall," 104–106; Green, *University of South Carolina*, 286. Trezevant, *Trezevant Family*, 103–104, says that Hamden left the college as a sophomore in 1821–22 and that no further information was available.

Others besides Arthur Wigfall were also interested in preventing the duel. Some of Brook's relatives—including his cousin Pierce M. Butler, who said that the community could not afford to lose one or both of the two promising young men—initiated a move to end the difficulty peaceably and honorably. They succeeded in obtaining a board of honor which included Wade Hampton, Franklin Elmore, and other eminent men of the state. Wigfall and Brooks were already on the field of honor near Limestone Springs for the issuance and acceptance of the challenge when the board of honor intruded and induced them to suspend proceedings until there was an opportunity to effect a reconciliation.[25]

After an investigation the board reported that the abusive language that Brooks had heard Wigfall use about Glover was uttered prior to the reconciliation between Wigfall and Glover, whereas they both had the impression that Brooks meant that the offense had taken place after their adjustment. Thus the board decided that Wigfall's charge that Brooks had lied was no longer applicable. Further, the board recommended that offensive newspaper articles, including certain ones by the elder Brooks, should be mutually withdrawn. Wigfall objected to the interjection of the name of Whitfield Brooks into the settlement, saying that if he was to be included, then *all* of his articles offensive to Wigfall had to be withdrawn. The board agreed to this stipulation and induced Colonel Brooks to consent to the revised report. The conclusion was hardly the one that Wigfall wished, but he felt constrained to accept it, he said, lest he appear bloodthirsty in the eyes of the many South Carolinians who were interested in the settlement. Maxey Gregg, Wigfall's second, wrote to assure Manning that Wigfall's conduct had been "marked by spirit, & a generous moderation." Wigfall was a noble fellow, said Gregg, and he would come out successful in every difficulty.[26]

25 Others of the Brooks family who were involved were A. P. Butler and Maximilian LaBorde. P. M. Butler to Hammond, July 2, 6, 8, 18, 1840; M. LaBorde to Hammond, July 8, 1840; Maxey Gregg to Manning, August 4, 1840; A. P. Butler to Hammond, July 24, 1840, all in Hammond Papers.
26 Edgefield *Advertiser*, July 30, 1840; Gregg to Manning, August 4, 1840, Wil-

Wigfall's difficulties with the Brooks clan were just beginning. While he was in the country awaiting the challenge for the Brooks duel, he was denounced in Edgefield by Brooks's uncle J. P. Carroll for a breach of confidence. According to Carroll, Wigfall had divulged confidential remarks that Carroll had made about congressional candidates while he, Dr. Burt, and Wigfall were drinking freely of wine. Wigfall regarded such matters seriously. Indeed, on an occasion that involved Hammond shortly before this, Wigfall had been quite scrupulous in preserving such a trust. As he left Limestone Springs, he announced his intention of attending to Carroll. Some of the same people who had instigated the previous adjustment induced mutual friends of Wigfall and Carroll to obtain explanations satisfactory to both of them. Thus, this phase of the conflict between Wigfall and the Brooks family also ended with a confrontation.[27]

But Wigfall soon heard that Preston Brooks was saying publicly that his and Wigfall's trouble had been settled by Wigfall's backing down on every issue. Wigfall responded by publishing in the *Advertiser* the Limestone Springs adjustment and his version of how it came about. Preston was out of town, but Colonel Brooks published a scurrilous contradiction of Wigfall's account. Wigfall promptly challenged the colonel to duel. The elder Brooks refused. In keeping with the *Code Duello*, Wigfall then informed the colonel that he would be posted that afternoon as a scoundrel and a coward. Carroll, Brooks's brother-in-law, and Thomas Bird, his young nephew, decided to ask Wigfall to reconsider. When they reached the courthouse, however, they found that Wigfall had already posted the notice and was guarding it. Carroll tore the placard down. Bird, perhaps thinking that Wigfall was about to shoot Carroll, drew a pistol and fired at Wigfall

liams-Chesnut-Manning Collection; Wigfall to A. Burt, July 31, 1840, Armistead Burt Papers, Duke University Library.

27 Carroll to Hammond, July 8, 9, 1840, M. LaBorde to Hammond, July 13, 17, 1840; A. P. Butler to Hammond, July 24, 1840, Hammond Papers; Wigfall to Manning, March 10, 1840; Wigfall to A. Burt, July 31, 1840, Burt Papers; Columbia *South Carolinian*, reprinted in the Edgefield *Advertiser*, August 27, 1840.

but missed. Wigfall then also drew, fired, and missed. But on the second exchange of shots, only Bird missed. He died two days later. As Bird fell, Carroll denounced Wigfall as a cold-blooded murderous scoundrel, whereupon Wigfall immediately challenged him to duel. They were to meet five days later. By that time murder charges had been filed against Wigfall for the killing of Bird. In the meantime Preston Brooks had returned and he also challenged Wigfall, who of course accepted.[28]

Carroll and Wigfall met on an island in the Savannah River near Augusta, Georgia. Both shot with extreme suddenness and missed. Representatives of the protagonists persuaded Carroll to concede that had he not been so excited, he would not have used such abusive language to Wigfall and that they should forget the incident. Wigfall agreed; his main quarrel was with Preston Brooks.[29]

One week later on the same site, Wigfall had his opportunity to face Brooks over pistol sights. Again both duelists missed with their first shots. But rancor ran too deeply for the seconds to effect any adjustment in this controversy. Both felt that blood had to be shed. In the second round of shots both duelists went down wounded, Brooks shot through the hip, Wigfall through the thigh. Only then did they agree to accept arbitration and a published settlement by a board of honor—which was more favorable to Wigfall. He grudgingly announced that he was satisfied. In reality, he was not. He said privately that he had wanted to ruin the entire Brooks family. Probably he would have carried the conflict further, could he have done so without appearing blood-thirsty. Many in the state were already hostile to him for his kill-

28 Edgefield *Advertiser*, October 22, 27, 1840; Columbia, South Carolina, *Southern Chronicle*, November 5, 1840; Wright, *Southern Girl*, 31–32; U. R. Brooks, *South Carolina Bench and Bar* (Columbia, South Carolina, 1887), 106–107; Carroll to Hammond, November 1, 7, 1840, Hammond Papers; Wigfall to Manning, April 25, 1841.

29 Carroll to Hammond, November 7, 1840, Hammond Papers; "Articles of Agreement to Govern a Meeting of Honor Between Messrs. Carroll and Wigfall," (n.d.) in Williams-Chesnut-Manning Collection; Augusta, Georgia, *Chronicle and Sentinel*, reprinted in Edgefield *Advertiser*, November 12, 1840.

ing of Thomas Bird, even though a grand jury had returned a
"No Bill" decision and the Court of General Sessions had dismissed the charge of murder in March, 1841.[30]

It would not be surprising if many people had lost interest in
the gubernatorial campaign during all the shooting. Wigfall did.
He contributed little to the newspaper campaign after July, 1840,
while he was involved in the more violent aspects of politics. The
actual election was rather anticlimactic. Richardson was the one-
sided choice of the legislature in the December election. Hammond got his turn as governor the following term. And for the
term after that, the governor was Colonel Brooks. Other prin-
cipals in the 1840 election who later became governors of South
Carolina were Manning, Pickens, and Hampton. The election of
Governor Brooks is an indication of Wigfall's failure to ruin the
family as he had wanted. Furthermore, his special nemesis, Preston Brooks, was later elected as Edgefield District's representative to the United States Congress where he gained notoriety for
his caning of Massachusetts Senator Charles Sumner on the floor
of the Senate in 1854. It was perhaps necessary for Brooks to
carry the cane because of the hip wound he suffered in his duel
with Wigfall.

For his services, Wigfall was appointed aide-de-camp with the
rank of lieutenant colonel on Governor Richardson's staff, but
this was small payment for what his first essay into politics and
his first, and last, newspaper editing had cost him. Professionally
and financially, he was nearly ruined. The social standing which
he had built so proudly was greatly diminshed. The hostile atmosphere, generated mostly from his killing of Bird, was so intense that it helped induce Wigfall to leave his beloved South
Carolina and move to Texas in 1846. But even there he could not
escape his past. Years later, on the plains of Texas, he "saw" Tom
Bird. Other ghosts of these violent years rose to haunt Wigfall
throughout his life.[31]

30 Augusta *Chronicle and Sentinel,* reprinted in Edgefield *Advertiser,* November
12, 1840; Wigfall to Manning, April 25, 28, 1841; M. L. Bonham to Hammond,
June 15, 1841; Carroll to Hammond, June 12, 1841, both in Hammond Papers.
31 J. W. DuBose, *The Life and Times of William Lowndes Yancey* (Birmingham,

Wigfall's reputation as a violent man grew out of proportion to fact in his later years. He did nothing to embellish nor discourage these false stories about himself, but capitalized upon his purported "willingness to shoot people who disagreed with him," using it as a bluff to intimidate many political opponents and critics, who were fearful of triggering Wigfall's temper and bringing his pistols into play. This is probably why one recent historian said that "Wigfall had wounded or killed eight dueling opponents." [32] Actually he wounded only one, Preston Brooks. The one man Wigfall killed, Thomas Bird, died not in a duel but as a consequence of a challenge.

His duel with Preston Brooks was Wigfall's last, but he remained a firm believer in the *Code Duello* as a factor in the improvement of both the morals and the manners of a community. Holding that it engendered courtesy in both speech and manner, he continued to encourage his friends to abide by the code. He urged one friend, John Cunningham, to duel a man by the name of McGowan. Wigfall seemed to delight in telling how he served as second to Cunningham, arranging for the weapons (rifles) and the number of paces, *etc.* He went into a particularly detailed description of how the rifle ball entered McGowan's ear and how the lower part of his skull was "much fractured." But he would recover, said Wigfall, and the duel had done much to raise Cunningham's prestige.[33]

Dueling had not raised Wigfall's reputation in any sense acceptable to the community. Soon after his confrontation with the Brookses, he moaned that the cursed family had cost him more than they were worth. Wigfall's involvement in publishing feuds, his preoccupation with honorable settlements, the public resentment over his killing of Bird, and the period of incapacitation while recuperating from his wound had virtually demolished his law practice. In October, 1841, a year from the time he had killed

Alabama, 1892), 676; D. C. Ray to C. W. Lord, June 9, 1925, and M. L. Bonham to C. W. Lord, May 18, 1925, cited in Lord, "Young Louis Wigfall," 112.

[32] W. A. Swanberg, *First Blood: The Story of Fort Sumter* (New York, 1957), 110.
[33] Wright, *Southern Girl*, 33; Wigfall to A. Burt, April 7, 1844, Burt Papers.

Tom Bird, Wigfall returned to court. Although still weak, he believed that physically he had recovered entirely.

Financially, however, it would be many years before he recovered from his irresponsibility. It was not until he was about to be married that he began to give much thought to his finances. Then he had to admit that he had been exceedingly careless with money and had gone in debt much more than he had realized. He found that after paying for a house and furniture in preparation for his marriage, with all the money he had and all that he would get by his marriage, he would still owe over $1,300. Four hundred dollars of that, Wigfall had borrowed from Manning over the previous eighteen months. The other $900 Wigfall said he could arrange with people who would wait with him.[34]

His wife-to-be, Charlotte Cross, knew his situation and seemed perfectly willing to live according to their means. But her willingness made the necessity that much more bitter to him. He had, he said, suffered much from sickness, but much more from anxiety of mind. Wigfall knew who was to blame:

> I seek no sympathies nor need
> The thorns which I have reaped of the tree
> *I planted*—they have torn me and I bleed—
> I should have known what fruit would spring
> from such a seed.[35]

Wigfall's problems prevented his making many arrangements for his wedding. About all that he had time and energy to do was to prepare himself for the wearisome trip to the home of his bride in Providence, Rhode Island, where the wedding took place in November, 1841. In Manning's collection of letters there are none in which Wigfall mentions his betrothed, that is, nothing about Charlotte Cross specifically. He had, however, in a letter written nearly three years earlier, generalized about what kind of wife he wanted, and Charlotte fitted the description of this dream wife remarkably well. Wigfall had said that if he

34 Wigfall to Manning, July 22, October 17, 24, 1841.
35 Lord Byron, *Childe Harold*, canto IV, stanza 10, quoted in Wigfall to Manning, July 22, 1841.

married, he would want some woman who had been reared in the "same circle" with himself. Charlotte Cross, Wigfall's second cousin on the Trezevant side, was from a wealthy family in Rhode Island and had spent much time in Charleston. He declared that his wife would have to be not a mistress to him, but a companion and a friend. Judging by his comments and by the observations from family friends, Charlotte was of inestimable value to her husband. She exerted a moderating influence upon his social life, and was probably responsible for his having no more duels after he married. His marriage only cut down rather than ended his drinking, but there is not even a hint that she ever scolded him for it. Charlotte Wigfall had no moderating influence upon his imprudent expression of political views, however. Indeed, she evidently had the same views and characteristics. Their children also displayed this Wigfall frankness. Some, but not everyone, found this an admirable family trait.[36]

Wigfall said that his wife should also be intelligent and well educated, a woman who could speak English and *"feel poetry."* Again Charlotte fulfilled the requirements, proving capable of supplementing her children's education and holding her own among her social clique in Washington and Confederate society, which included Mary Chesnut.

A necessary but difficult test for any prospective Mrs. Wigfall was that she had to "admire" her husband. Charlotte seems never to have lost respect for her husband, not even in the tribulations during their early marriage or during the still darker days that came with the collapse of the Confederacy. Thus, she met another of her husband's early specifications; she was a woman who could share both poverty and honor.

Once, in early 1839, Wigfall cheered himself by taking time out from his studies for the bar examination to dream of how happy he might be in his ideal marriage. He related this dream

---

36 Wigfall to Manning, February 22, [1839], April 19, 1841; Trezevant, *Trezevant Family,* 104; T. C. DeLeon, *Belles, Beaux and Brains of the Sixties* (New York, 1907), 152–53; Wright, *Southern Girl,* 33; Russell, *Diary,* 62–63; Chesnut, *Diary,* 106.

to his alter ego, John Manning: "I'll build a comfortable little house & get me a pretty wife. . . . And then I'll have a spare room for my friend & his lady & when they come I'll . . . introduce them to *my* lady & show them a pretty little boy . . . & when they ask him what his name is he shall answer 'John Manning Wigfall, Sir.' Ma foi! I'll be a happy fellow yet!" [37] Once Wigfall thought his dream was being realized. But it degenerated into a nightmare in which his home was sold at an insolvent debtor's sale, and his curly-haired son John Manning Wigfall was dead at the age of three.

One reason Wigfall was not able to pay his debts as he had hoped, was because of medical expenses for his son. Wigfall had built up his law practice slightly, and brought in some additional income by "riding circuit," following a mobile court around the country. But this was not enough. His son had been afflicted with "a most distressing disease of the skin" since he was two weeks old. Dr. Burt could do nothing to relieve the boy, and he advised Wigfall to try the effect of salt air. Charlotte and the baby stayed in Charleston for several months but to no avail.[38]

Wigfall hoped that the settlement of his father-in-law's estate would bring enough to placate his creditors, but it did not. Frantically he tried to make some arrangement that would relieve him of his embarrassment. But even Manning refused to take up a note for Wigfall when he could not make the payments. He thought again, more seriously, of moving to the West for a new start. Texas looked inviting to Wigfall, but he decided that he could and should build a successful life in South Carolina.[39]

Wigfall tried desperately to get a mortgage on his property in Edgefield which would pay enough to prevent its being sold to satisfy debts. He did succeed in borrowing a little money from

[37] Wigfall to Manning, February 22, [1839].
[38] *Ibid.*, April 19, 1843.
[39] *Ibid.*, July 29, October 1, December 15, 1843. In 1846, at the time Wigfall lost all of his possessions for nonpayment of debt, Manning established a South Carolina College scholarship which he secured by depositing in the bank the sum of $5,000. See Green, *University of South Carolina*, 305. If Wigfall knew of the scholarship, he did not mention it in his correspondence. But his letters to Manning became fewer and less personal after that.

William Yancey, and his practice was improving, but he had another mouth to feed. Another son, Francis Halsey Wigfall, was
born in November, 1845. Wigfall succeeded only in delaying,
not preventing, the realization of his fears. In a series of three
sheriff's sales in May, June, and July of 1846, the Wigfalls lost
virtually everything they had. Part of that time Wigfall was in
the custody of the sheriff for nonpayment of debt as suits were
being brought by some of his creditors. The family possessions
that were sold at ridiculously low prices included their home,
carriage, three horses, four slaves, piano, guitar, music books, and
even their child's chair, wagon, and crib. After the sale of his
property, there were still unsatisfied debts against Wigfall. These
were legally marked off as *Nulla Bona*.[40]

Even though his debts were more severe than ever, and his
small son was dying, Wigfall became more interested in politics
than before. As a delegate to the state Democratic convention
he helped draw up resolutions for the campaign of 1844. To the
South Carolina delegates the paramount question of the times
was the addition of Texas to the Union. In their resolutions they
concluded that grounds upon which annexation was being resisted compelled them to consider the annexation of Texas as
necessary to the maintenance of slavery which was guaranteed to
them by the Constitution. Wigfall spoke at the convention in
support of the resolution and for James K. Polk, the Democratic
nominee for President, but mostly he spoke against Henry Clay,
the Whig candidate, and his high-tariff policy.[41]

Like most South Carolinians, Wigfall was strongly opposed
to the protective tariff. His creed, he said, was the last two pages
of George McDuffie's speech in the United States Senate in re-

40 Wigfall to Manning, September 7, 1839, January 3, 1844, June 25, 1845; Wigfall to Yancey, July 20, 1864, University of North Carolina Archives; Wigfall to
A. Burt, December 8, 1845, Burt Papers; Edgefield *Advertiser*, July 7–October 7,
1846. The description, price, and name of the buyer of the Wigfall property fills
eleven double-spaced typed pages when transcribed. See Sale Book T., 159, 161–68,
April 10, June 6, 1846, in Sheriff's Office, Edgefield Court House; and Deed Book
EEE, 62, Clerk of Court's Office.
41 Edgefield *Advertiser*, June 5, 1844; Wigfall to Manning, n.d., but *ca.* June,
1844.

ply to protectionists' arguments. In the speech to which Wigfall referred, Senator McDuffie expounded the standard southern arguments of the supremacy of their civilization—Negro slavery, agriculture, and natural resources—over the northerners' manufacturing and wage slavery. Claiming that he never felt the national government but by its oppressions, McDuffie threatened that unless there was a speedy adjustment of the tariff the Union would soon be shaken to its foundations.[42]

It was because of the tariff issue that Wigfall first lost faith in Polk. In a letter written for the benefit of Democratic protectionists in Pennsylvania, Polk indicated that he might equivocate on the tariff. While political leaders in South Carolina looked upon Polk's letter as campaign propaganda, Wigfall was extremely excited and seemed convinced that all Edgefield was equally so. While in Charleston he told Franklin Elmore that Edgefield would denounce Polk and begin agitation for immediate action by the state. Elmore doubted that and wrote to Calhoun that Wigfall was too much inclined for such a course to be a good judge of what others thought about it.[43] This was so and proved to be true of Wigfall in a number of instances.

Soon Calhoun heard even more disquieting news about Wigfall. Francis Pickens informed the senator that reports were circulating that the Nullifiers might lose South Carolina because of the actions of some of their friends there. Pickens pointed specifically to Wigfall, who was saying that Robert Barnwell Rhett, editor of the Charleston *Mercury*, had split from Calhoun because he had been bought off by the promise of the presidency. And furthermore, Wigfall was openly for disunion, Pickens reported to Calhoun, whose hope was that sectional

42 Wigfall to A. Burt, April 7, 1844, Burt Papers; Senator George McDuffie, "Speech on the Tariff in Reply to Messrs. Evans and Huntington," January 19, 1844 in *Miscellaneous Pamphlets Pertaining to United States History from 1828–1858* (Washington, 1844), No. 54, pp. 10–11.

43 F. H. Elmore to Calhoun, July 30, 1844, in Chauncey S. Boucher and Robert P. Brooks, "Correspondence Addressed to John C. Calhoun, 1837–1849," *Annual Report of the American Historical Association, 1929* (Washington, 1930), 242–43.

problems could be solved by resorting to nothing more serious than nullification.[44]

Wigfall, about sixteen years ahead of the majority of South Carolinians, was an avid secessionist by 1844. And, as Elmore said, he was so much inclined that way that he thought everyone else should be also. His secessionist speeches, however, met with some sharp criticism by relative moderates. A month before the election of 1844, Wigfall instructed his militia unit upon the issues of the times. Some critics attacked the speech, saying that he should speak more against the tariff and less for disunion. But Wigfall found some support: "Many Officers of the Seventh Regiment" wrote a letter, published in the Edgefield *Advertiser*, in defense of their commander. Wigfall's speech, they said, was one of intrinsic merit, and one that embodied in forcible language those "principles which for the last eighteen or twenty years it has been the pride of South Carolina . . . to cherish." [45]

There was such a controversy over just what Wigfall had said that it gave him an opportunity to publish his speech in the *Advertiser*. He made it clear at the outset of his address that he had only the smallest interest in the election of 1844. This was because, regardless of what the Whigs and Democrats said, neither party would redress the wrongs perpetrated upon South Carolina. They would not lower the tariff, nor would they work to annex Texas. And the slave states needed Texas for the increase in the slave population. The excess slaves could not stay in the older states, Wigfall declared, because they could not support them. If new slave territory were not added, it would not be long, ten to twenty years, before slaveowners were forced to free their slaves. Northerners would claim, said Wigfall, that slaveowners would have no more right to complain than a thief who was forced to give up stolen goods. But Wigfall took refuge from such a charge in an old southern saw: If southerners owned

44 Pickens to Calhoun, August 10, 1844, *ibid.*, 243.
45 Letter of "Many Officers of the Seventh Regiment," in Edgefield *Advertiser*, September 11, 1844.

stolen property, the fathers of their northern brothers were thieves. Wigfall piously thanked God that South Carolina was never engaged in the slave trade.[46]

In the same letter, Wigfall raised other questions important to southerners: "When our negroes are free, of what use would our land be to us?" That was not all. If the Negro population, at least equal in number to the white, were freed, would they, the blacks, Wigfall asked, "be willing to live amongst us, deprived of all civil rights?" If they would, would northerners permit it? Wigfall insisted they would not. One of the peculiarities of the people of the North, as Wigfall saw it, was impertinent meddling; therefore, he warned his fellow South Carolinians, they would be forced to vote with their Negroes and to sit with them in the legislature—or to exterminate them. He bluntly stated that if Texas were not admitted into the Union and if the protective tariff were continued, Carolinians would be forced first to free their Negroes and then fight them within twenty-five years.[47]

There was no question in Wigfall's mind that the South had to keep the institution of slavery. But this conviction apparently did not arise from any idea that the South had the cheapest labor system. This was disclosed by his efforts to impose his views of secession upon those southerners who wanted manufacturing established in their section. The South could not manufacture without protection against the North, argued Wigfall, because both capital and *labor* were cheaper there.[48] Furthermore, northerners had the advantage of superior skill and experience. Again the alternatives were clear to Wigfall, and this is the point at which he was driving: unless southerners were ready to dissolve the Union, they had to give up the idea of manufacturing.[49]

[46] Louis Wigfall, "Answer to the Letter of Many Officers of the Seventh Regiment," in Edgefield *Advertiser*, September 25, 1884.

[47] *Ibid.*; see also, Wigfall to A. Burt, April 7, 1846, Burt Papers.

[48] If Wigfall's "Creed," as voiced by McDuffie, embraced the senator's statement that "the labor of African slaves . . . is the cheapest labor in the world for its efficiency . . .," he contradicted himself. This could be partially reconciled if Wigfall thought that slave labor could not be used efficiently in factories.

[49] Wigfall, "Answer to the Letter of Many Officers of the Seventh Regiment."

What was to be done? Wigfall pondered the course that some southerners were talking about—united southern action, or "The Bluffton Movement," launched by a handful of secessionists who hoped to arrange a convention of delegates from all the slave states in order to promote a united front of southerners to dissolve the Union rather than abandon Texas. This aroused much opposition from moderates and unionists, and the movement would soon fail. Wigfall reviewed the possibilities of such a program at its outset and announced his conclusion that it would not work. Those who talked of such united action, he said, forgot that other southern states did not dislike the tariff as much as South Carolina did, nor were they so interested in Texas as Carolinians were.[50] South Carolina had to act independently.

But act how? Wigfall confessed his decided preference for secession over nullification. There were, he said, many reasons which might be urged for this preference, but he contented himself with mentioning just one—his belief that secession would be more likely to prove peaceable than would nullification. In answer to any charge of being a disunionist, Wigfall replied: "I love the Union, I believe, . . . as much as it loves me, or those amongst whom I live. Let those feel horrified who please at this sentiment. 'The sacredness of the Union' and 'the divine right of kings' are arguments invariably resorted to when tyranny becomes so intolerable that no others can be urged." And who had consecrated the Union? Wigfall asked. He answered that not one drop of martyrs' blood had been shed for the Union; it was "for liberty our fathers bled," and union came long after liberty was achieved. If South Carolinians surrendered liberty for the sake of union, then they were blind fools.[51]

In a dual purpose effort to buttress his argument that secession was more likely to prove peaceful than nullification, and to

---

Wigfall wanted not only manufacturing, but also a strong merchant marine. Wigfall to A. Burt, April 7, 1846, Burt Papers.

[50] Wigfall, "Answer to the Letter of Many Officers of the Seventh Regiment"; *Niles Register*, LXVI (March–September, 1844), has an account of the united South movement of this time.

[51] Wigfall, "Answer to the Letter of Many Officers of the Seventh Regiment."

undermine allegiance to the Union, Wigfall called to the attention of his readers and listeners the nullification crisis of 1832–33. How could he, asked Wigfall, forget seeing the Union flag floating over the arsenal at Augusta, Georgia, where federal regiments were assembled for the purpose of invading their own district and destroying their homes? [52] But not many people other than the "many officers" agreed with Wigfall. His solutions were too drastic for the 1840's, even for South Carolina.

Despite his continued preference for secession rather than nullification, and although he was outside Calhoun's circle of intimates, Wigfall respected the Carolina senator's political views and opposition to the Whigs. Beside their basic agreement on states' rights and the problems of the South, Calhoun's and Wigfall's notions about the Oregon and Texas problems were quite similar. Before the outbreak of the Mexican War, Wigfall said he would regard a war over Texas (with Mexico) or Oregon (with Great Britain) as the most unfortunate event to befall the South. Like Calhoun, he feared that a war would agitate the slavery question and would bring a heavy national debt which would be an excuse for protectionists to raise the tariff. Furthermore, Wigfall believed that a war with Great Britain would decrease southern cotton sales to the English, and they would probably start cultivating cotton in their eastern empire. Moreover, such a war might allow Great Britain, who had abolished slavery in her empire, to make war on slavery in the South. In such a case, Wigfall was sure, the northern Abolitionists would join with the British in attacking the South. [53]

Nevertheless, Wigfall feared that a war with Great Britain was inevitable someday because of her aggression and avowal to produce emancipation throughout the world. He was anxious to postpone this as long as possible, however, and thus hoped for a peaceable settlement of the Oregon question. He said, two years before the treaty actually came about, there never was a more

[52] *Ibid.*
[53] Wigfall to A. Burt, April 7, 1844, Burt Papers; Margaret L. Coit, *John C. Calhoun: American Portrait* (Boston, Sentry Books, 1961), 439–44, 447.

propitious time to make a settlement. And while some individual Democrats were talking of challenging Great Britain with the slogan of "54°40' or fight!" (thus including in their Oregon claim a strip of Canada along the Pacific coast to the southern tip of Alaska), Wigfall counseled a moderate course—compromise along the 49°. After Polk was elected, he did compromise at the 49°, as he had probably intended all along.[54]

The conflict over Texas was not settled so peaceably, and it caused a small rift between the senator and Wigfall. To Calhoun, the Mexican War was one of aggression by the United States. Wigfall, however, had changed his mind after the war started. At an Edgefield Democratic Party meeting to consider support of the Mexican War, he spoke in favor of the war, but he also took advantage of a frail opportunity to defend Calhoun. Francis Pickens' resolutions approving of the Mexican war as a means of protecting the rights of Americans and annexing Texas were adopted unanimously and contained no mention of Calhoun. One delegate, however, in speaking for the resolutions, took the opportunity to criticize Calhoun for his failure to speak out in favor of the war. Another delegate, J. Abney, thought that everyone there except the critic regretted the attack, but only Wigfall spoke out. Instead of merely replying to Calhoun's censor, Wigfall assailed the resolutions and, in a scathing oration, offered a resolution praising Calhoun, seeing "nothing to condemn and everything to approve" in his actions.[55]

Abney was sure that if a simple resolution complimenting Calhoun had been offered without any speech by Wigfall, it would have passed instantly. Those present refused to pass Wigfall's resolution, although he argued for it with great ability, said Abney, because of the spirit and temper in which Wigfall offered the resolution. Another delegate described Wigfall's resolution as a firebrand thrown in to disturb the harmony of the meeting.[56]

54 Wigfall to A. Burt, April 7, 1884, Burt Papers.
55 J. Abney to A. Burt, June 6, 1846, Burt Papers; resolution in the Hamburg *Journal*, June 3, 1846, reprinted in Edgefield *Advertiser*, June 10, 1846.
56 Abney to Burt, June 6, 1846, Burt Papers; Hamburg *Journal*, June 3, 1846, reprinted in Edgefield *Advertiser*, June 10, 1846. W. P. Brett of Edgefield testi-

It is difficult to see what good effect Wigfall hoped to produce unless it was an improvement in his relations with Calhoun.

Through Armistead Burt, Wigfall advised Calhoun that more opposition would develop against him if he continued to oppose the war. Although he did not take Wigfall's advice, Calhoun's counsel was sought by Wigfall. Even after he had left the state, he hopefully asked Calhoun if he could not persuade South Carolina to strike the first blow to rally the South.[57] Twelve years later it did.

Wigfall loved South Carolina, but he fell into two categories of migrants to Texas—those who were in debt and those who had killed someone. Not that he was escaping legal prosecution for either—his bankruptcy had satisfied the law, but not all of his creditors; the grand jury had exonerated him of any guilt in his killing of Tom Bird—but the community had not forgiven him.

While Wigfall was urging annexation of Texas, he was probably considering the possibility of going there. At least twice during earlier difficult times he had thought of moving to Texas. In 1839 he said that if he decided to leave South Carolina—nothing but the direst necessity would ever cause him to do so—he would be a candidate for the South Carolina legislature before he left. He thought it would be easy to be elected, and it would, he said, give a young man in a new state some reputation to have been a South Carolina legislator. Wigfall hoped, however, to be able to pay his debts and stay in the Palmetto State. But if not, he would go west, "Texas perhaps." In 1843, however, when his reputation had been ruined, his financial problems had become acute, and his son ill, Wigfall spoke to his wife and three of his

---

fied over a year later that Wigfall changed his mind in regard to Calhoun's course and said in the presence of Pickens and others that Calhoun should have voted for the war. Deposition of Brett, October 9, 1847, in F. P. Pickens Papers, Duke University Library.

57 Wigfall to A. Burt, July 7, 1846, Burt Papers; Wigfall to Calhoun, June 10, 1848, January 4, 1849, in Boucher and Brooks, "Correspondence Addressed to Calhoun," 440–41, 493–95; Calhoun to Thomas G. Clemson, January 30, 1847, in J. Franklin Jameson (ed.), "Correspondence of John C. Calhoun," *Annual Report of the American Historical Association, 1899* (Washington, 1900), II, 717; Crallé, *Works of Calhoun*, IV, 413, 420.

closest friends of moving west, this time without raising the possibility of first being elected to the legislature.[58] By 1846 his problems were worse, his older son was dead, any possibility of a political career in South Carolina was ruined, and Texas, the new frontier state, was more attractive than ever. He decided to move.

Wigfall had contacts in Texas who could help him. His cousin James Hamilton, who had been governor of South Carolina, had moved to Texas some years earlier. Hamilton saw great potential in the Lone Star Republic and wrote to the President of Texas of a desire to attract other people to come. It may have been Hamilton who arranged Wigfall's move to Texas. Hamilton did arrange a law partnership for his cousin with a promising young attorney named William B. Ochiltree in Nacogdoches before Wigfall left South Carolina.[59]

Sometime in the early fall of 1846, less than a year after Texas had been admitted as a state to the Union and about a year before the Mexican War was concluded, Wigfall boarded a ship bound for Galveston. Probably Charlotte and little Halsey did not go with him but went instead to stay with Mrs. Wigfall's parents in Providence, Rhode Island. There, in April of the next year, the Wigfall's first daughter, Louise Sophie, was born. Soon afterward, however, the Wigfall family was united in Texas for their fresh start in a new state.[60]

[58] Wigfall to Manning, February 22, [1839], December 15, 1843.

[59] J. Hamilton to President Mirabeau B. Lamar, December 3, 1840, in Lamar Papers, V, 452, Texas State Library; Galveston *News*, February 19, 1874. Another of Wigfall's cousins, James Hamilton Trezevant, was already a successful lawyer there, probably in the Richmond, Texas, area and was elected to the Texas Legislature in 1847. Trezevant, *Trezevant Family*, 34–35.

[60] Galveston *News*, February 19, 1874; United States Census, 7th Census, 1850, microfilm in University of Texas Archives. Perhaps it was to give him a greater sense of starting anew, or to make it sound more aristocratic, that he changed the spelling of his name from "Lewis" to "Louis." Book L, 531, State of Texas, Harrison County Clerk's Office, Harrison County Court House, April 27, 1853.

Chapter III

To Preserve
the Union—of 1787

RAPID CHANGES had come about in Texas in the twenty-five years before Louis Wigfall arrived there in 1846. Successively a Spanish territory, a Mexican territory and part of a state, and an independent republic, Texas had come into the Union only the previous year. Still greater transformations were to come for the Lone Star State in the fifteen years before civil war. About the time that Wigfall moved there, the population, including slaves, was only 135,000. By 1860 the number of Texans had more than quadrupled—to over 604,000. Since most of the immigrants were from the older southern states, they brought with them their ingrained attitudes and social institutions, including slavery. It was only gradually, however, that the majority of Texans were forced to pay attention to the sectional dispute that was raging to the north and east of them. Despite frontier conditions Texas was a relatively prosperous state in the 1840's and 1850's, and Texans were generally apathetic to divisive sectional issues. Jacksonian nationalists such as Sam Houston were more listened to than were sectionalists such as Wigfall. During the mid-1850's, however, Texans began to feel threatened. Seizing the opportunity, Wigfall led strident extremists in "alerting" Texans to the dangers about to beset them. Gradually, the din of fire-eating sectionalism overpowered even the most persistent voices of nationalism.

Even the politically ambitious Wigfall had to pay some attention to the mundane matter of earning a living. If he were truly going to start over and stay out of debt, he had to turn his attention to the practice of law. Grudgingly he did so; it was over a year, in early 1848, before he became active in organized politics.

Both of Wigfall's law partners, William B. Ochiltree and Thomas J. Jennings, were active in state affairs. Jennings served as attorney general of Texas from 1852 through 1856. Ochiltree was even more widely known. He held several offices in the government of the republic, and about the time that Wigfall arrived in Texas was making an unsuccessful bid for Congress as a Whig candidate. It was hardly to be expected that Wigfall, who was becoming an active and vocal Democrat, would long remain partners with an active Whig. Soon after coming to Nacogdoches, Wigfall moved to Marshall and established his own law office.[1] The rapidly growing town, seat of Harrison county, on the northeastern border of the state, was the homebase for Texans advocating states' rights and a strict interpretation of the Constitution. Most of the residents in the county were slaveowning cotton farmers who had moved there from the older South. During the decade before the Civil War, Harrison had more slaves than any other county in Texas. And again, as in South Carolina, the white population of Wigfall's home county was outnumbered slightly by slaves. On the eve of the war Harrison was not only one of the largest counties (1,500 square miles), it was the third most populous and one of the wealthiest in Texas.[2]

Wigfall's reputation as an attorney grew rapidly and soon spread beyond the county. His place in the legal profession was secured by his ability and knowledge despite his begrudging attention to his practice. Soon he was in demand as a trial lawyer

---

1 Wigfall to Calhoun, June 10, 1848, in Boucher and Brooks "Correspondence Addressed to John C. Calhoun, 1837–1849," pp. 440–41; Wigfall to O. M. Roberts, in Oran Milo Roberts Papers, University of Texas Archives; Wright, *Southern Girl*, 20; Galveston *News*, February 19, 1874.

2 Walter Prescott Webb and H. Bailey Carroll (eds.), *Handbook of Texas* (Austin, 1952), II, 148; Wright, *Southern Girl*, 11; *Texas Almanac for 1857* (Galveston, 1856), 69–70.

over all of East Texas. Indeed, in the estimation of a contemporary, William Pitt Ballinger, Wigfall was a great lawyer. One young attorney said that he heard Ballinger state to Samuel F. Miller, a Justice of the United States Supreme Court, that Miller had never had a lawyer before him who was intellectually superior to Louis T. Wigfall, nor one better prepared to present an able argument upon any question of law.[3]

Wigfall's success as a lawyer, however, did not terminate his financial problems. In March and November of 1848 he borrowed a total of $548 from a William R. Smith of Galveston. In 1853 he had enough cash to buy 388 acres of land near Marshall. But unprofitable investments in railroads drained his resources, and he was again plagued by creditors. Two years after he bought it, Wigfall lost the land for nonpayment of debts.[4] He was never again solvent for more than a few weeks at a time.

Wigfall's first concern was politics, not law or investments. Probably as he expected, he arrived in Texas in time to help organize the Democratic Party there. Although the Democrats dominated the first legislature of the state (1845–47), holding 55 of 86 seats, it was not because they were organized but because they were less disorganized than was their opposition. As reflected in their representation in the first state legislature, the opposition was made up of four Whigs, four Jeffersonian Republicans, two Tyler men, one each of various descriptions such as a Polk man, a Tariff man, an Anti-Tariff man, a Locofoco, a Nullifier, a Texan, and fourteen "undefined." [5]

In 1846, before Wigfall arrived, there was an effort by some Texas Democrats to organize their party. Both Whigs and Democrats held state conventions that year and from time to time

3 Norman Goree Kittrell, *Governors Who Have Been, and Other Public Men of Texas* (Houston, 1921), 149–50. Perhaps the value of Judge Ballinger's testimony is enhanced by the fact that he had never been a Democrat and had opposed the secession of Texas. Webb and Caroll (eds.), *Handbook of Texas*, I, 104, 780; see also Wigfall to O. M. Roberts, December 9, 1841, in Roberts Papers; Executive Records, III, No. 277, p. 385, in the Texas State Library.

4 Book A, 441; Book O, 382, District Court Records, County Clerk's Office, Harrison County Court House, Marshall, Texas.

5 Austin, *Texas Democrat*, May 20, 1846.

thereafter, but with insignificant results until the mid-1850's. Politics were largely personal until this time. Most Texans were Democrats and felt no need to organize, for they felt no threat from other political parties and they had no interest in national politics until then. It was probably not at all difficult for Wigfall to become a leader in the Democratic Party. He attended a Galveston County Democratic meeting in February, 1848, at which time he was named chairman of the committee on resolutions. As chairman he presented and defended the committee's resolutions before the convention.[6]

These resolutions, concerned primarily with the sectional storm fomented by the Wilmot Proviso, reflected the attitude that Wigfall professed continually for the rest of his life. The Proviso had grown out of the prospect of acquiring territory as a result of the Mexican War. David Wilmot, an antislavery Democratic representative from Pennsylvania, added a stipulation to a Polk Administration bill for $2 million to facilitate territorial negotiations with Mexico. If accepted, this Proviso would have prohibited the existence of slavery in any part of any territory acquired from Mexico. Wilmot's bill precipitated a far-reaching debate on the issue of whether Congress had constitutional authority to prohibit slavery in the territories.

The resolutions formulated by Wigfall's five-man committee and passed by the Galveston Convention in 1848 reiterated the southern argument. In his defense of the resolutions, Wigfall explained the nature of the "federal" government, denying that it was "national." The Constitution was, he said, a creation not of the people but of the states. The Constitution was, therefore, a compact entered into by the states. The federal government was not a party to the compact but was rather a creation of it, an agent of the states. It was created with specific powers for specific purposes—which did not include the authority to abolish

6 *Ibid.*, April 15, 1846; Rupert Norval Richardson, *Texas: The Lone Star State* (New York, 1943), 175; the Houston *Telegraph and Texas Register*, January 20, 1855; Anna Irene Sandbo, "Beginnings of the Secession Movement in Texas," *Southwestern Historical Quarterly*, XVIII (July, 1914), 44; Galveston *News*, October 30, 1855.

slavery in the territories. The Wilmot Proviso was therefore unconstitutional.[7]

Furthermore, since he believed all territories of the United States belonged to all the states for their common use, Wigfall repudiated squatter sovereignty—the moderate concept of allowing the people of a territory to decide for themselves if their territory would allow slavery. Until a territory became a state, he argued, *no* agency had any authority to keep citizens and their property (slaves) from entering. When the territory became a state, it could, if it chose, prohibit slavery. There was, then, said Wigfall, no such thing as squatter sovereignty. And southerners could not trust any northerner, not even northern Democrats, who accepted squatter sovereignty. Indeed, Wigfall doubted that southerners could trust any northerner on any issue.[8]

Still, not many Texans were interested in such matters in 1848. It was not until the mid-1850's that they became concerned. It was then that the 1848 Galveston resolutions and Wigfall's speeches were reprinted and circulated. Had it not been for the lack of political organization in Texas in the late 1840's, it is doubtful that Wigfall could have vaulted into a position of leadership so soon, if at all. To some he was simply the most rabid states' rights man in the Lone Star State. But to others he was gaining a reputation as the clearest expounder of the doctrines of John Calhoun.[9]

According to what he wrote to Calhoun, Wigfall relied upon the Old Nullifier's views and wanted to get them directly. He needed them, he said, to govern his course, especially in regard to the 1848 election. In Wigfall's own estimation, Lewis Cass, the Democratic candidate, was objectionable because of his support of squatter sovereignty. But the Whig candidate, Zachary Taylor, was dangerous because his views on that issue were unknown.

[7] Galveston *News*, October 30, 1855; *Texas Republican*, December 24, 1859.

[8] *Texas Republican*, December 24, 1859.

[9] Charles William Ramsdell, *Reconstruction in Texas* (New York, 1910), 13; Francis Richard Lubbock, *Memoirs: Six Decades in Texas* ... (Austin, 1900), 258; Sandbo, "Beginnings of the Secession Movement in Texas," 45–46; *Texas Republican*, December 24, 1859.

Was there anything to hope for from Taylor, Wigfall inquired of Calhoun.[10] Neither could Calhoun accept Cass or Taylor. He proposed that South Carolina boycott the 1848 election and take the lead in organizing a "Southern Party" to insist upon slavery in the territories. If they could not get it, then perhaps they should secede. This eventually culminated in the Nashville Convention of 1850. Nevertheless, Texas Democrats in their first national convention sent delegates pledged to support Cass, and Texas went for Cass, giving him 10,688 votes to 4,509 for Taylor.

Soon after the election, Wigfall sent Calhoun a copy of resolutions adopted at a public meeting in Marshall. These state sovereignty resolutions simply called public attention to southern rights under the Constitution and attacked Senator Houston and President James K. Polk for not defending those rights, but Wigfall used this as a "pulse" to conclude that *all* Texans were ready to hazard as much for the United States Constitution as they had for the Mexican Constitution of 1824. Thus, to Wigfall, the situation was shaping into a war such as Texas had recently fought with Mexico. Again Wigfall projected his position to others as he explained it to Calhoun. It seemed to Wigfall that Texans felt that the last hope of the southern states was to stand upon the Constitution and declare that while willing to preserve the Union of 1787, they would not allow its perversion.[11]

Although Wigfall surely had his mind made up, he asked Calhoun what should be done if Congress insisted on making free states of California and New Mexico. He felt that any such attempt to deprive southerners of their share of the territories would warrant any risk in objecting to it. Wigfall believed, to his chagrin, that Texas would not take the lead in opposition to the application of the Wilmot Proviso in New Mexico and California. But he felt that Texas would "willingly and almost unanimously" follow the lead of any other state. Again, as he had done in South Carolina, Wigfall projected his own sentiments as being

10 Wigfall to Calhoun, June 10, 1848, in Boucher and Brooks, "Correspondence Addressed to John C. Calhoun, 1837–1849," pp. 440–41.
11 *Ibid.*, January 4, 1849, pp. 493–95.

the opinions of the great majority of his state. But certain that Calhoun would want to know the feeling of "the people in this section" upon the "exciting issues," Wigfall sent him the Marshall resolutions. If they were not accepted in other parts of the state, Wigfall was sure it would be because the people were not aware of the dangers pending. Wigfall intended to inform them.

Wigfall and Calhoun were not personal friends. Their correspondence was formal and infrequent. One can only suppose from the tenor of Wigfall's letters that Calhoun replied. Wigfall seems to have been quite humble in asking forgiveness for having taken the liberty of writing the great southern spokesman. But it seemed to him that the time was rapidly approaching when the South would have to act, and he wanted "to be in the right position" when it did.[12]

At the same time Wigfall was seeking the advice of Calhoun, another Texan, Sam Houston, was attacking that same man's policies in the Senate. While serving as one of the first Texas senators he had already clashed often with Calhoun. To Houston the course pursued by Calhoun led to the same end as the course of the abolitionists—the destruction of the Union.[13] Houston was a strict constructionist constitutionally, a Texan jealous of the rights of his state, a slaveowner who accepted the institution and even believed in the right of secession. But he was convinced that secession was unwise, that the brightest future for Texas and the other southern states lay within the framework of the Union. His popularity in the North for criticizing Calhoun's policies pleased Houston because he was ambitious for the presidency and knew that he would have to have northern support to be elected.[14]

12 *Ibid.*
13 Houston to James Gadsden, September 20, 1849, in Amelia W. Williams and Eugene C. Barker (eds.), *The Writings of Sam Houston, 1813–1863* (Austin, 1938), V, 99. After the senatorial elections in the Texas Legislature in 1845, Thomas J. Rusk drew the six-year term; Houston drew a two-year term, 1845–47, but was reelected for the 1847–53 term.
14 Llerena Friend, *Sam Houston: The Great Designer* (Austin, 1954), 202–203, 297; James Knox Polk, *The Diary of a President, 1845–1849* . . ., edited by Allan Nevins (New York, 1929), 194–95; Walter Prescott Webb, *The Texas Rangers* (Boston, 1935), 197.

The first Wigfall-Houston clash came in the 1849 gubernatorial campaign when Houston backed George T. Wood. The colorful Houston spoke in Marshall for Wood, but his speech was aimed mostly against Calhoun's call for a southern convention. Wigfall defended Calhoun and countered by arraigning Senators Houston and Thomas J. Rusk as recreant to Texas and to the entire South. Wigfall hit especially hard at Houston's vote on the Oregon bill. Although Houston never wavered in his opposition to the Wilmot Proviso, he voted for the organization of Oregon under the Ordinance of 1787 which also prohibited slavery. Wigfall echoed Calhoun's charge that Oregon had become a free territory only with the help of Sam Houston and Thomas Hart Benton (Dem.–Missouri), the only two Senators from southern or western slave states to vote for the admission of Oregon. Newspapers gave the exchanges between Wigfall and Houston a great deal of attention, some suggesting that Wigfall was foolish for attacking Houston at the zenith of the latter's popularity. Many Texans still thought of Houston as the Hero of San Jacinto and the President of Texas.[15]

That same year, however, Wigfall had enough support to be named to the lower house of the Texas Legislature to complete the term of the Harrison County representative who had resigned. He was one of five nonlegislative delegates selected by the Texas Legislature to attend the Nashville Convention of southern radicals who met in 1850 and who asserted the right of secession. He did not go, probably because he was named to the legislature and preferred to attack Houston from there.[16] Until the end of his term in December, 1850, Wigfall used this new fulcrum of greater leverage to further his secessionist ideas and to topple the nationalism of Houston. Early in 1850 he helped to

[15] Austin, *Texas State Gazette*, September 15, 1849; Friend, *Houston*, 163, 191, 196–97; Richardson, *Texas*, 241; Webb and Carroll (eds.), *Handbook of Texas*, I, 845–47; L. T. Wigfall, *Speech in Reply to Houston and Rusk*, in *Texas Republican*, November 8, 1849, also in pamphlet form (Marshall, 1849); *Texas Republican*, November 24, 1859.

[16] *Members of the Legislature of the State of Texas from 1846–1939* (Austin, 1939), 11.

secure a legislative resolution condemning Houston for laxity in
protecting Texas' interests. Then he spoke in numerous East
Texas towns to urge that county meetings be held to approve the
resolutions.[17] But Wigfall's onslaughts had little effect on Houston's popularity, even after the Old Warrior voted for every part
of the Compromise of 1850.

This compromise, resulting from moderates' concern over
growing sectional antagonism, involved primarily the issue of
slavery in the territories, but also involved were some matters
affecting Texas even more directly. Kentucky Senator Henry
Clay introduced a series of resolutions as a formula for settling
sectional differences. This culminated in five congressional bills
which, after eight months of some of the bitterest debates in the
political history of the United States, comprised the Compromise
of 1850. California was admitted as a free state, and New Mexico
and Utah were each organized as territories, utilizing the concept
of squatter sovereignty in regard to slavery there. This was strong
medicine to many southerners, but especially to Texans because
in the "Texas and New Mexico Act" of the compromise, the
Lone Star State was to relinquish her claims to the upper Rio
Grande area which was declared to be a part of New Mexico.
The payment of $10 million by the United States to Texas for
the abandonment of her claims was little sugar for such a bitter
dose, some Texans thought. Further, the slave trade was abolished in the District of Columbia, a wedge that abolitionists had
been trying to drive for some time. The concession to the South
was a more stringent fugitive-slave code, placing fugitive-slave
cases under federal jurisdiction.

Moderates in all sections hoped that this had finally settled
the controversy. But extremists in the North and South took exception to parts of it. Abolitionists condemned the Fugitive Slave
Act. And although most southerners accepted the settlement, fire-
eaters such as Wigfall resented the incorporation of squatter
sovereignty and looked upon the compromise as conditional. The
"Georgia Platform," subscribed to by many extreme states' right-

17 *Texas Republican*, March 14, April 28, 1850.

ists, pledged acceptance of the compromise only so long as the North honored the Fugitive Slave Act.

Some Texans were upset over the compromise. The hotbed of Texan discontent was located, as usual, in Marshall, Wigfall's hometown. There was a demonstration there which, as described by one who attended, was "Anti-Everything." Many there were convinced that Houston and other senators and representatives had sold out.[18] The "South Carolina Resolutions," therefore, found some support in the Texas Legislature. These proposals defended the right of secession and renewed the call for a meeting of southern states to discuss their common problems. Some Texas legislators were so incensed with the Compromise of 1850 that they wanted to send delegates to such a meeting to work for southern secession. But the majority refused and termed a southern convention unwise at that time.[19]

Wigfall, who had spoken passionately in support of the Texas claims for the upper Rio Grande, found fresh ammunition against Houston, the only southern senator who had voted for every item of the compromise. As usual, Wigfall thought his own views were those of the majority, but he had little success; despite his anti-Houston acrimony, the Old Hero was elected to a third senatorial term in 1853. And the efforts of Wigfall and other Democratic Party leaders notwithstanding, the Texas Democrats remained disorganized in the early 1850's.[20] In 1854, however, Congress passed a momentous act which dimmed Houston's star and helped to pave the way for the culmination of Wigfall's secession sentiments.

After allaying the problem of slavery in the territories, Congress concerned itself with the problem of railroads in the territories. This came with the desire for a "transcontinental" line, linking some point on the Mississippi River with some point on the Pacific coast. While this matter was less volatile than slavery,

18 J. K. Holland, October 3, 1850, as quoted in Friend, *Houston*, 212.
19 Webb and Carroll (eds.), *Handbook of Texas*, II, 587.
20 *Ibid.*, 845–47; Nichols, *Disruption of American Democracy*, 10–11; Winkler, *Platforms of Political Parties in Texas*, 24, 34, 36; Sandbo, "The Secession Movement in Texas," 49–50.

it was nevertheless a complex sectional issue. A southern transcontinental route had certain advantages over any the North had
proposed. For one thing, a track laid from New Orleans to California would pass through states and organized territory, but in
the North lay the vast, unorganized "Nebraska" territory. In
order to meet this southern competition, Illinois Senator Stephen
A. Douglas introduced a bill to organize Nebraska. To get necessary southern support for the measure, a provision was included
which would end the prohibition of slavery in the northern part
of the Louisiana Purchase. The final version of the bill organized
the two territories of Kansas and Nebraska and repealed the part
of the 1820 Missouri Compromise which had prohibited slavery
in the Louisiana Purchase north of 36°30'. Many southerners
accepted the bill with alacrity, thinking that it repudiated the
congressional intervention with slavery in the territories as stated
in the Missouri Compromise. In doing so, however, they acqui-
esced to Douglas' principle of "popular sovereignty," a more
dignified term for squatter sovereignty which was incorporated
into the Kansas-Nebraska Act of 1854. Southerners felt that while
Nebraska would probably become a free state, Kansas would be
a slave state.

    Seldom if ever had a congressional act had such immediate and
momentous effects. In brief, it reopened the controversy over
slavery in the territories, with bitterness flowing afresh and more
vehemently than ever. Within a year it would lead to the formation of a new political party (Republican), cause the death of
one of the two old parties (Whig), and set in motion the forces
that would divide the other one (Democratic) along sectional
lines.

    Few people had the prescience to discern the enmity which
would ensue. Sam Houston did. Once more out of step with his
southern colleagues, he opposed the Kansas-Nebraska Act because the repeal of the Missouri Compromise line would result
in "discord and civil broil." [21] But in Texas, where Wigfall again

────────────

21 Speech in the United States Senate, February 14–15, 1854, in Williams and

led the attack against him, Houston lost much of his popular following. The Texas Legislature passed a resolution censuring his opposition to the Kansas-Nebraska Act. As Llerena Friend, Houston's biographer, has said: "Texas had written finis to Houston's senatorial career," even though his term would run to 1859.[22]

Wigfall could not see these dangers; he was busy warning Texans of the threats to their sectional interests. But not even after the Kansas-Nebraska Act did all Texans heed the strident call of Wigfall's radicalism. Houston still had the support of some staunch unionists, including Independent Democrats, some Whigs, and many of the Know-Nothings.

The Know-Nothing, or American, Party was to figure prominently in Wigfall's rise in state politics. Originally a secret organization opposed to Catholicism, immigration, and just about anything that the party decided was "foreign," in the late 1850's the Know-Nothings were still antiforeign, but they stressed more and more their unionist principles. Houston, no Free Soiler and too nationalistic to identify with the southern Democrats, cautiously affiliated with the Know-Nothings. When asked about his relations with them, he said he "knew nothing" of it, but that he agreed with many of their principles.[23] The Know-Nothings reached the zenith of their brief career in 1855, when Houston backed their gubernatorial candidate Lieutenant Governor D. C. Dickens, who nevertheless lost to Elisha M. Pease by four thousand votes.

During the 1855 campaign more Texans followed the anti-Houston trend. Twenty-two of the ninety-nine counties in 1855 adopted resolutions endorsing states' rights and slavery and censuring Houston's stand on the Kansas-Nebraska Act. Some reso-

Barker (eds.), *Writings of Houston*, V, 502; and *Congressional Globe*, 33rd Cong., 1st Sess., 339.

22 *State Gazette*, December 8, 1855; Friend, *Houston*, 232, 241–42.

23 Ray Allen Billington, *The Protestant Crusade: A Study of the Origins of American Nativism* (New York, 1938), Chap. 15; *State Gazette*, October 6, 1855; Williams and Barker (ed.), *Writings of Houston*, VI, 111–54, 159–64; Friend, *Houston*, 235–36, 243, 245, 296.

lutions even requested the state legislature to ask for the resignation of Houston so that he could be replaced with a states' rights senator.[24] Undoubtedly, Wigfall wanted the job. He certainly took exception to the way Houston was doing it.

Wigfall was finally striking effective blows against Houston. As analyzed by one observer, Houston's opposition included many men of exceptional ability, but only one or two approached his effectiveness on the hustings. One of these was Louis T. Wigfall. And none of the Old Hero's opponents was more obnoxious to him than was Wigfall.[25] His attacks against Houston and the Know-Nothings were too effective for them to ignore. At first their defense was subtle and oblique. A Know-Nothing newspaper, the *Texas State Times,* denounced all "newcomers in Texas politics," lamenting that the times had sadly changed; a tide of new men, and with them new measures, had been constantly rolling into Texas. And much of the primitive patriotism of the country was being supplanted by a set of politicians who knew, or cared, but little about the hardships of the men of former days. The *State Times* thought it worthwhile to point out to Texas voters that a large majority of those who were attempting to mold public opinion were also those who had sat down to the banquet after all the dangers and the toil of preparing it were over. Wigfall continued to denounce the Know-Nothings, calling upon all "good and true" Democrats to take an "open and bold position against this new party," and debating Know-Nothing speakers, even in Louisiana.[26]

Throughout 1855, the year before the election, Wigfall played a major role in uniting and organizing the Democrats in Texas, rallying them into a vocal states' rights association. Writing for

[24] *State Gazette,* October 6, November 17, 1855; Sandbo, "Beginnings of the Secession Movement in Texas," 51–52.

[25] Charles A. Culberson, "General Sam Houston and Secession," *Scribner's Magazine,* XXXIX (May, 1906), 590; Lubbock, *Memoirs,* 258–59; Clarksville, *Northern Standard,* June 2, 1855.

[26] Austin *Texas State Times,* June 30, 1855; Wigfall, J. T. Mills, O. M. Roberts, P. Murrah, and J. P. Henderson to Senator T. J. Rusk, July 3, 1855, Thomas J. Rusk Papers, University of Texas Archives; *Texas Republican,* September 29, 1855.

the Committee of Invitations of the Democracy of Harrison County, he invited Judge O. M. Roberts to attend the great rally for the party in November, 1856, adding that on the success of that party "rests our last hope of preserving the Union." [27] Wigfall was even willing to support a northern Democrat, James Buchanan of Pennsylvania, for the presidency in order to defeat the Know-Nothings.

Indeed, Wigfall treated the Know-Nothings as a greater threat than the two-year old antislavery Republican Party. He wholeheartedly attacked Millard Fillmore, the Know-Nothing candidate, while virtually ignoring the Republicans. Fillmore, who had been President (as a Whig) after Taylor died in 1850, was flayed for his acceptance of the Compromise of 1850 and for other antisouthern policies. Wigfall's efforts against Fillmore were evidently effective. The Marshall *Texas Republican* credited "Wigfall's incessant clamor" for the wane of Know-Nothing strength in Harrison County and for Buchanan's winning the county by a majority of sixty votes.[28]

After the 1856 election Wigfall's reputation as a "Know-Nothing fighter" was made. Democratic strategists turned to him for advice upon how to attack the Know-Nothing candidates in the Texas elections of 1857. That year Wigfall was successful not only in helping elect other Democrats, but was himself elected to the state legislature as senator from Harrison County.[29]

Wigfall was also selected that year as a delegate to the Texas Democratic convention in Waco to prepare for the election. To be successful in this first open struggle between the states' rights Democrats and Houston for the support of the people, the Democrats would have to maintain their party's momentum from the presidential election of the previous year, and they would have to promote even greater unity amongst themselves. Wigfall contributed in both respects. By this time he was adept at arousing

---

27 Wigfall to Rusk, October 11, 1855; October 11, 14, 1856, Rusk Papers; Wigfall to Roberts, October 11, 1856, Roberts Papers.

28 *Texas Republican*, October 11, November 8, 1856.

29 W. R. D. Ward to John H. Reagan, January 3, 1857, John H. Reagan Papers, Texas State Archives; *Members of the Texas Legislature*, 28.

concern amongst the voters, and he was able to submerge some of his most divisive radicalism. A fellow delegate at Waco, Francis Lubbock, said that Wigfall helped stir enthusiasm with an able and loudly applauded speech on states' rights. Later in the convention he made what Lubbock described as "conciliatory remarks" which were effective in promoting unity in the Democratic ranks.[30]

In 1857 it was easy for Wigfall to work in good faith to persuade the Texans to support the stated principles of the national Democratic Party. The Texas Democratic Committee on Platforms, with him as a member, agreed that the cardinal doctrines of the party were set forth in the 1856 national Cincinnati Platform, which endorsed the Virginia and Kentucky Resolutions and stated that Congress had no power to interfere with slavery.[31] Only states could decide on such domestic institutions, said the national Democrats. The people of a territory could decide upon the issue of slavery only when they drew up a constitution for statehood.[32]

Two months before the Waco Convention met, a southern majority on the United States Supreme Court had written into constitutional law, in *Dred Scott* vs. *Sanford*, the complete Calhoun interpretation of the Fifth Amendment and slavery in the territories. Slaves were property which Congress had to protect; only states could prohibit slavery, said the Court. Most southerners were jubilant, but Wigfall continued to deny the power of the Supreme Court to interpret the Constitution, maintaining that this was a right of each state.[33]

States' rights Democrats had had their way at Cincinnati in 1856. They had their way at Waco in 1857, simply reaffirming the Cincinnati Platform which was now supported by the Dred

---

30 Lubbock, *Memoirs*, 209.
31 The resolutions by Thomas Jefferson and James Madison in 1798 and 1799, explaining that the federal government had only delegated powers.
32 "The Slavery Pronouncement of the American Democracy, Cincinnati, 1856," quoted in Nichols, *Disruption of American Democracy*, 507–509; see also Winkler, *Platforms of Political Parties in Texas*, 75–76.
33 Lubbock, *Memoirs*, 209.

Scott decision. They also obtained their choice for the 1857 Democratic gubernatorial nominee—H. R. Runnels.[34]

Wigfall, now generally recognized in Texas as a leader of the radical states' rights Democrats, turned his talents to helping Runnels defeat Sam Houston in the governor's race. Houston, running as a unionist and Jacksonian Democrat but with Know-Nothing support, based his campaign upon his record in the Senate. Wigfall met him on these grounds. The Old Warrior refused to debate in the strict sense of the word—indeed, he refused to speak from the same platform with anyone opposing him. But Wigfall followed him, speaking immediately after Houston and attacking his arguments point by point.[35]

The General reacted in characteristic Houston fashion, maligning his opponents. Wigfall, J. P. Henderson, W. S. Oldham, Francis Lubbock, and others were all criminals who had fled to Texas, said Houston. Wigfall had swindled his law clients and had escaped South Carolina to avoid the penitentiary. Along with these libelous charges, Houston resorted to what one observer termed "bawdy-house vulgarity" which "turned the stomachs" of some listeners.[36] Hitting closer to the truth, Houston denounced Wigfall as a murderer and soon developed a pet name for him. Appearing at Tyler, Houston closed his speech, for example, by telling his audience that the speaker following would be a "murderer named Wiggletail," and warned his listeners not to stay unless they were fond of lies. Wigfall, however, stuck to the issues and, compared to Houston's fulminations, carried on a high-level campaign. And his oral onslaughts were effective. Houston's affiliation with the Know-Nothings hurt him, but his defeat was generally accredited to Wigfall. He was the only man

34 Winkler, *Platforms of Political Parties in Texas,* 75–76.

35 A. W. Terrell, "Recollections of General Sam Houston," *Southwestern Historical Quarterly,* XVI (October, 1912), 118–19; Richardson, *Texas,* 117.

36 Houston's Speech at Austin, July 7, 1857, in Williams and Barker (eds.), *Writings of Houston,* VII, 28; Marquis de Lafayette Herring to O. M. Roberts, June 15, 1857, Roberts Papers. Although Herring was prejudiced against Houston, Llerena Friend, Houston's biographer, said that this Herring letter "may be a fairly accurate description of many of the Houston campaign speeches of 1857." Friend, *Houston,* 251.

who ever bested Houston at this kind of rough-and-tumble stump speaking. It was the only defeat that Houston suffered in a major contest. Runnels and the regular Democrats won an overwhelming victory in 1857.[37]

It is not surprising that Wigfall should have had a strong voice in the Democrats' 1858 state convention. He helped formulate the platform, introduced it, and defended it before the convention. Again pointing with pride to the Cincinnati Platform, Wigfall viewed with alarm the recent events in the United States Senate which had created in southern minds serious apprehension that Congress was soon to repudiate the great doctrine of its nonintervention with slavery in the territories.[38]

He was in the meantime enhancing his reputation as a radical with his activities in the state legislature. At every opportunity he hammered at states' rights, slavery, and the tariff issue. Even in his thirteen-page eulogy of his cousin James Hamilton, Wigfall spent five pages denouncing the Compromise Tariff of 1833, and most of the remaining pages were devoted to other problems of the South. As usual, he prescribed bold remedies for these sectional ills. Even the Kansas question could be settled satisfactorily to southerners, he said, if they stood firmly for their rights.[39]

Kansas was by this time on the verge of civil war. Abolitionists in Massachusetts had organized to promote the settlement of antislavery groups in Kansas in order to make it a free state. Returns of the various confused elections indicate that the free staters were probably in a slight majority. But Wigfall decried their means, denied their majority, and defined majority rule as dangerous revisionism anyway. "Modern statesmanship" had discovered, he said with contempt, that a constitution not ratified

37 Terrell, "Recollections of General Sam Houston," 119; Lubbock, *Memoirs*, 256; Galveston *News*, February 19, 1874; Webb and Carroll (eds.), *Handbook of Texas*, I, 971; Winkler, *Platforms of Political Parties in Texas*, 40.

38 *State Gazette*, January 16, 1858.

39 "Wigfall's Speech on Republican Government," *Debates of the Seventh Texas Legislature*, November 25, 1857, pp. 79–82. Lubbock thought it "a speech of wonderful eloquence" and quoted part of it in his *Memoirs*, 229–30.

by a popular vote was no constitution. If that were true, Wigfall argued sophistically, then none of the original thirteen states had constitutions. "Modern statesmen" had also discovered the doctrine "that sovereignty does not reside in the people—in the whole people, but in a part—i.e. a majority." According to this argument, he continued, sovereign power could only be exercised at the ballot box. Wigfall concluded from this that since the Declaration of Independence was made by the Continental Congress, which had not been elected by the people at the ballot box, Americans were still subjects of Britain. Southerners had to oppose this fallacious reasoning by abolitionists, warned Wigfall.[40]

It is significant that prior to the 1850's the United States *was* generally referred to as a confederacy or a republic, not as a democracy. "Democrats," "Democratic Party," or "American Democracy" as the party was officially renamed in the 1850's, were merely political labels. But as northern leaders, representing the more populous states, became frustrated by southern control of the national government, they demanded majority rule through representative democracy. Wigfall and most other southern leaders could see only northern domination in this, and they resisted it as a dangerous demand for mob rule. Thus, Wigfall became a party to that apparent paradox wherein Democrats were opposing democracy.[41]

Mob rule and abolitionism had to be met in Kansas, Wigfall warned; southerners had to refuse to allow Congress to admit Kansas with a free-soil constitution. Wigfall's remedy lay in a threat of secession. In a fine example of the thinking that spelled doom for the slave states, Wigfall advised them to say "with perfect good humor—cooly and deliberately—that out of this blessed Union they will go" if Kansas were admitted with a free-state constitution, and such an event would never happen. He challenged the southern "Union savers" with the declaration that the

40 "Col. Wigfall's Reply to an Invitation to Attend a Dinner in Honor of M. L. Bonham," Dallas *Herald*, December 8, 1858. See also "Wigfall's Speech on Republican Government."
41 See Nichols, *Disruption of American Democracy*, 7.

Union was in no danger but from them. Their timidity had invited aggression, and such a policy might induce the North to commit some act of rash folly that would precipitate dissolution. Never would the North knowingly and deliberately force such an issue, continued Wigfall; let them know of the danger, and they would back down. If "we can but to ourselves be true neither we nor the Union are or will be in any danger," he said; the constitution was sound, it was up to southerners to enforce it. What should they do? As Wigfall analyzed the situation, the South had to have Kansas. It was necessary to preserve slavery in Missouri, northern Texas, ad infinitum.[42]

More and more Texans were heeding Wigfall's advice. In the ten years since his arrival in Texas, he had risen to a position of leadership in state politics, riding the crest of southern uncertainty and sectionalism. In a decade of doubt—when the country was feeling the first effects of having doubled in size in the previous ten years, when the South was afraid of losing its favored position in the growing nation—Wigfall's brand of dynamic dogmatism offered political and emotional shelter to many Texans. Through states' rights they could curb the power of a federal government they no longer controlled, and they could at the same time get their "fair share" of the territories.

The extreme states' rightists, or regular Democrats, were strongly entrenched in the state by the end of 1857. They had elected their governor, won most of the lesser offices, helped elect a successor to Houston for the Senate—two years before the General's term expired—and they had sent one of their most radical members, J. P. Henderson, to the Senate to succeed Rusk, who had committed suicide in 1857. It had been a good year politically for Wigfall and the rest of the regular Democrats.

It was not a good year financially for Wigfall. In a suit against him, a court decided that he still owed the 1848 debt to one William R. Smith of Galveston. Smith charged that the payment had often been demanded but remained wholly unpaid. The

42 "Col. Wigfall's Reply to an Invitation."

court ordered Wigfall to pay $1,010 for the $548 he had borrowed at 10 percent interest in 1848.[43] This was not the end of the debt problems which continued to plague him even after he became a United States Senator. But the most important thing to Wigfall was undoubtedly his political fortune, and this was to flourish richly.

In the minds of many the two strongest voices among the regular Democrats were those of Henderson and Wigfall, both ultraradicals. It was Wigfall who had nominated Henderson for the Senate. When Henderson died before serving a year of his senatorial term, Wigfall's influence in the party became stronger than ever. The Dallas *Herald* began to chant the name of Wigfall for the Senate. No man in the state was better fitted for the position, said the *Herald*. As a political debater he was without a superior, and he was "perhaps more thoroughly conversant with the theory of our complex system of government that any other man." With his fine education, extensive reading, and elegant address, he would vault at a bound into the front rank of those "younger intellectual giants" (other southern extremists) who were redeeming the United States Senate from its retrogression. Wigfall might have faults, the *Herald* admitted; he might commit errors of judgment "and be not altogether orthodox in politics," but he could be pardoned for the sake of his talent.[44]

The *Herald* had pointed up Wigfall's basic obstacle to being elected. By mid-1858 too many Texans thought his politics so unorthodox as to preclude him a place in the nation's government. Many had never embraced all of what he advocated, and further, Texas was undergoing a conservative reaction in late 1858 and early 1859. Unfortunately for Wigfall, he chose this time to press two ultraradical programs: the revival of the foreign slave trade and filibustering in Latin America for more

[43] Book A, 441, District Court Records, County Clerk's Office, Harrison County Court House, Marshall, Texas.

[44] Dallas *Herald*, July 3, 1858, and similar praise in most later issues, especially in February 9, 1859, till his election. Governor Runnels appointed Matt Ward to serve as temporary senator until the legislature named a successor.

slave territory. This was disquieting to many Texans who were unwilling to risk additional sectional strife for such issues.[45]

The Dallas *Herald* was getting little support in its drive to send Wigfall to the Senate, though he was now courting voters. Even the *Texas Republican* in Marshall was for the moderate John H. Reagan until he leveled a blast at Wigfall which editor R. W. Loughery thought unjustified. When Reagan labeled those men who supported the slave trade and filibustering as disunionists in a class with abolitionists, the *Republican* turned to Wigfall as their champion. The paper had not been averse to Wigfall before this and had given attention to his campaign. After one Wigfall speech, the *Republican* reported that for nearly two hours "the eloquent speaker" had the undivided attention of the large audience made up of persons from practically every part of the country. Wigfall had taken this occasion to diagnose the sickness of the country. After pronouncing that the slavery question was not the real disease—but merely the exhibition of it—he discoursed at length on the Missouri Compromise and the Kansas struggle to show how expansion in the territories was the actual ill. Somehow Wigfall decided that more expansion was the remedy. He regarded the acquisition of Cuba as a political necessity and a slice of Mexican territory not objectionable. The South could and would colonize these new areas, having plenty of slaves to spare, said Wigfall.[46]

If the South had enough slaves, what then of the foreign slave trade? Wigfall piously decided the best way to Christianize Africa was "to catch Africa and bring it here," for the cotton field or the rice plantation was the proper place for the Negro. There all of his physical wants would be cared for, and he would "be brought under the saving influence of Christianity." Surely, said Wigfall, the 1808 Congressional Act prohibiting this trade was unconstitutional. The question should be examined and debated,

45 William L. Yancey to Wigfall, April 16, 1858, Wigfall Family Papers; Earl W. Fornell, "Agitation in Texas for Reopening the Slave Trade," *Southwestern Historical Quarterly*, LX (October, 1956), 245–59; *Texas Almanac for 1858*, pp. 132–33.
46 *Texas Republican*, April 22, 29, May 6, October 1, 1859.

and then the states would be prepared to take advantage of the circumstances.[47]

The Texas Democrats never espoused these programs, but the party came under suspicion because of Wigfall and a few other radicals. Because of this and other centrifugal forces in the Democratic Party, some of the moderates were apprehensive about the coming elections in August, 1859. Ironically, the crushing defeat of the Know-Nothings had in one way worked ill for the regular Democrats. With the disappearance of the Know-Nothing Party, many of its leaders returned to the Democratic Party. And here were sown seeds for division, for many of them changed their church but not their religion. Wigfall and his policies were no more palatable to them in 1859 than in 1855. And by 1859 the ex-Know-Nothings were reorganized within—but not assimilated by—the regular Democratic Party.[48]

To many voters the central issue in the 1859 gubernatorial campaign, between Houston and Runnels again, was union or disunion. Runnels, while not as strong for disunionism as Wigfall, was not nearly so adverse to it as Houston. Houston, still hoping to save the Union and become President, sought the governorship as a Jacksonian nationalist on the Independent ticket, for the Union and against reopening the foreign slave trade. Some of the pro-Houston Democrats, many of them ex-Know-Nothings, called themselves National Democrats.

Wigfall tried to pour oil on the troubled waters that threatened to overturn the Texas Democratic Party. In his own county he was successful in healing the breach between Pendleton Murrah, a strong states' rightist, and John Reagan, a moderate.[49] And finally deferring to the threat of a Houston victory, Wigfall tried to belittle the slave trade as an issue. On the floor of the legislature he spoke not of filibustering or slave trade but of such

[47] *Ibid.*, April 22, 1859; see also speech delivered in Galveston, May 14, 1859, in Dallas *Herald*, June 1, 1859.

[48] See Austin, Texas, *Southern Intelligencer*, April 6, 1859.

[49] Dallas *Herald*, June 15, August 10, 1859; John H. Reagan, *Memoirs: With Special References to Secession and the Civil War*, edited by Walter Flavius McCaleb (New York, 1906), 71.

issues as higher education. Perhaps in an effort to draw attention
from a divisive national controversy by creating a milder, non-
political state issue, Wigfall proposed a bold plan for the cap-
stone of public education in Texas. As chairman of the Senate
Committee on State Affairs, he recommended a state university
where the lectures would be free to all of both sexes. Furthermore, there would be wide selection of courses and no particular
course of study would be prescribed. Although his recommenda-
tions were well-received by some newspapers and hailed by one
of his friends in the legislature as "able and eloquent," most Texans remained preoccupied with the elections, and Wigfall never
pursued the matter further.[50] He was forced instead to turn directly to the slave trade issue, trying to belittle it as academic and
impracticable for anyone to discuss. To his disappointment, however, it was widely discussed and became a divisive question
throughout the state. He had, in fact, helped to split his party by
bringing up the issue in the first place. Houston made the most
of this advantage over a divided opposition, and he and many
other conservatives were elected. Although the Democrats maintained a slight majority in both houses of the legislature, the
southern trend to more moderate politics was underway in
Texas. Wigfall and his radicalism were clearly repudiated. And
yet, before Houston's inauguration four months later, Wigfall
was elected to the United States Senate.

John Brown's raid on Harper's Ferry triggered this dramatic
shift in the trend of Texas politics. Southerners seemed unwilling to realize that Brown's raid was condemned by a great majority of northerners; they were ready to believe that the North
was peopled by abolitionists who agreed with Ralph Waldo
Emerson when he hailed Brown for making the gallows as glori-

[50] "Report of the Chairman of the Committee on State Affairs on the Propriety
of Establishing a State University," quoted in *Texas Republican*, July 30, 1859;
Lubbock, *Memoirs*, 227–28. A site had been set aside for a university in 1838 and
financial and administrative provision made in an 1858 act, but sectional excitement, secession, Civil War, and Reconstruction prevented the establishment of
the University of Texas until 1881. Webb and Carroll (eds.), *Handbook of Texas*,
II, 821.

ous as the cross. Despite sincere public denunciations for the raid by many party leaders, southerners rested responsibility for the raid upon the Republican Party.[51] Brown's raid could not have been more effectively timed for greater impact. It was ample evidence to southerners that their institution of slavery was doomed should "Black Republicans" gain enough power. It was no longer just a "cold war"; many southern states began to arm for violent conflict.[52]

The result in Texas was to nullify the recent trend to moderation in state politics. There had seemed to be little hope for the extremists that their man Wigfall could be selected over a moderate such as Reagan. Wigfall's newspaper support had not enlarged appreciably. The *Texas Republican* reported that several papers had "spoken favorably" of him and so had "prominent politicians" throughout the state.[53] But the *Republican* and the Dallas *Herald* remained his principal boosters.

On the eve of a meeting of Harrison County Democrats to endorse a candidate for the Senate, the *Republican* eulogized Wigfall. After listing the prerequisites for the office, the Marshall paper announced that both Wigfall and Reagan met these qualifications. But "in point of intellectual ability and information," Wigfall had no superior in Texas, and he had given uniform and fervent support to the Democratic Party. On the other hand the *Republican* had this startling observation: *Reagan* had "unnecessarily produced discord in the Democratic ranks . . . thereby aiding in defeat of the state ticket in the late election." [54]

Harrison County Democrats did indeed endorse Wigfall, paying high tribute to him in a list of resolutions. The day after

---

[51] For the most lucid and able defense of John Brown, see Louis Ruchames (ed.), *A John Brown Reader* . . . (New York, 1959); also Martin Duberman (ed.), *The Antislavery Vanguard* . . . (Princeton, 1965).

[52] James G. Randall and David Donald, *The Civil War and Reconstruction* (2nd ed.; Boston, 1961), 124–26, 166; Nichols, *Disruption of American Democracy*, 279, 353, 420.

[53] Dallas *Herald*, October 12, November 23, 1859; Ben H. Proctor, *Not Without Honor: The Life of John H. Reagan* (Austin, 1962), 114; *Texas Republican*, October 1, 1859.

[54] *Texas Republican*, October 8, 1859.

this was reported by the *Republican,* John Brown struck at Harper's Ferry. Surprisingly the *Republican*, the mouthpiece of ultraradical Harrison County, at first discounted reports that the raid was an abolitionist movement. But as time went by, the *Republican* editor took note of the great concern that Brown had created in the area and in all of Texas. In the spring of 1860 the paper resorted to a grim riddle-pun: "With what instrument does the South propose to sever the bonds of National Union?— The Acts [ax] of John Brown." [55] The raid was also the ominous "ax" which demolished the support of moderates in the Senate campaign of 1859.

A week before Brown's raid, J. W. Throckmorton, an astute analyst of Texas politics, advised Reagan that he had a chance of being selected senator. Governor Runnels and his friends would first canvass for Matt Ward, but on finding him without much strength, predicted Throckmorton, they would then throw their support to Colonel Wigfall. Should Reagan's name be before the legislature, Throckmorton thought he would get more votes than anyone else, but no one would have enough to be elected on the first ballot. There would not be enough independents to elect Houston, but they would be the deciding factor in the election.[56]

But Reagan's name was not before the legislature when they selected a senator. He had realized that his chances were shattered in the shock waves of Brown's raid. Even so, Throckmorton was correct in much of his analysis. Runnels' support did switch to Colonel Wigfall; more than one ballot was necessary; and the Houston men nearly did control the election. They could have, if they had been successful in their efforts to unite Wigfall's opposition. But because of John Brown, regular Democrats were determined to send to Congress "the most violent partisan in the state" as Judge O. M. Roberts said.[57]

55 *Ibid.*, October 15, 29, December 3, 10, 17, 24, 1859, January 1, May 5, 1860.

56 Throckmorton to Reagan, September 9, 1859; see also Reagan to William Alexander, October 3, 1859, both letters in Reagan Papers.

57 O. M. Roberts, "Poltical, Legislative, and Judicial History of Texas," in Dudley G. Wooten (ed.), *A Comprehensive History of Texas* (2 vols.; Dallas, 1898), I, 58.

Some legislators opposed Wigfall for his radicalism, and others, even some regular Democrats, could not swallow all their constitutional qualms. The constitutional obstacle to Wigfall appeared to many to be insurmountable when they considered Section 24 of the Bill of Rights in the 1845 Texas Constitution: "No member of either house shall, during the term for which he is elected, be eligible to any office or place the appointment to which may be made in whole or in part by either branch of the legislature." [58] Even the prospect of Wigfall's resignation from the legislature failed to satisfy many strict constructionists who pointed out that the prohibition was effective for the *entire term* for which he was elected (through February, 1860). Leaders of the regular Democrats decided upon two stratagems to overcome the opposition to Wigfall. For one, the pro-Wigfall House Judiciary Committee reinterpreted the constitutional provision so as not to apply to the election of senators. Previously, this had been construed as applying to the election of United States senators, and some, such as Judge Roberts, wondered if it did not apply to senators, then to whom did it apply? [59]

When it became known that some regular Democrats would not vote for Wigfall, the pro-Houston national Democrats sought to nominate a regular Democrat less objectionable to them. Their plan was to defeat Wigfall by combining their votes with those of the regular Democrats who would not vote for him. But the regular Democratic leaders had a stratagem for this also. On November 14 they called a party caucus in which they officially nominated Wigfall for the Senate. This meant that dissident Democrats who had pledged to their constituents to support the party had to break their pledges or vote for Wigfall—or perhaps not vote at all. The Wigfall camp hoped for the latter alternative. Their champion could not hope to muster a majority of the entire legislature, but if enough of his opposition stayed away— because of caucus pledges or the reaction to John Brown's raid—

[58] *Ibid.*, 57–58. See also *Texas Republican*, December 3, 10, 1859; Dallas *Herald*, December 7, 21, 1859.
[59] Roberts, "Political, Legislative, and Judicial History of Texas," 58.

Wigfall might get a majority of the votes cast. Probably Brown was the more important factor in keeping anti-Wigfall legislators away from the election. As Judge Roberts said, in deference "to the expressed wishes of a very large majority" of Democratic voters who wished to have a radical senator to deal with radical abolitionists, many of the objectors failed to attend the joint electoral session.[60]

When December came, the opposition still had not agreed upon a candidate. Certain that Wigfall could not be elected on the first ballot, they could nominate several and then perhaps unite behind the strongest. And in order to keep Wigfall from getting a majority, they hoped to be able to force the abstainers to vote.[61] Thus, the opposition's battle plans were somewhat uncertain on election day, Monday, December 5.

That Monday, as the hour for convention drew near, the Texas legislators milled about in the capitol, many of them still campaigning. In heated exchanges, Wigfall supporters argued that northern extremism required extreme countermeasures. Wigfall's opponents remonstrated against his radicalism and his constitutional ineligibility. The halls buzzed with the news that Wigfall had that day tendered his resignation from the legislature.[62]

Just before 11 A.M. the joint session convened and the legislators gathered in the House chambers. One admirer of Wigfall cites an incident which occurred at this point to show that Wigfall was not a demagogue but an "aristocrat of aristocrats." Ballinger reported that Wigfall stood with a friend in the capitol hall and as the legislators filed in to vote, Wigfall said: "A lot

60 *Ibid.*; *Proceedings of the Joint Session, Eighth Texas Legislature, in the Election of U.S. Senator,* Monday, December 5, 1859, p. 2.

61 Houston *Telegraph* and *Texas Republican,* December 3, 1859.

62 Governor Runnels to Texas Senate, December 5, 1859, Executive Records, III, No. 277, p. 385. A second letter, Governor Runnels to Texas Senate, December 28, 1859, *Journal of the Senate, Eighth Texas Legislature,* 311, confuses the matter somewhat. Both the December 5 and 28 letters say that Wigfall resigned that day. There seems to be no doubt, however, that Wigfall resigned December 5 before the balloting began. This is confirmed by the *Proceedings of the Joint Session, Eighth Texas Legislature,* 9–10; and by Lubbock and Roberts who were closely concerned with events of the election. See Lubbock, *Memoirs,* 258; Roberts, "Political, Legislative, and Judicial History of Texas," 58.

of those fellows are fine specimens of legislators to be vested with the power of electing a gentleman" to the United States Senate. Then, so the story goes, the friend warned Wigfall that he was being very indiscreet since those men held his political fate in their hands. Wigfall is said to have replied: "I don't care a d—n. The fact remains that a whole lot of 'em are copperas breeched hayseeds and have no business here." Possibly the story is true in essence; other friends of Wigfall thought that his outspoken frankness prevented his holding higher posts than he did.[63]

As soon as the electoral session convened, the tactics of Wigfall's opposition became apparent—to delay until they could require the presence of the abstainers. One of the opponents ordered a roll call of the members. Then another moved to adjourn till the next day. But a majority of the members there were evidently in favor of getting the business over with. They stayed in session, and nominations were finally secured. Wigfall and five others were nominated. The results of the first ballot were:

	TOTAL	HOUSE	SENATE
Wigfall	59	43	16
Others	62	47	15
	121	90	31

No candidate having a majority, a second ballot was taken—with the exact results as the first.[64]

Before a third ballot could be ordered, the opposition began delaying again. They asked for roll calls, then demanded adjournment because of the absence of some members, or that the abstainers be brought in by the sergeant at arms. When each of these was voted down, they asked for a reconsideration of the vote. Soon Speaker of the House D. K. Taylor of Cass, a strong supporter of Wigfall, began declaring such motions out of order. Then the national Democrats appealed the decision of the chair, taking more time. When they cited a rule which could, they

[63] Kittrell, *Public Men of Texas*, 150; DeLeon, *Belles, Beaux, and Brains of the 60's*, 152–53.
[64] *Proceedings of the Joint Session, Eighth Texas Legislature*, 1, 13–14; *Journal of the House of Representatives, Eighth Texas Legislature*, Monday, December 5, 1859, pp. 174–75.

argued, require the absent members to be brought in, Taylor interpreted the rule as not applying to joint sessions, and he was again sustained by a majority.[65]

It was clear that though Wigfall did not have a majority, neither did his hard-core opposition. Each side accused the other of factionalism and "tricks." A typical lament of the opposition was voiced by Ben Epperson, a Throckmorton supporter and staunch unionist, who protested indignantly that the first two ballots demonstrated that Wigfall did not have a majority, and yet his election was about to be consummated. And were it not for the favoritism of the Speaker of the House, this would be impossible. The Wigfall camp contended that all proceedings were fair. Besides, they asserted, their party had been so overwhelmed in the recent election that the place of United States senator was the only mite which was left for them. They seemed determined to sit there until they got their man elected.

The first ballot had been taken a little after 11 A.M. At 5:20 P.M.—six hours, numerous motions, and thirty-eight roll calls later—the third ballot was taken.[66] Wigfall's vote from House members remained the same, but three representatives who had voted for opposing candidates did not vote at all in the third ballot. This, and the switch of a single senator from Ward to Wigfall, gave him a bare majority:

	TOTAL	HOUSE	SENATE
Wigfall	60	43	17
Others	58	44	14
	118	87	31

The Speaker then announced that Louis T. Wigfall was duly elected as Senator from Texas to the Congress of the United States.[67]

Immediately upon this announcement, a scene of wild confusion ensued. At length, order reigned and Wigfall was sum-

65 *Proceedings of the Joint Session, Eighth Texas Legislature*, 1–7.

66 Matt Dale's account of the election, in the *Trinity Advocate*, quoted in *Texas Republican*, December 24, 1859.

67 *Proceedings of the Joint Session, Eighth Texas Legislature*, 13–14.

moned. He then addressed the crowd "in strains of burning eloquence" for about twenty minutes. As one newspaperman described the scene: "The lion was aroused, and he surpassed himself." Vowing his acceptance of the Constitution and the Cincinnati Platform, Wigfall pledged his support to Buchanan as long as he did the same. But anyone who did not follow a strict construction of the Constitution was no Democrat, he warned.[68]

There was strong irony in Wigfall's basing his political life on a strict interpretation of the federal Constitution and his being elected to the Senate at the cost of a gross infraction of the Texas Constitution by ignoring his constitutional ineligibility.[69] But perhaps he could rationalize it; he could best serve the people if he were in the Senate. Here he could aid the Democratic Party, "the only party which could successfully oppose the . . . Black Republicans who were marching down upon [the South]." [70]

Criticism of Wigfall in Texas did not die, however, even after he was in Washington. In the Texas House the constitutional repercussions continued, with thirty legislators endorsing a resolution attesting to his ineligibility. Some critics probably agreed with Sam Houston, who regarded Wigfall as "a little demented either from hard drink, or from the troubles of a bad conscience." But Houston had great faith in his country; he exclaimed at the news of Wigfall's election: "Thank God this country is so great and strong that it can bear even that." Others were not so sure.[71] The continued criticism of Wigfall is additional evidence that he could not have been elected had it not been for John Brown.

Louis T. Wigfall and John Brown, though at opposite extremes of the sectional spectrum, had much in common. Both fol-

---

68 Dale's account in *Texas Republican,* December 24, 1859.

69 There was also in the 1845 Texas Constitution a prohibition against legislative membership for those who engaged in dueling. But it did not apply to the period before the constitution went into effect, so Wigfall was not ineligible on this count.

70 Dale's account of Wigfall's acceptance speech in *Texas Republican,* December 24, 1859.

71 *Journal of the House of Representatives, Eighth Texas Legislature,* January 16, 1860, pp. 408–12; Houston to A. J. Hamilton, March 17, 1860, in Williams and Barker (eds.), *Writings of Houston,* VII, 527; Chesnut, *Diary,* 71.

lowed their causes to the neglect of family and fortune. Though his background did not harbor the prevalent strain of insanity that Brown's did, Wigfall was a fanatic on the subject of states' rights and was unreasonably enthusiastic in devotion to his cause. He was ideally suited, however, by ability, temperament, training, and experience to take advantage of the conditions in the country, in the South, and in Texas. These conditions inevitably led him to a position of influence. Three days after John Brown was hanged for his cause, Louis Wigfall was elected to go to Washington and champion his.

Chapter IV

Grasping the Spears

THE THIRTY-SIXTH CONGRESS, 1859–61, was the most exciting—
and most disappointing—in the history of the United States.
Meeting in almost continuous session, taking time out only for
the 1860 campaign and election, spokesmen for both the North
and the South hurled insults back and forth. It was in the halls
of Congress that hopes for a rational settlement were buried
under an avalanche of irresponsible emotionalism. The seeds of
disunion had already been sown by the time Wigfall took his
seat as the freshman senator from Texas in December, 1859.
Epitomizing southern beliefs in white supremacy, slavery, states'
rights, and opposition to the protective tariff, Wigfall was the
most pugnacious, and one of the most destructive, of a number
of radical congressmen—northern and southern—who intensified
sectionalism to the point of civil war.

The day of Wigfall's election to the Senate, December 5, was
also the opening day of the Congress to which he was elected.
He was in Washington before legislative business began, however, because the House of Representatives took two continuous
months to elect a Whig-Republican as Speaker. The Senate was
no closer to a consensus. The Democrats were stronger here,
having thirty-eight of sixty-six seats, but they were divided into
as many as five blocs. And ten of the thirty-eight Democrats had
ambitions to become President, an aspiration which hampered

cooperation among them. Wigfall and other radicals might accomplish much if they worked together.[1]

Wigfall ignored the tradition that freshmen senators should say little, and despite his relegation to two of the less important committees, Private Land Claims and Post Offices, he seized numerous occasions to demonstrate his southernism. Soon he had earned a reputation for his ready, natural eloquence; his ability as a quick, bitter debater; his acerbic taunts; and his readiness for personal encounter. He was known, too, for his consistent attendance on the floor of the Senate—an attendance record all the more notable considering that his debates did not end in the halls of Congress. He also frequented bars and gaming rooms, seeking out adversaries even there.[2]

Wigfall was particularly disputatious toward New England congressmen and carried on a special vendetta against those from Massachusetts. Senator Henry Wilson of that state lit Wigfall's short fuse by attacking southerners in Congress who had succeeded in obtaining in the Compromise of 1850 more territory for Texas than Wilson felt was rightfully hers and paying her $10 million to take it. Further, Wilson said, Senator Sam Houston had admitted that Texans had only a mere claim, not a right, to the territory. Wigfall immediately voiced firm doubt that Houston had ever said any such thing. The Texas title to that land was staked upon "the bloody field of San Jacinto," thundered Wigfall, and he launched into a dramatic version of the Texas fight for independence, the Mexican War, the Treaty of Guadalupe-Hidalgo, and the Compromise of 1850. In a theatrical climax Wigfall produced and read extracts from Houston's 1850 Senate speeches in which he defended the Texas land titles that Wilson had questioned. Thus, a few days after his arrival in the capital, Wigfall vied with a Massachusetts senator, as both contributed to the mounting sectional tensions. And in the exchange, the Texan gained stature, if not respect, as he dem-

1 Nichols, *Disruption of American Democracy*, 282, 388, 461–62.
2 Russell, *Diary*, 63.

onstrated how Wilson "was mistaken in the position he had assumed." [3]

The following week he created still greater consternation in the North by attacking another Massachusetts senator, their lamented hero Daniel Webster, for his nationalistic interpretation of the Constitution. *All* the difficulties the country labored under, averred Wigfall, stemmed from a misapprehension of some of the most distinguished leaders as to the form of government of the United States. The best example he could offer was Webster; if there was a single thing about which "the godlike Daniel" was more profoundly ignorant than any other man, it was the Constitution of the United States. When northern senators responded to this with amused smiles, Wigfall warned that if the Union were ever to be destroyed, it would not be over slavery but nationalism. [4]

Developing his attack upon Webster, Wigfall attempted to set all the nationalists straight. There was no such thing, he instructed them, as a "national" government; there was only a *federal* government, and there was no majority rule in that. All this had been argued many times, but Wigfall's interpretation of "separation of powers" may have piqued interest if only for the sake of curiosity. Ignoring the federal judiciary, he explained that the separation was among *three departments of the legislature,* the House, the Senate, and the *President* of the United States. In an effort to prove three of his extreme states' rights views at once, Wigfall explained the veto process to show: (1) how the President was less an executive than a negative legislator; (2) how there was no majority rule; and (3) how there was no national government. When both houses had passed any bill, it then went to the President. If he disapproved of the bill, it was sent with his objections back to Congress where the veto could be overridden by a two-thirds vote in each house. In this process, Wigfall could see proof that there was no national government,

3 *Congressional Globe,* 36th Cong., 1st Sess., 593–602.
4 *Ibid.,* 675; reprinted in *Texas Republican,* April 14, 1860.

because whether the veto was sustained or overridden, the names of those voting yea or nay were entered in the journals. Thus, every man who voted on a presidential veto would have his name published and stand before his constituents on that question. Consequently, the Constitution ignored the idea of *national* popular majorities, concluded Wigfall. There was no nation of the United States; there were thirty-three nations which had confederated. Congress had only the powers that the states had delegated to it when they ratified the Constitution. Thus taught Wigfall, who proudly announced at the end of his lesson that he was "one of the straitest of the sect of State-rights men." [5] As Wigfall undoubtedly expected, his pedagogical admonition was not well received by his northern colleagues, but he seemed never to tire of repeating it during his eighteen months as a United States senator.

The political framework within which Wigfall attacked Wilson and Webster was actually the initial stage of the election of 1860, formalizing platform issues. Senator Albert G. Brown of Mississippi, who was even more radical than Wigfall and less acceptable to the leaders of the Democratic Party, sought his place in the political sun by introducing a set of radical resolutions. The most controversial portion of Brown's resolutions was the demand for an immediate congressional code to protect slavery in the territories, thus denying Douglas' popular sovereignty. Urging the adoption of his resolutions in the Senate and their incorporation into the Democratic platform, Brown set off extensive debate. Jefferson Davis, who aspired to fill Calhoun's shoes, could scarcely afford to appear less devoted to southern rights than his fellow Mississippian; but Davis also hoped to fill the presidential chair and did not want either the Union or the Democratic electoral votes divided between the North and South. After giving Brown a tongue-lashing, Davis offered his own less-

[5] *Congressional Globe*, 36th Cong., 1st Sess., 676. At this state of the conflict Wigfall was "straiter" than other Texas delegates, and he found it difficult to confer with them on the subject of what action Texas should take in the sharpening controversy. Wigfall to Hon. Thomas M. Isbell, February 6, 1860, Miscellaneous Letters of the South Carolina Collection, University of South Carolina.

radical resolutions. He brought Calhoun up to date by accepting the principle of federal protection of slavery in the territories, but Davis said that a slave code was not *yet* necessary. He read the southern situation correctly. A majority of southerners including Wigfall, supported the Davis Resolutions, but northern senators would accept neither the Brown nor the Davis proposals.[6] Thus, a vitriolic debate was opened upon the constitutional and political aspects of slavery in the territories and upon the nature of the Union. In such a situation Wigfall was at his forensic best.

A typical Wigfallian exchange was with Jacob Collamer (Rep.–Vermont), one of those to whom it was clear that the constitutional authority of Congress to "make all needful Rules and Regulations" for the territories included the power to prohibit slavery. Collamer pointed out that Congress had done so in the Missouri Compromise of 1820. But, he argued, the Mexican War, the annexation of Texas, and the Kansas-Nebraska Act, which repealed the Missouri Compromise, were successful parts of the conspiracy of slavocrats to expand their evil institution. Wigfall was quick to reply, but he started, as he often did, with deceptive calmness. He asked Collamer, "just as a matter of curiosity," what he understood to be the "principle" of the Compromise of 1850 concerning congressional intervention in Utah and New Mexico. Collamer replied that there was nothing said in the compromise about that. Wigfall then declaimed that since nothing was said about congressional power to establish or prohibit slavery therein, "any principle" in the compromise had to be that Congress should not legislate in regard to slavery in the territories. When Collamer objected that Wigfall was drawing a conclusion, Wigfall replied cutely that he was merely asking for information, "You see I am a new Senator yet, and do not understand these questions." As Collamer started to reply, Wigfall left the chamber. When he returned much later, he suggested that Collamer yield the floor since he had been talking for three hours. "Only two-and-a-half hours," shot back Collamer,

6 *Congressional Globe,* 36th Cong., 1st Sess., 658–59, 1048.

who kept talking for another hour-and-a-half about how the founding fathers had planned the eventual abolition of slavery.[7]

To such abolitionist theories Wigfall replied that "the fathers, as they are called," never sanctioned any such principles. Even though he was willing to admit that Jefferson, Madison, and Washington "supposed" that slavery was an evil, Wigfall maintained that they still did not believe the federal government had the right to abolish it anywhere. Wigfall refused, however, to cite the principles and practices of these men for his proof, as some southern spokesmen did. In this instance Wigfall did not even point out that all three of the presidents mentioned had been slaveowners. Specifically, and characteristically, he refused to pin his "faith to anybody's sleeve," or to claim that "because Calhoun, or Jefferson, or Monroe, or Adams, or Clay voted in a particular manner, therefore, *ipso facto*, the proposition is established that I am right. These gentlemen all differed from themselves at different periods, . . . It is useless to go back, in a Government like ours . . . . We must put every proposition in the crucible of argument, and there try its truth." Nevertheless, Wigfall used Jefferson's denunciation of the Missouri Compromise to argue against the idea that Congress had authority to keep slavery out of the territories or anywhere else. Besides, he continued, slavery was *not* a moral wrong, but rather the destruction of property (in slaves) was a moral wrong. Therefore, according to the Texan, Congress had acted not only unconstitutionally but immorally in the part of the Compromise of 1850 which abolished the slave trade in the District of Columbia.[8]

Thus, Wigfall agreed with the principle of the Davis and Brown resolutions. But while he delighted in baiting northern Republicans, he said he desired unity among northern and southern Democrats. He thought Brown's proposal useless agitation which would only benefit the Republicans by dividing the Democrats. If the Republicans in 1860 were successful, it would mean the destruction of the Union because they would try to abolish

[7] *Ibid.*, 1048–60.
[8] *Ibid.*, 1488–89.

slavery; therefore, if northern Democrats wanted to preserve the Union, Wigfall warned, they should unite with southerners behind Davis' resolutions. Any fears for Democratic unity on the eve of their national convention were justified. The issue of slavery in the territories was splitting the southern and northern Democrats. Just three days after Wigfall voiced his fears, a House debate on that issue degenerated into a shoving, name-calling melee, and one southern congressman said later that he had cocked his revolver in his pocket, determined to sell his blood at the highest price.[9]

The degree of sectional animosity and refusal of senators from one section to understand the problems of another section is reflected in Wigfall's effort to obtain federal aid to protect Texas frontiers. Citing examples of Mexican and Indian atrocities, Wigfall argued that it would be more economical for Congress to spend one million dollars early to protect the border than to wait and pay ten million for the destruction of property—"life you cannot pay for." Wigfall was convinced that he was getting a runaround, for members of the executive department told him that they were unwilling to do anything until Congress had passed an appropriation bill, and when he went to Congress he was told that they were unwilling to grant money until the President asked for it.[10]

When Wigfall finally presented his request for $1,100,000, his opposition coalesced. If the opponents of Wigfall's senatorial election in the Texas Legislature had not taught him anything about obstructive parliamentary tactics, William Pitt Fessenden (Rep.–Maine) certainly did. Especially galling to Wigfall was Fessenden's charge that if Texas borders were actually threatened, the Texans should defend themselves as the people of his state of Maine had done when they were invaded by troops from Canada. Then, while Wigfall was electioneering for his bill, it was referred to the Military Affairs Committee through some

[9] *Ibid.*, 1488–90; *Texas Republican*, April 28, 1860; Nichols, *Disruption of American Democracy*, 286.
[10] *Congressional Globe*, 36th Cong., 1st Sess., 874–75

northern "parliamentary legerdemain" which he did not understand at all. But to his greater amazement, before he "could turn
around and see what was done," Committee Chairman Jefferson
Davis had the bill back on the Senate floor with a favorable
report.[11]

Speaking for his bill, Wigfall introduced a Texas newspaper
report he had just received. One recent day, according to the
report, four Texas communities had been attacked by Comanches. Nine settlers were known dead, more were feared dead,
four women had been captured and "abused in the most brutal
manner," and two of them had been scalped. Seemingly unable
to speak without venting his hatred of Yankees, Wigfall hurt his
own cause by saying that though the Republicans might have
"peculiarities" and "sympathies for a class of the human family
[slaves] that mislead them as to some matters," they would not
vote against his bill.[12]

Fessenden was not convinced; he still wondered why Texans
suffered and waited till they were organized and paid by the national government. Exuding sarcasm, Wigfall thanked the Maine
Republican for his suggestion and allowed that: "The people
of Texas, of course, are avaricious; of course they are timid; in
their veins there run not those warm currents that course through
the veins of the people . . . in Maine, who so gallantly defied the
British . . . on an occasion of which I have not been informed!
Those frontiermen . . . live from five to . . . twenty miles apart.
No man dares to be out of sight of his house . . . [lest] savages
come in behind them and murder [their] women and children."
The only practical mode of dealing with the problem, said Wigfall, was to establish posts along the Rio Grande and the northern
frontiers and to attack the Indians when they were most vulnerable.[13]

After three more days of invective-swapping with northern
senators, Wigfall was so angered that he threatened them, "You

11 *Ibid.*, 938–39, 943, 945, 1009.
12 *Ibid.*, 1009.
13 *Ibid.*, 1010.

will not get any tariff if you reject this." When he finally brought it to a vote, the bill got the support of a majority voting, but there was no quorum present. It took Wigfall several more days of repeated efforts to get another vote. Then his frontier bill passed the Senate, 41–11, but was rejected in the House. Though he tried again several times, the bill never became law.[14]

Nor did Wigfall succeed in getting federal aid for the Southern Pacific Railroad through the Southwest. In this effort the Senate was treated to the unusual spectacle of "one of the straitest of the State Rights sect" asking for federal land and funds and then tripping himself up so completely that he had to vote against parts of his own bill.

For all the furor of the Kansas-Nebraska Act, Congress had been unable to agree on a transcontinental railroad route. Wigfall, apropos of his theories of letting each section go its own way, proposed a bill to finance a northern track and a southern track, each with a parallel telegraph line. The Southern Pacific line would extend from New Orleans through Texas. The northern road would begin at some point on the Missouri River. Both would reach California. The directors would receive extensive land grants along the right-of-way, and they would get a federal loan of $70 million upon almost indefinite terms.[15]

Although Wigfall argued that the federal government had no right to charter a company of any kind, it could donate land and contract for the transportation of the mail, making advance payment for it. And this was, according to its caption, one purpose of his railroad bill.[16] Nevertheless, some of his colleagues reproved him, especially when he denied the power of the federal government to grant land under a homestead bill. This issue of

14 *Ibid.*, 1011–12, 1021–22, 1060–63, 1075, 1086, 1100, 1118–20, 1142–44, 2888, 2934–35; *Texas Republican*, March 10, 1860; Dallas *Herald*, March 28, 1860.

15 *Congressional Globe*, 36th Cong., 1st Sess., 658, 668, 1528; *Texas Republican*, April 21, 1860.

16 "A bill to provide for the . . . transportation . . . of mails, troops, munitions of war, military and naval stores between the Atlantic States and California, and for other purposes." *Congressional Globe*, 36th Cong., 1st Sess., 1528. Wigfall had argued similarly while a member of the Texas Legislature; see his speech in Marshall, Texas, April 19, 1859, in *Texas Republican*, May 19, 1859.

free land, centering around proposals for homesteads of 160 acres, had been debated in Congress since the mid-1840's, but it was not until 1852 that Andrew Johnson (Dem.–Tennessee) pushed a bill for it through the House, and then it was not considered by the Senate. In 1858 it met a similar fate, but only by the deciding vote of Vice-President John C. Breckinridge (Dem.–Kentucky). As the Northeast and the West combined in favor of free land, the South lost ground.

Wigfall and his attitude were representative of southern opposition to another homestead act presented in 1860. Johnson pleaded for its passage as "a great measure calculated to . . . elevate the condition of the common men and advance the great cause of civilization." But his nemesis Wigfall lampooned it as a bill providing land for the landless, homes for the homeless, "and leaving out the important matter . . . of niggers for the niggerless."

Wigfall then launched into the most disorganized speech of his senatorial career, a four-hour extemporaneous filibuster (he never spoke from notes and castigated those who did) in which he discoursed with sarcastic humor on a potpourri of subjects including the reopening of the African slave trade.[17] This foreign trade would make the government an eleemosynary establishment, because it would lead to the Christianization of Africa without endangering the clergy. (According to Wigfall's droll reckoning, three preachers were eaten to every convert made by missionaries going to Africa.)

Returning briefly to the homestead bill, Wigfall declared that public lands belonged not to individual citizens or to the federal government but to the states, which simply let the federal government administer the land as a trust. Congress had no more power to give 160 acres than it did to give 160 *dollars* to every poor man in the country. Then he was off on another tangent. As far as the government's holding land for the purpose of admitting new states, it did not have any manifest destiny to spread

17 *Congressional Globe*, 36th Cong., 1st Sess., 1298–1303.

"blatherskiting Americanism." That was a false doctrine advo cated by New England.

As usual, Wigfall had some choice invective for New Englanders, who he charged, looked upon the government as a cow. The South had been feeding the beast, and New England had been milking it. By federal legislation they had been able, without work, to get rich, while the South had become poor. Reallizing this, they would not dare push the South into dissolving the Union. The northeastern people would starve if they did, crowed Wigfall; Seward and others who talked of the "irrepressible conflict" would be so unpopular in the North that they would have their heads taken off close to their shoulders.

After reassuring his colleagues that he rose not to make any threats, Wigfall announced his belief that no Black Republican would ever be inaugurated President of the United States—let war come, "and if we do not get into Boston . . . before you get into Texas, you may shoot me." The North could not conquer the South, declaimed Wigfall belligerently. As he looked around at the northern senators, he saw only one who had ever witnessed the firing of a gun, but he pointed out several southerners who had served well in war. Furthermore, the only source of northern money was in the South, Wigfall scoffed. The South could ship its tobacco and sugar in other than northern ships. But more important, he chided, "Cotton is King"; and the North did not have enough money to pay the navy to blockade southern ports. If necessary, Europe would help the South because Europeans had to have southern cotton. The South just might confederate with England, Wigfall hinted. The northern and southern states had confederated for "certain purposes," he said, but the North had broken the bargain and then had tried to fool the South with "twaddle" that the Union was of divine origin. That would no longer do, he declared.

Some proponents of the homestead bill frequently countered Wigfall's constitutional objections with pointed questions about the constitutionality of his railroad bill. His most able critic on this issue was George Pugh (Dem.–Ohio). Pugh asked the Texas champion of states' rights to inform the Senate where in the Constitution or the "famous Kentucky or Virginia resolutions" he had discovered that the federal government had any more authority to provide railroads in Louisiana, as well as in the territories, than it had to bestow lands upon the landless. Wigfall replied that while the government had no authority to carry on any system of internal improvements, it could provide for carrying mail and soldiers. But Wigfall hedged; if he could not show this true beyond a doubt, he would vote against his own bill. Pugh would not let up. Republican senators must have been delighted as he termed Wigfall's interpretation of the Constitution more latitudinarian than the Federalists ever dreamed.[18]

Touching on a sore but valid sectional point, Pugh wondered how the homestead bill could either encourage or discourage the settlement of slaveholding communities. Responded Wigfall, "one hundred and sixty acres is not enough to work a negro." And he insisted, exaggerating greatly, that the bill was anti-southern because the South had no pauper citizens; the non-slaveholders of the South being landholders "ninety-nine times out of a hundred." The purpose of the bill was to "free-soil" the territory of the United States with the outpourings of the jails and the poor houses. And Wigfall did not want states being built up with such inhabitants who believed they were beneficiaries of the federal government.[19]

As his constitutional arguments weakened, Wigfall's reasoning went further afield. His colleagues were slow to take him seriously when he announced that poverty was a crime and the homestead bill would encourage crime. Had not God declared that "he who will not provide for his own family is worse than an infidel"? Wigfall had little use for that class who did nothing but eat, sleep, and die. The "capitalists" were the producers. A "capitalist" by his description was a man who lived by his honest toil, his skill, and his brains, even though he owned no land or slaves. Such a man would not take a handout of a free home. The

18 *Ibid.*, 1528–33.
19 *Ibid.*, 1533, 1539, 1658–59.

proper solution, said Wigfall, was to dispose of the lands to the states in which they lay, leaving the states to use them as they saw fit. He and C. C. Clay (Dem.–Alabama) introduced bills to accomplish that.[20]

Wigfall might have admired Andrew Johnson as one of the "capitalists" since he had worked his way up from an illiterate tailor, but he was on the wrong side of the political fence. To embarrass the self-educated Tennessean, the Texan called attention to Johnson's protest against his more learned colleagues' high-flown usage of Greek and Latin phrases. Wigfall asserted that education was necessary for any avocation, be it law, medicine, "or tailoring." Politicians especially should be educated. And, as "history was philosophy teaching by example," no man ought to enter politics unless he had studied history.

Wigfall implied that had Johnson known more about history, he would not have alluded to Calhoun as a mere politician. In defending Calhoun, Wigfall referred to Arnold Winkelreid, a Swiss who had battled the oppresive Austrians until he stood in the last gap in which liberty could be defended. Speaking, as usual, without notes, he extolled the heroic Winkelreid:

> He, of battle martyrs chief,
> who to recall his daunted peers,
> for victory shaped an open space
> by gathering with a wide embrace
> into his single breast, a sheaf
> of fatal Austrian spears.

Undoubtedly, Wigfall saw not only Calhoun, but also himself as the martyr, "Springing out from the ranks," grasping the enemy spears and opening a way "through which his countrymen marched to liberty and independence." [21]

Despite the efforts of Wigfall, Clay, and other southerners, the Senate and House passed the homestead bill in May, 1860. But President Buchanan vetoed it, and cotton-state senators prevented the two-thirds majority necessary to override a veto.

20 *Ibid.*, 1534–36, 1537, 1538, 1656, 1659.
21 *Ibid.*, 1657, 1658.

Thus, southerners were no more sympathetic to needs of northerners than their northern brethren were to Texans' needs for frontier defense. One southern senator said he felt that no two nations on earth were ever more distinctly separate and hostile than were the North and South.[22] The Democratic National Convention opened the next day, April 23, in Charleston, South Carolina, and demonstrated this hostility.

As the 1860 election approached, political, economic, and religious trends were interacting to force the future of the United States to flow rapidly into new channels. Politically, the Democrats were dividing their forces, North and South, in the face of the new northern party—the Republicans—which was growing stronger. Economically, the Panic of 1857–60 had sectional effects. Northern manufacturing, on the threshold of the industrial revolution, felt the restless urge of progress and the need for favorable federal legislation to stimulate their economy. But the South read the panic differently. The slave states, having suffered little from the financial chaos, were more convinced than ever that cotton was king and that southern civilization, based upon slave labor, was superior. Even the religious upheavals in the country from 1840 to 60 had taken sectional directions. The North became more liberal and rationalistic, and abolitionism became a moral crusade, while the South became more conservative and evangelical. It all formed a pattern; the North had become progressive and equalitarian and the South had followed the planter class into orthodoxy. Jeffersonian liberalism and the skepticism of earlier southern generations were gone.[23] Both sections viewed the 1860 campaign, as one farmer succinctly put it, as "no less than a contest for the advancement of the kingdom of heaven or the kingdom of Satan . . ."; each, of course, having its own ideas about who was on which side.[24]

[22] James H. Hammond to Major Hammond, April 22, 1860, Hammond Papers, University of South Carolina, quoted in Nichols, *Disruption of American Democracy*, 287.

[23] *Cf.* Nichols, *Disruption of American Democracy*, 139; and Francis Butler Simkins, *A History of the South* (New York, 1956), Chap. 11.

[24] Letter to Abraham Lincoln, undated, quoted in Robert W. Johannsen (ed.), *The Lincoln-Douglas Debates of 1858* (New York, 1965), 9.

The Democratic Party could not withstand the sectional results of the rechanneling of economic, religious, and political
forces. Northern and western Democrats had become even more
dissatisfied with their obstructionist southern brethren who had
prevented federal aid for internal improvements, free homesteads, and a protective tariff. The southern Democrats had their
own grievances, such as the exorbitant price of slaves and in-
debtedness to northern banks and merchants, to goad them into
radical action.

All of the conflicting interests of the North and South were
focused on the issue of slavery in the territories. To northern
businessmen and industrialists, the western lands meant new
markets, raw materials, and the completion of what Columbus
had been seeking—a direct route to the Orient. To northern
farmers, the West meant cheaper land and opportunity to expand. To northern abolitionists, the territories were the first line
of attack upon slavery. To all northerners, western lands meant
an opportunity to increase the number of free states and congressmen to outvote the slave states, thus passing legislation favorable
to the North. Conversely, southerners considered the western
lands as their first line of defense for their civilization.[25]

The northern demands coalesced as the Republican platform
of 1860. The extreme southern sentiment was embodied in the
"Alabama Platform," which asserted that the Democratic Party
had to demand federal protection for slavery in the territories. Northern Democrats countered with a "Douglas Platform"
which sought refuge in a form of the old Cincinnati policies,
evading the question of positive federal protection of slavery in
the territories, but declaring vaguely that the party would abide
by Supreme Court decisions.

The Douglas Democrats constituted a majority of the delegates at the national convention, but the radicals undoubtedly
drew strength from the environment of Charleston, the heart of
southernism. Partial control of the party slipped to fire-eaters

25 *Cf.* Johannsen, *Lincoln-Douglas*, 5–6, Nichols, *Disruption of American Democracy*, 287.

such as William L. Yancey of Alabama, and Robert Barnwell Rhett of South Carolina. (Wigfall's name had been presented as a delegate, but for some reason it had been withdrawn almost three weeks before the convention.) [26] With Yancey as their spokesman, the Deep South states presented the Alabama Platform as their ultimatum. Nevertheless, the Douglas Democrats pushed their plaform through. Most of the cotton-state representatives then walked out. The remaining delegates, unable to decide what to do, adjourned to reconvene in Baltimore six weeks later.

During that time, two other parties met, drew up platforms, and nominated candidates. The Constitutional Union Party, composed of Whig and Know-Nothing remnants, nominated John Bell of Tennessee on a platform against sectional parties and for upholding the Constitution. The Republicans nominated Abraham Lincoln and skillfully drew up a platform to appeal to the East and West as well as to the North, reaffirming the Wilmot Proviso—but also the right of states to control their respective domestic institutions—supporting federal aid for internal improvements, a transcontinental railroad, a homestead act, and a protective tariff. It denied congressional authority to protect slavery in the territories or to give it legal status there. Despite the threats presented by the opposing parties, most of the bolting Democrats remained as intractable as ever.

After the failure of the Charleston convention, Congress itself became more of a confused political convention than a legislative body. After an evening in Washington with Wigfall, Davis, and General Joseph E. Johnston, John Manning reported that everything was in confusion there: "Nobody knows anything about anything." [27]

Wigfall and other radicals were doing nothing to bring order or to salve feelings. The southern walkout represented just such defiant, concerted action as he had preached for years. He re-

[26] Dallas *Herald*, April 18, 1860.
[27] Manning to his wife, May, 1860, Williams-Chesnut-Manning Collection.

fused to join the efforts of nine of the more moderate southern senators to get the straying delegates back into the fold. Wigfall cooperated zealously, however, with a cabal to discredit Douglas.[28] Gulf-states senators, led by Davis and Judah P. Benjamin (Dem.–Louisiana), attacked Douglas with such invective that they cowed most of the northern Democrats. Douglas was in poor shape to reply. Disheartened by personal as well as political troubles, he was drinking so heavily that his managers tried to keep him from the Senate floor. Only Pugh of Ohio stood up for him. When Pugh charged southerners with causing the rupture at Charleston, Wigfall countered with the assertion that Douglas, Pugh, and their like were the rebels from the true Democratic Party.[29]

After pronouncing Douglas politically dead, having died from a surfeit of printer's ink, Wigfall performed a two-day filibuster as a funeral oration. In an astonishing projection of his own faults to others, he charged that southern "compromise efforts" had been met by the inflexibility of the Douglas clique. "Rule or ruin, that is the game they play," he accused. Democrats had to have a man for whom they could all vote, lest a Republican win. And Wigfall warned, "disunion is imminent if a Republican is elected." They were a party fraught with all sorts of heresies against the Constitution, the Kentucky and Virginia Resolutions, and human nature, Wigfall admonished. Instead of states' rights men they were woman's rights men, and human rights men. "They think a woman a man with a petticoat on, and a negro a black white man; that everyone is created free and equal." Wigfall marvelled, why should it not be considered an "act of aggression" upon the South if a Black Republican were elected President? Such diligence for the southern cause won him high rank among the statesmen of America, said the Montgomery, Alabama, *Advertiser*; the Dallas *Herald*, the *Texas Republican*,

28 *Texas Republican*, June 2, 1860; Nichols, *Disruption of American Democracy*, 309–10.
29 Nichols, *Disruption of American Democracy*, 310; *Congressional Globe*, 36th Cong., 1st Sess., 2244–49.

and even the more moderate Clarksville, Texas, *Northern Standard* agreed.[30]

Wigfall also worked with a majority of other Democratic senators against Douglas' popular sovereignty theory by speaking and voting for the Davis Resolutions as the gleeful Republicans egged on the family quarrel.[31] Thus, Douglas, the leading Democratic contender for the presidency, was repudiated by his Democratic colleagues on the eve of the Baltimore convention and the election of 1860.

After sectional lines were more clearly drawn in the party platforms, campaigning by senators became extremely intense and sometimes personal. One Republican campaign pamphlet moved Wigfall to protest. In a speech published by the Republican Congressional Committee, Kingsley S. Bingham (Rep.–Michigan) asserted that Wigfall had said in the Senate a few days earlier that southerners had only to threaten the northern senators with secession and "the timid creatures will . . . bite the dust, and kiss the rod raised to chastise them." The Texan disavowed the use of such language anywhere, anytime, and asked Bingham his authority for it. Bingham's defense was that he had cut it from a newspaper and supposed it correctly reported. On numerous occasions Wigfall had denounced the practice of "clipping speeches from newspapers," and he was especially indignant at Bingham. Under pressure, Bingham was unable to name the newspaper. Triumphantly Wigfall proclaimed, "the Senators will draw their own conclusions." [32]

Wigfall clashed headlong with Republican Senators William H. Seward, Wilson, and Collamer during the debate over the admission of Kansas as a state. Prefacing his remarks with his usual didactics on the nature of the Union, Wigfall objected to the admission of Kansas because of the nature of its population;

---

30 *Congressional Globe*, 36th Cong., 1st Sess., 2276–78. Douglas did offer to withdraw but his managers would not let him, Montgomery *Advertiser*, May 14, 1860; Dallas *Herald*, May 16, June 20, 1860; *Texas Republican*, June 16, 1860; *Northern Standard*, July 14, 1860.

31 *Congressional Globe*, 36th Cong., 1st Sess., 2321–24, 2347, 2349, 2350–52.

32 *Ibid.*, 2455. *Cf.* Wigfall's statement on p. 65, concerning the use of threats.

they were not law-abiding people—most of them came from New England, especially Massachusetts. Using "Beecher's Bibles" (Sharp's rifles which Boston Congregationalist minister Henry Ward Beecher said would do more good than the Bible to keep Kansas free), they came to "free-soil" the territory. To thwart this, Congress had passed the Kansas-Nebraska Act. But it was not carried out because of free-soiler obstructionism, explained Wigfall. His remedy was more direct—some rope, a battery of artillery, and a squadron of cavalry, for outlaws and traitors had been allowed to gain a possible majority, while good men had been driven out. Again he closed on a dire note: Had the northern Democrats remained steadfast to the party, Kansas would have been protected and there would have been better hopes of saving the Union than he saw in the future.[33]

If the Democrats in their Baltimore convention were worried about saving the Union from the Republicans, they did not act like it. When the northern Democrats secured the nomination of Douglas, the southerners walked out again, followed by more Gulf-states' delegates than at Charleston. Ten days later, the Baltimore delegates nominated Vice-President John C. Breckinridge for President and Jo Lane of Oregon for Vice-President. Their platform incorporated the Davis Resolutions' call for federal protection of slavery in the territories when needed. The southern delegates had demanded what they knew they could not have from the northern Democrats. When they could not rule, they ruined—the Union as well as the party; for most should have realized, if they did not, that by dividing in the face of a determined northern party, they were assuring the election of a Republican, even while announcing that such an event would mean secession of the South.

Some southern Democrats, however, thought they had a slender chance of defeating Lincoln. Perhaps the election would be so close that no presidential or vice-presidential candidate would receive a majority in the electoral college, meaning that the elec-

---

[33] *Ibid.*, 2622–24; a vote was delayed to take up the army bill; also in *Texas Republican*, June 30, 1860.

98   LOUIS T. WIGFALL

tion of the President would then be decided in the House of
Representatives, with each state having one vote. Here again, it
was hoped, there would be no majority, thus producing a dead-
lock. The vice-presidential contest would be decided in the pre-
dominantly Democratic Senate, which was likely to select Lane
over the Republican Hannibal Hamlin if it got a chance. Since
no President had been selected, Lane would become President
by default. So far had reason fled some of the southern leaders.[34]

Though their chances were slender, southern Democrats cam-
paigned desperately. After all, their way of life within the Union
was at stake. The threat did not breed unity, however. The conflict in Texas is an example of how southern states were torn by
factional struggles. Sam Houston, running for President on a
nationalist ticket of his own, was determined to defeat the radical
southerners' bid to carry the state for Breckinridge and Lane.
Wigfall, just as determined, conducted a forceful campaign
across the state for his favorites. The South had to vote for
Breckinridge and Lane, he warned. If southern men refused to
sustain their platform, northern men could never be induced to
believe that the South felt any real interest in the issues. Douglas
would not carry any state, Wigfall predicted; he would not even
be strong enough to divide the vote and send the election into
the House of Representatives. The people would decide between
Lincoln and Breckinridge. But the Constitutional Unionists
were dangerously misleading the North; the free-soilers were led
to believe that the South felt no real interest in the slavery question and that Lincoln could be elected with safety.[35]

The impact of Wigfall's warnings was intensified by rumors
of slave uprisings causing near panic in large areas of Texas and
other southern states. Two "northern agents" were captured and

34 Wigfall speech at Jefferson, Texas, July 28, 1860, in *Texas Republican*, August 4, 1860; Nichols, *Disruption of American Democracy*, 338–39; Murat Halstead
in Allan Nevins, *The Emergence of Lincoln* (2 vols.; New York, 1950), II, 211.
35 Wigfall speech at Jefferson, Texas, July 28, 1860, in *Texas Republican*, August 4, 1860; speech at Marshall, Texas, August 1, 1860, in *Texas Republican*,
August 11, 1860; see also Wigfall to John Marshall (editor of the *Texas Gazette*),
August 27, 1860, in *Texas Republican*, October 20, 1860.

hanged in Fort Worth for allegedly attempting to foment a slave insurrection and plotting to poison the wells of the slaveowners. And on August 5, the day after Wigfall spoke in Jefferson, Texas, the town of Henderson, fifty miles away, was burned—by northern arsonists, Texans were sure.[36]

While Wigfall was in Marshall for the election on August 3, a story spread that a young lady had been "killed by the negroes." Actually, she had simply fled her home after becoming suspicious that they were about to revolt. Other events and numerous fires continued to provoke fears of Negro uprisings through November, and more could be expected if Lincoln were elected, the *Texas Republican* warned. The summer of 1860 was an extremely dry one in Texas, and dry summers usually brought fires. But under the combustible political conditions, Texans saw sinister incendiarism in every blaze. Even small villages had twenty-four-hour guards, which sometimes included Wigfall during the six weeks he was campaigning in Texas. When Congress reconvened in December, Wigfall was quick to air his views on the "terrorism." He blamed this on an association which he said was named the "Mystic Red," comprised of members of the Methodist Church North and the John Brown men, and their purpose was, Wigfall told the Northern senators: "to carry out the irrepressible conflict, to burn our towns . . . to bring free-soil northern capital in. and thus get possession of Texas, and make it a free state." [37]

Wigfall and Breckinridge would have met more opposition in Texas than they did, had it not been for the panic there. Even so, the unionist press in Texas took Wigfall to task for such things as his "startling doctrine that we have no nation here." [38]

36 Herbert Aptheker, *American Negro Slave Revolts* (New York, 1943), 353–58; Clement Eaton, "Mob Violence in the Old South," *Mississippi Valley Historical Review*, XXIX (June, 1942), 351–71; Nichols, *Disruption of American Democracy*, 363–64; *Journal of the Secession Convention*, 7.
37 *Texas Republican*, August 11, 18, November 10, 1860; *Congressional Globe*, 36th Congress, 2nd Sess., 74.
38 *Intelligencer*, October 10, 1860; see also the *Harrison Flag* (Marshall, Texas), as quoted in *Texas Republican*, August 11, 1860; *Journal of the Secession Convention*, 7; Friend, *Houston*, 311.

But such opposition was slight; the little support that Douglas had in Texas, dwindled before the election, and in mid-August Houston withdrew from the contest. Thus, the 1860 Texas vote was an overwhelming victory for the prosouthern faction.

CANDIDATES	POPULAR VOTES
Breckinridge	47,548
Bell	15,463
Douglas	410
Lincoln	0

But the national results were another story. Breckinridge carried the South, but this was only 18 percent of the national popular vote, worth 24 percent of the electoral vote. Lincoln was elected with 59 percent of the electoral votes, though he had only 39.8 percent of the popular vote. He would have been elected even if his opposition had combined their totals. His strength was centered in the populous North where the electoral vote was heaviest.[39]

The southern cause was not immediately lost. The congressional returns indicated that Republicans did not control the House, and the Supreme Court was essentially the same one which had rendered the Dred Scott decision. But these Justices would not live forever; new ones would be appointed by the Republican President. Articulating the general argument used by fire-eaters to justify secession, Wigfall refuted the belief that the South controlled the Senate. There were eighteen free states; free Kansas would soon come in, he said, and then there would be nineteen free states with thirty-eight senators. With the few changes to come March 4, there would be a tie of thirty-four votes each for the North and South, then their "Black Republican Vice-President" would break the tie. They could pass pronorthern legislation, and Lincoln could appoint abolitionists to office. But there would not be many southern Democrats in the Senate by then, Wigfall warned.[40]

[39] Richardson, *Texas*, 245; W. Dean Burnham, *Presidential Ballots, 1836–1892* (Baltimore, 1955), 71–84, 888.
[40] *Congressional Globe*, 36th Cong., 2nd Sess., 75. *Cf.* Kenneth M. Stampp, *And*

Wigfall's constituents in his home county of Harrison attended a mass meeting November 24 and voted unanimously for resistance to Black Republicanism.[41] In other Deep South states the feeling was much the same. The disunionists had lost a fair election, but they would not accept the results. Wigfall, and even more moderate southern leaders, refused to fill a minority role behind the Republicans.

When Wigfall answered the opening roll call for the second session of the Thirty-sixth Congress, he was convinced that he would not be there for its close. Indeed, on that very day, December 3, 1860, preparations were made in Texas to call a secession convention. An overriding tone of "no compromise" was established by northern as well as southern radicals at the outset of the session and became more pronounced through the next five months of sectional umbrage. In defiance of the South, northern senators pushed the homestead bill, while Wigfall, Davis, Lane, Brown, and others brought their charges against the North. Buchanan's pusillanimous State of the Union Message, denying the right of secession but doubting his authority to do anything about it, brought odium upon him from Wigfall, Seward, and others of both sides. Wigfall warned that Buchanan's course, too, would bring war. To please Wigfall, the President would have to accept secession and help convince northerners of its legitimacy.[42]

While most senators of the cotton states caucused to agree on ways to dissolve the Union, their moderate colleagues, mostly from the tobacco states, planned ways to save it. The moderates decided to cast their program in the form of proposed constitutional amendments to be introduced by John J. Crittenden of Kentucky. Lazarus Powell, also of Kentucky, was to move for the formation of a Senate committee of thirteen which, the Union

the War Came: The North and the Secession Crisis, 1860–61 (Baton Rouge, 1950; paperback, Chicago, 1964), 136. Kansas was admitted to the Union the next month, January, 1861.

41 *Texas Republican,* December 1, 1860; see also Ramsdell, *Reconstruction in Texas,* 14–15.

42 *Journal of the Secession Convention,* 7; *Congressional Globe,* 36th Cong., 2nd Sess., 12–14, 283–89; Stampp, *And the War Came,* 56; Jesse L. Keene, *The Peace Convention of 1861* ... (Tuscaloosa, 1961), 28.

Democrats hoped, would endorse their program. It was a bad omen for them when the introduction and then the vote on the Powell Resolution were delayed by the bitter debates between Wigfall and other fire-eaters against Senator John P. Hale (Rep.– New Hampshire) and other radical Republicans.[43]

Wigfall not only disagreed with the "Union savers," but even instructed some of his disunionist colleagues on the justification of secession. After all, it was difficult, even for senators, to discuss secession intelligently, he said, when they had no well-defined ideas upon the subject. Paternalistically the seasoned secessionist lectured his less-learned colleagues on the rights of states. Some were saying that secession was a *revolutionary* right, but this was not true, said Wigfall. Any state had the right to withdraw from the Union at any time for any cause, or for no cause other than that she just wanted to. Later in the same speech, however, he appealed to "that great . . . right of revolution," warping it to his purpose as meaning: "If this government does not suit us, we will leave it." [44]

At a caucus of southern senators held December 8, Wigfall was with a large majority who agreed that the time had come to exercise the right of secession and to begin a new union. Although some of the Texas delegates still hoped for compromise, he declared to the caucus that Texas would secede within thirty days (it was actually fifty four). On the Senate floor, Wigfall was explaining that the South only meant to say that: "A man who is distasteful to us has been elected, and we choose to consider that as a sufficient ground for leaving the Union, and we intend to leave the Union." [45]

Occasionally Wigfall expressed a hope that the separation would be peaceable, but more often he equated it with war, once vowing that if war came, its concluding treaty would be signed in Boston's Faneuil Hall. If the North really wanted peace, he

43 *Congressional Globe*, 36th Cong., 2nd Sess., 6, 316; Nichols, *Disruption of American Democracy*, 393, 394.
44 *Congressional Globe*, 36th Cong., 2nd Sess., 12, 13.
45 *Texas Republican*, December 22, 1860; *Congressional Globe*, 36th Cong., 2nd Sess., 14.

said, they could save the Union by appeasing the South with constitutional amendments to protect slavery in the territories. But for these to mean anything, they would have to be ratified unanimously by the northern states to demonstrate a conciliatory spirit. Northern senators would have to urge the amendments, cease preaching the "irrepressible conflict," do away with their abolition societies, stop calling southerners cut-throats and slandering their women, and then *beg* southern senators not to secede until an honest effort could be made. Only then, said Wigfall, could there be prospects for the South's consideration of the amendments. When the Republicans laughed at him, Wigfall called upon Powell and other "Union-savers" to see the contempt that was expressed in every Republican senator's face when serious peace proposals were made.[46]

Certainly Wigfall did not expect the northerners to accept his one-sided bargain; he was simply trying to dissuade southerners from supporting Crittenden's amendments. In reports to Texas, Wigfall had belittled them as being intended only to divide southerners.[47] Turning back to the Republicans, he promised that the southerners would have what they wanted, though they would have to leave the Union to get it. South Carolina would show the way. In a conclusion which brought applause from the galleries, Wigfall thundered at the Republicans that South Carolina might be made a graveyard of freemen, but it would never be the habitation of enslaved white men.

When Senator Horatio King (Dem.–New York) smiled at this threat, Wigfall predicted that he would laugh out of the other side of his face before the matter was terminated. King said later that comparatively few persons either in the North or West anticipated any "serious trouble," regarding the threats of the secessionists as only a repetition of what they had said on former occasions, "and all for political effect." [48]

46 *Congressional Globe*, 36th Cong., 2nd Sess., 56–58, 71–72, 74.

47 Wigfall to Judge Leslie Thompson, December 7, 1860, in Galveston *News*, and *Texas Republican*, January 5, 1861.

48 *Congressional Globe*, 36th Cong., 2nd Sess., 85–86; Horatio King, *Turning on the Light* (Philadelphia, 1895) 86–87.

But the fire-eaters were serious. In mid-December another
caucus of cotton-state congressmen adopted a manifesto prepared
by Wigfall and Senator James L. Pugh of Alabama. By signing
this "Southern Manifesto," six other senators and twenty-three
representatives agreed with Wigfall that:

> The argument is exhausted. All hope of relief in the Union . . .
> is extinguished, and we trust the South will not be deceived by ap-
> pearances or the pretense of new guarantees. In our judgement the
> Republicans are resolute in the purpose to grant nothing that
> will . . . satisfy the South. We are satisfied the honor, safety, and
> independence of the Southern people require the organization of a
> Southern Confederacy.[49]

The manifesto was well-timed. It reached South Carolina in
time to be circulated among the delegates of the secession convention and was widely quoted and discussed throughout the
Deep South during important local elections. It was extremely
significant that after the signing of the manifesto, most of the
southern moderates seemed convinced that they could not stop
the secession movement. They turned their attention to nego-
tiating for a more satisfactory position for the South when it got
back into the Union.[50]

Under this pall of pessimism, Senator Crittenden presented his
compromise proposals to reestablish the Missouri Compromise
line (36°30′) and extend it to the Pacific, and—during territorial
stages—prohibit slavery north of the line while allowing slavery
south of it. New states, however, would be admitted with or
without slavery as they wished. If fugitive slaves were not returned from free states, they would be paid for. A majority of
the Democrats, northern and southern, favored these resolutions,
and they were submitted to Powell's Committee of Thirteen on
December 20. But President-elect Lincoln let it be known that
he was unwilling to compromise on the issue of slavery in the
territories. Republicans on the committee blocked the compro-

[49] Wigfall and others, "To Our Constituents," December 14, 1860, in *Texas Republican*, January 12, 1861.
[50] *Texas Republican*, January 12, 1861; Nichols, *Disruption of American Democracy*, 399.

mise, justifying their action by pointing to the Wigfall-Pugh Manifesto as a resolute expression of southern secessionism. Indeed, it was too late; on that day South Carolina announced her secession from the Union.[51]

During the next few weeks of frantic appeals by Crittenden, Douglas, and other moderates, the radical fire-eaters and Republicans drew the sections farther apart. Both had determined on their courses, and both tried to blame it on the other. Many Republicans agreed with Lincoln when he said: "The tug has to come and better now than later." [52] Perhaps they felt that acceptance of disunion or compromise would have split the Republicans, and they were relying upon the unionists in the South to prevail. Lincoln calculated the risk of violence, but the tug was certainly greater than he anticipated.

On January 16 the Republican senators were able to pass (25–23) an *anti*-compromise resolution as a substitute for Crittenden's amendments because cotton-state senators boycotted the session or, like Wigfall, refused to vote, saying the Republicans were opposed to compromise anyway.[53] Thus, conciliation was thwarted by fire-eating southerners and inflexible Republicans as well.

There is a story related by some of Wigfall's contemporaries and accepted by some historians that Wigfall made a desperate effort to avoid war by conniving to kidnap the President of the United States. *The Diary of a Public Man*, supposedly a day-to-day journal by an anonymous but knowledgeable figure of the time, includes an account of an alleged talk with someone referred to only as "B—," who said that Wigfall had called together a few "choice spirits" and proposed that they kidnap Buchanan. This would allow Vice-President Breckinridge to become President, and the South would feel secure against being trapped into a war. According to the story, Wigfall had laid his plans care-

51 *Congressional Globe*, 36th Cong., 2nd Sess., 274, 279–80; Stampp, *And the War Came*, 134–37, 153; Nichols, *Disruption of American Democracy*, 402.
52 John G. Nicolay and John Hay (eds.), *The Complete Works of Abraham Lincoln* (12 vols.; New York, 1894), VI, 77–78.
53 *Congressional Globe*, 36th Cong., 2nd Sess., 275, 279–80, 326–27, 409.

fully, but he needed Secretary of War John Floyd, a Virginian, to help get Buchanan out of Washington. When Wigfall went to Floyd's house on Christmas night to enlist his aid, Floyd refused. Supposedly, Wigfall lost his temper and—if the rest of the story be true—he lost his nerve; the plot was never attempted. A confidant of Lincoln, Ward H. Lamon, relates a strikingly similar story but gives no hint as to where he obtained the information. Though the *Diary of a Public Man* has proved useful in corroborating events in Washington during this period, the story of Wigfall's kidnap plot is almost certainly a fabrication by someone. The Texan and the South were afraid of what Lincoln would do, not what Buchanan would do. Further, Wigfall was not interested in saving the Union even before South Carolina had seceded, and still less inclined that way after his natal state had left the Union. Two days after South Carolina seceded, and three days before he supposedly approached Floyd with the plot, Wigfall announced emphatically from the Senate floor, "We are going out." "Public Man" himself, although describing Wigfall as having "the eye of a man capable of anything," expressed incredulity upon hearing of the plot, and two months later he denounced Wigfall as a "desperado" who took it for granted that the Union had failed.[54]

Indeed, Wigfall had been convinced for some time that the Union had failed, and he was becoming more effective in persuading others. On January 4, proclaimed by Buchanan as a day for fasting and prayer for the Union, Wigfall and other secessionists met and decided to advise their states to secede at once. Pointing to the inflexible policies of the Republicans, the dis-

[54] Frank Maloy Anderson, *The Mystery of "A Public Man"* (Minneapolis, 1948), 143, 159; Ward H. Lamon, *Recollections of Abraham Lincoln 1847–1865*, ed. by Dorothy Lamon Teillard (Washington, 1911), 264–65; *Congressional Globe*, 36th Cong., 2nd Sess., 200. Nichols, *Disruption of American Democracy*, 421, accepts the story; and Swanberg, *First Blood*, 110, uses part of "Public Man's" story and qualifies part with "he was said to have gone to Secretary Floyd's house with a typically Wigfallian proposition." Frank Maloy Anderson, who has made a close study of the "Public Man," has concluded that this is one of the "almost certainly sheer inventions" of the *Diary*; see his *Mystery of "A Public Man,"* 177, 197–98.

unionists again proclaimed that all hope of justice within the Union was gone. Wigfall and a few others said they would stay in Washington only to keep Buchanan's hands tied and to keep watch on the Republicans.[55]

The southern radicals, especially Wigfall, were encouraged when Texas and Louisiana held convention elections, on January 7 and 8 respectively, which indicated that those states were "going sesesh" despite significant Union sentiment there. Other news from Texas, however, was less pleasant for Wigfall. His finances back home were in such poor shape that on January 1 some of his property in Marshall was sold to satisfy $750 of his debts.[56] But he could vent his frustration upon his enemies, who were plentiful in Washington, and he could gain satisfaction by telling himself he was neglecting his finances to serve his section, by spying on the unionists.

Since most of the cotton-state senators were convinced by December 20 that secession was coming, they insisted that Federal troops be withdrawn from forts in the South. As late as January 4, Secretary of the Interior Jacob Thompson of Mississippi was assured by Buchanan that no troops would be sent to reinforce the forts. The next day a relief expedition was dispatched to Fort Sumter in Charleston Harbor. Soon after it sailed, the watchful Wigfall cabled Governor Pickens: "The *Star of the West* sailed from New York . . . with . . . troops and provisions. It is said her destination is Charleston." Thus warned, Charleston was ready for the *Star of the West*. When it reached there on January 9, it was fired upon and turned back. That same day Wigfall attacked Buchanan's policy with a characteristically sarcastic speech which he hoped would "produce peace and harmony and good feeling on both sides of the chamber." [57]

55 *Texas Republican*, January 19, 1861; Nichols, *Disruption of American Democracy*, 430, 433–34.

56 *Journal of the Secession Convention*, 7; Book T, 4, County Clerk's Office, Harrison County Court House, January 9, 1861.

57 Wigfall to F. W. Pickens, January 8, 1861, *War of the Rebellion: A Compilation of the Official Records of the Union and Confederate Armies* (130 vols.; Washington, 1880), I, 253. At about the same time, Secretary Thompson also found out about the expedition and wired Pickens. This is the same Pickens who was an

Secessionists had cause to feel well. Also on January 9, Mississippi announced her secession from the Union. The next day Florida departed, and the day after that, Alabama. By January 31, all of the states of the Deep South were out except Texas and there were few cotton-state senators left; thus Wigfall said it was incumbent upon himself to speak in defense of those states which had seceded, or certainly would. Regardless of what some said, declared Wigfall, the Republicans and the southern Democrats represented popular opinion in their respective sections. Southerners wanted to secede; northerners wanted war and would save the Union only by the bayonet.[58]

The old Union was dead, Wigfall announced; but, he predicted, a new one would soon be formed in Montgomery, Alabama, by the seceded southern states. He only regretted that Texas would not be out soon enough to join that government. Actually, Texas was "out" in time. While Wigfall spoke, preparations were made for the convention vote. The next day the vote was cast, 166–7 for secession. But Texas delayed official announcement until after the voters at the polls confirmed the convention vote, 44,317–13,020, on February 23.[59]

Wigfall blamed the dissolution of the Union partially upon Douglas and his popular sovereignty concept and partially upon Republicans who had deluded their people about congressional authority to abolish slavery. But Wigfall saved his unkindest words for the "southern traitor" Andrew Johnson of Tennessee, whom he assailed as having done more than any other living man to produce disunion.[60] It had been necessary, said Wigfall, for the southern states to secede because northern treachery and southern treason put them in peril. Johnson's role was that of a bugler, urging the radical members of the Republican Party to

opponent of Wigfall in the gubernatorial campaign of 1840. Charleston *Courier*, January 23, 1861, cited in Swanberg, *First Blood*, 146; *Congressional Globe*, 36th Cong., 2nd Sess., 284–89.

[58] *Congressional Globe*, 36th Cong., 2nd Sess., 664–66.

[59] *Ibid.*, 666; Richardson, *Texas*, 246–48; Ramsdell, *Reconstruction in Texas*, 17, 19.

[60] *Congressional Globe*, 36th Cong., 2nd Sess., 781–82.

greater encroachments. If they freed the slaves, who would suffer in the South? Wigfall was sure it was the masses whom Johnson said he had been trying to aid. When the day came that 4,500,000 African slaves were loosed in the South, slaveowners, being men of substance, would leave the country. The poorer nonslave-holders would be the ones to fight it out with the freed slaves. That was why, said Wigfall, the nonslaveholders of the South sup-ported secession.[61]

Thus, Wigfall claimed, Johnson erred when he said that south-ern politicians did not have popular support, that they were moved only by ambition. Wigfall, perhaps again protesting too much, denied any ambition—surely not for the presidency—he would rather be the keeper of "a miserable railroad tavern" than President. It was Johnson, countered Wigfall, who hungered for the presidency. He had adopted the Black Republican platform, ingratiated himself with the "very worst of the northern popu-lace." Knowing that he could not get a vote in the South, John-son deliberately drove the Deep South out. He had even proposed a constitutional amendment which stated that every alternate four years the President must be a southerner. And when the amendment was not adopted, said Wigfall, Johnson had broken up the Union so that he might become President of what was left. But if any President tried to enforce unionist laws in the South, as Johnson was advocating, there would be war. Wigfall had come there, he said, to plead for peace, but as things had developed, he was indifferent about it. If they wanted war, they should be warned of King Cotton and the fact that it would be easy to maintain a southern army in the populous North.[62]

Some Republicans were talking as if they wanted war. Maybe "a little blood letting was necessary," intimated Zachariah Chan-dler of Michigan, speaking for the radical Republicans.[63] After quoting Thomas Jefferson's 1787 letter about the tree of liberty

---

61 *Ibid.*, 782, 787–88.
62 *Ibid.*, 782, 788, 789–91.
63 *Ibid.*, 1370, 1372. Mary Boykin Chesnut had two weeks earlier, on February 15, 1861, expressed her fear that bloodletting was the inevitable remedy in her *Diary*, 3.

needing to be refreshed from time to time with the blood of patriots and tyrants, Chandler declared that civil war was not so bad as anarchy. He would never consent to compromise with traitors who had flouted the laws of the United States, and he would rather join the Comanches than live under a government that did not enforce its laws. Wigfall expressed his fervent hope that Chandler would reconsider the last threat because the Comanches had "already suffered much from their contact with the whites." [64]

Nevertheless, the states of the Deep South had left the Union. "Texas went out to-day [March 2]," crowed Wigfall. "We have dissolved the Union; mend it if you can; cement it with blood." Triumphantly, Wigfall trumpeted his most insulting taunt to the North: "The *Star of the West* swaggered into Charleston harbor, received a blow planted full in the face, and staggered out. Your flag has been insulted; redress it, if you dare. You have submitted to it for two months, and you will submit to it forever." [65]

Northern newspapers found the presence in Washington of such "cool, audacious, traitors" as Wigfall difficult to understand, and they furiously urged loyal Republican senators to expel him. Republicans were doing something. A committee of five representatives began, on January 26, investigations of rebel activity in Washington. On February 14 they issued a reassuring report, even though they had found evidence that the "Breckinridge and Lane Club" of the District of Columbia was armed and drilling. Wigfall was said to be connected with it, but it was not known exactly how.[66]

Wigfall was in fact the head of these operations, and he was becoming more active in spying. On February 20 he warned Governor Francis Pickens of another expedition being planned for

[64] *Congressional Globe*, 36th Cong., 2nd Sess., 1371, 1372.

[65] *Ibid.*, 1373. March 2 was the day that Texas had declared independence from Mexico in 1836; in 1861 it was the day that she formally declared her independence from the United States. Ironically it was also Sam Houston's birthday. Thus, it was to be expected that Wigfall would commemorate the occasion.

[66] "Treason at Washington," New York *Tribune* (n.d.), in *Texas Republican*, February 23, 1861; *Official Records*, LIII, 133; LII, Pt. 2, p. 27; LI, Pt. 2, p. 8; Nichols, *Disruption of American Democracy*, 491.

an attempt to reinforce Sumter. On the day before Lincoln's inauguration, Wigfall tried to goad Republicans into betraying whether they would try to recapture all the forts taken by the Confederate States. But Senator Lyman Trumbull (Rep.—Illinois) replied that Wigfall would learn about the policies of the incoming administration the next day from the eastern steps of the Capitol.[67]

Eight slave states were still in the Union when Lincoln was inaugurated. Although Texas had announced her secession two days earlier, Wigfall and John Hemphill, the two Lone Star State Senators, were still in Washington. Jointly they announced their determination to wait for an official notification of the secession of their state before leaving the Union capital. (The *Texas Republican* reported that it was thought that their continued presence would be useful to the cause of the South.) Thus Wigfall was there to hear his analysis confirmed by the new President; Lincoln made it clear that he would save the Union but not by compromise. Wigfall and the other slave states' representatives agreed that Lincoln's Inaugural Address was hostile.[68] He telegraphed Governor Pickens: "Inaugural means war." At the same time, Wigfall warned against hasty, independent action by South Carolina; it was desirable to have a show of unity: "Do not permit any attack on Sumter without authority of Government of Confederate States." But Federal reinforcements would be sent soon, he was sure.[69]

Whether it was coincidental or satirically staged by Wigfall, in a "seventh of March" Senate speech he countered all of the nationalistic and pacifistic principles of Daniel Webster's great "seventh of March speech" on its eleventh anniversary. Wigfall charged that Lincoln was not dealing in facts; the Confederate

[67] Wigfall to Pickens, February 20, 1861, *Official Records*, I, 257; *Congressional Globe*, 36th Cong., 2nd Sess., 1381.

[68] *Congressional Globe*, 36th Cong., 2nd Sess., 1441; *Texas Republican*, March 6, 1861; Lincoln "First Inaugural Address," *Journal of the Senate*, 36th Cong., Special Sess., 402–404. The Dallas *Herald* printed the speech on April 4, 1861, from a copy sent to them by Wigfall.

[69] Wigfall to Pickens, March 4, 1861, *Official Records*, I, 261–63; see also *Congressional Globe*, 36th Cong., Special Sess., 1436.

States would not leave Sumter in United States hands. If the United States wanted peace, they had to give up the fort. Lincoln talked about peaceable enforcement of laws and collection of revenues; if he were to send a fleet into Liverpool, England, and try to collect taxes and enforce United States laws, Wigfall asked, would the British government be held responsible for the bloodshed that would ensue? The Crittenden resolutions might have saved the Union a few months earlier, but now the Union was dead, pronounced Wigfall. There might be reconstruction; he doubted it. "If you were to [let the South] write their own Constitution . . . , they would not live under this Administration." The question , he thought, was not of saving the Union but of saving the peace. The United States could keep the peace by withdrawing Federal troops from the South, acknowledging the Confederate States of America, and meeting with its commissioners to divide up the territory, ships, army, and public debt, and by forsaking any plans to collect tribute from people who were no longer citizens of the United States. Then a treaty of commerce and amity could be negotiated. "And if you will reorganize your own government . . . as suits us, we may again confederate with you." But "send your flag into that country . . . , and war will ensue." [70]

One part of his tirade finally elicited information about Lincoln's plans for Federal strongholds in the South. When Wigfall charged that Douglas and Lincoln were masters of inactivity when it came to facing the problem of the forts, Douglas came to his feet with a statement which was revealing to the South and surprising to the North; Sumter had provisions for only thirty-one more days—by then a decision would be made. As Wigfall hinted pointedly, Douglas had been in consultation with Lincoln, so the information was worthwhile.[71]

Although Wigfall had stated it was a fact that seven states (Texas was the seventh) had seceded, although Texas was officially represented in the Confederate States government, al-

---

[70] *Congressional Globe,* 36th Cong., Special Sess., 1439–41.
[71] *Ibid.,* 1442.

though Wigfall had been named as one of the Confederate
delegates, and although he had announced in the United States
Senate that he was a foreigner who owed his allegiance to another country, both Wigfall and the other Texas senator remained in Washington. Wigfall blandly explained that they had
not been officially notified that their state had abolished the office
of United States Senator. When such action were taken, he said,
he would file that information with the President of the Senate.
Then, if his name was continued on the rolls, Wigfall said he
would probably answer and vote if it suited his convenience;
after all, he considered the Senate "a very respectable public
meeting." [72] Thus, he continued to attend, debate, vote, and an-
tagonize in the Senate throughout the special session which met
March 4 through 28.

Wigfall's "seventh of March speech" aroused new rounds of
criticism of him in the North and excited some Republican senators to an effort to get rid of him through the most stringent
parliamentary action open to them. One of the new Republican
senators, Lafayette S. Foster of Connecticut, proposed a resolution that since Wigfall had stated that he owed no allegiance to
the United States, that he be expelled from the Senate. After a
brief debate in which some border-state senators defended Wigfall against the charges of several Republicans, the resolution was
referred to the Judiciary Committee by the votes of Republicans
who did not want to precipitate any issue prematurely. According to James G. Blaine, they agreed to let the matter rest because
they were convinced that Wigfall's presence was helping rather
than harming the Union cause.[73]

Thus, Wigfall helped to assure war by stiffening the northern
will to resist southern secession and by strengthening southern
resistance to peaceful negotiation. He accomplished the latter not
only with the spoken word, but also by supplying soldiers and
guns. Sometime in February, Confederate President Jefferson

[72] *Ibid.*, 1439, 1442.
[73] *Journal of the Senate,* 36th Cong., Special Sess., 412; James G. Blaine, *Twenty
Years of Congress: From Lincoln to Garfield* (2 vols., Norwich, Conn., 1884–86), I,
288–89; *Congressional Globe,* 36th Cong., Special Sess., 1447–51.

Davis received a proposal from Wigfall that he be authorized to recruit a regiment in Baltimore. Shortly after the inauguration of Lincoln, Wigfall received Davis' approval for the plan. The Texan was authorized to draw upon the Confederate treasury for funds to raise the regiment and ship it to Charleston.[74] Union authorities became concerned about Confederate recruiting in Maryland, but they did not know that Wigfall was masterminding it. Nor did they know that he and Texas Ranger Captain Ben McCulloch were buying a thousand Colt revolvers and a thousand Morse rifles for Texas Confederates. By April 2, one shipment of them had already been sent to New Orleans. Also by that time Wigfall had sent between sixty-four and a hundred recruits to the Confederate forces at Charleston.[75] With his gift for rationalization, he certainly felt no guilt for these sub rosa activities. His spying, recruiting, and arms-buying had been conducted covertly but without any self-recognized expense to his integrity; his disavowal of the Union flag had been complete and public.

Less covertly Wigfall was meeting with the Confederate commissioners to Washington. Indeed, while the Senate was debating whether to expel him for his allegiance to a foreign government, Wigfall was dining and conferring with agents of that government, urging them to force Lincoln into immediate action against forts Sumter and Pickens so that the Confederacy could capture them before federal reinforcements could arrive. The commissioners, however, felt that they should give Secretary Se-

[74] L. P. Walker to Wigfall, March 5, 1861; and C. G. Memminger to Wigfall, March 4, 1861, both in Staff Officers File, National Archives; Walker to Wigfall, two letters, March 21, 1861, *Official Records*, I, 278; Wigfall to P. G. T. Beauregard, March 16, 1861, *Official Records*, I, 276; Walker to Beauregard, March 17, 18, 1861, *Official Records*, LIII, 134–35.

[75] General Charles P. Stone, "Washington on the Eve of War," in R. U. Johnson and C. C. Buell (eds.), *Battles and Leaders of the Civil War*, (4 vols.; New York, 1956), I, 7–25; *Journal of the Secession of Texas*, February 4–March 2, 1861, 125–27, 132; Wigfall to his son Halsey, March [1861]; Charlotte Wigfall to her daughter Louly, March 24, 29, 1861; Davis to Wigfall, April 12, 1861, all in Wright, *Southern Girl*, 33–34, 37; Ben McCulloch to Wigfall, April 2, 1861, and Wigfall to Colonel ———, April 9, 1861, both in Wigfall Papers, Library of Congress; *Official Records*, I, 276, 278; LIII, 134; LII, Pt. 2, p. 27; LI, Pt. 2, p. 8.

ward more time to achieve peaceful evacuation. Seward convinced many Confederates, including Wigfall, that Sumter would be evacuated.[76]

Near the end of the special session of Congress, the Wigfalls anticipated leaving Washington but were still uncertain as to when and how. Fearful of arduous travel and unpleasant confrontations, they sent their two daughters to stay with their maternal grandparents at Longwood, near Boston. As Wigfall's days in Washington drew to a close (he was still a United States Senator) , he surveyed the situation and confided to his son that the general impression there was that "we will have peace." The Texan continued, "Political matters are in *statu quo, ante bellum*. The war has not yet begun, but I believe it will before the *end of summer*." [77]

Thus Wigfall expected war to come, though not as soon as it did. It would have been asking too much of Wigfall to expect him to feel any guilt for his part in bringing on the conflict. As far as his personal politics were concerned, there was nothing concrete to indicate that he expected to rise any higher in the Confederate government than he had in the Union. Wigfall and the majority of southerners were convinced that their civilization had no future in the northern-dominated Union. Slavery was their *summum bonum* of morality, physical excellence, and moral purity;[78] to remain in the Union was to risk their peculiar institution. Wigfall surely expected personal recognition for his part in saving "the southern way of life." For seventeen years he had been preaching that the South would be better off outside the Union; now he had helped to bring it about.

Until about mid-March, 1861, he had seemed genuinely hopeful that the separation would be peaceable. In an effort to obtain what the South wanted without its having to fight for it, Wigfall

[76] *Texas Republican*, March 16, 1861; Wigfall to Beauregard; and Wigfall to Davis, March 11, 1861, *Official Records*, I, 273; Charlotte Wigfall to Louly, March 24, 29, April 2, 10, 1861, in Wright, *Southern Girl*, 35, and in Wigfall Papers.

[77] *Texas Republican*, March 23, 1861; Wigfall to Halsey, March—, in Wright, *Southern Girl*, 33–34.

[78] Russell, *Diary*, 39, 101.

resorted to the bluff, threatening the North with economic and physical ruination at the hands of King Cotton and southern armies. But the Republicans called his bluff; not only did they refuse to compromise the issue of slavery in the territories to prevent an attempt at secession, they even refused to divide the territories after the attempt, or indeed, even to allow peaceable secession at all.

The unfortunate trend in southern policy was the acceptance of the Wigfall brand of misguided southernism. He, and the South, completely misunderstood the North's commitment to the experiment in majority rule and to the Union. The Republicans were slow to realize that such fire-eaters as Wigfall were not merely bluffing, that they had sufficient public support in the South to attempt to carry out their threats. It is doubtful that the Republicans would have changed their policies appreciably had they realized the seriousness of the southern menace. As far as the ability and willingness of the leaders of that generation to compromise their economic and political differences, the Civil War was an irrepressible conflict between two distinct civilizations in one nation. If they could not compromise on the issue of slavery in the territories, they could compromise on nothing. For in it lay all the economic, political, and moral difficulties. And on that issue both sides were inflexible. Southerners felt that they had to expand slavery in the territories in order to perpetuate their civilization within the Union. Northerners felt they could not allow it. Reflecting the southern attitude, Wigfall spoke of this expansion of slavery into the territories as a constitutional right; northerners had become convinced it was a moral wrong.

Too many southerners were like Wigfall in failing to understand how they could share in the industrial revolution, how they could prosper economically and survive socially by ending slavery and incorporating freed Negroes into southern society. Wigfall's role was in compounding this misunderstanding by intensifying emotions, especially those of honor, petty pride, and fear. It was fear that did the most to drive the South out of the Union: fear of loss of property (slaves); fear of slave uprisings

(stirred by abolitionists); fear of the social and economic problems attendant upon freedom for over three million slaves in the
Deep South; fear of the emergence of submerged whites (Helper-
ism); and fear of losing political power to the more populous and
rapidly growing North. Wigfall helped persuade southern leaders that the time had come, while they still had the support of
the majority of white southerners, to cut the bonds of the Union.
He was among the few who realized that the severance would not
be without bloodshed. But he seemed to think there would be
little of that, that rather the war would be brief and would result
in a glorious victory for the Confederacy. He was wrong again.

Chapter V

In the Vineyard
of Southern Rights

WHEN LOUIS WIGFALL ARRIVED in Charleston on April 1, 1861, he was treated to a hero's homecoming. He embarked on a rigorous schedule of public speeches and an exciting dual role of civil and military leadership which was to last until February, 1862. In the spring of 1861 the Confederates, especially South Carolinians, were a confident people. The glorious reception of the Wigfalls in 1861 was a sharp contrast to their ignominious departure from South Carolina in 1846. On his return Wigfall was the object of numerous complimentary editorials and serenades, and a boat, the *Lady Davis*, was put at his command so that he could inspect the fortifications of Charleston harbor. In one of his numerous "fighting speeches," he told an emotional crowd that the honor of South Carolina had been vindicated whether the Federals in Fort Sumter were starved out or shelled out, but he warned the Carolinians that if they thought their independence was going to be gained without bloodshed, they were mistaken.[1]

Confident that military action was to come soon, Wigfall stayed close to General P. G. T. Beauregard, the Louisiana Creole in charge of the Confederate forces at Charleston. Charlotte Wigfall had expected to leave Charleston before April 7 for the Con-

1 Charlotte Wigfall to Louly, April 2, 1861, and Charlotte Wigfall to Halsey, April 7, 1861, both in Wigfall Papers; Charleston *Mecury*, April 5, 1861; Wright, *Southern Girl*, 35–36; Charleston *Daily Courier*, April 4, 1861; Chesnut, *Diary*, 32.

federate capitol in Montgomery, but there was no dragging her husband away while there was the prospect of an immediate attack upon Sumter. Most Charlestonians hoped, as did Charlotte Wigfall, that Major Robert Anderson and his Federal troops would be evacuated and the matter settled peaceably. But this hope faded as Federal relief expeditions were said to be heading that way. Mary Boykin Chesnut reported that "the only thoroughly happy person" she saw was Wigfall, the "Stormy Petrel"; the senator was "in his glory." He credited his "usual good luck" with bringing him to Charleston where he would have the privilege of seeing "the flashing of the guns." [2]

On April 10 he received an even greater honor; at Beauregard's request he took an appointment on the general's distinguished staff of volunteer military aides. The sword and red sash of their office became Charleston's highest badge of social prominence and was worn by such dignitaries as Wigfall's old friend Governor John Manning. During his first day as aide, Wigfall advised President Davis to order the capture of Fort Sumter. Such an order was necessary, urged Wigfall, because it was clear that Lincoln was preparing to strike. All was ready on the Confederate side, so any delay only favored the North. Further, such a bold stroke would surely bring Virginia in on the southern side. Davis replied to his "dear friend" that an order had already been issued which anticipated his wish so fully that he would probably think it an answer to his request. The order came from Secretary of War L. P. Walker the same day that Wigfall made the suggestion, and on the next day, April 11, Beauregard demanded the evacuation of the fort.[3]

2 Charlotte Wigfall to Halsey, April 7, 10, 1861, and Charlotte Wigfall to Louly, April 10, 1861, both in Wigfall Papers; Wright, *Southern Girl*, 35–36; Chesnut, *Diary*, 34. Wigfall to Colonel——, April 9, 1861, Old Records Division, Adjutant General's Office, United States Army, Washington, D.C.

3 Staff Officer's File of Brigadier General Louis T. Wigfall, War Department Collection of Confederate Records, Record Group 109, National Archives; Samuel Wragg Ferguson Memoirs, Louisiana State University Department of Archives and Manuscripts, IV, 1; Chesnut, *Diary*, 38; Wigfall to Davis, April 10, 1861, and Davis to Wigfall, April 12, 1861, both in Wright, *Southern Girl*, 37; Walker to Beauregard, April 10, *Official Records*, I, 297; Charlotte Wigfall to Louly, April 11, 1861, in Wright, *Southern Girl*, 37–38.

By April 11 the Confederacy had about six thousand men placed in a semicircle on the land side of Sumter. Wigfall was sent to Morris Island to bring order among the two thousand men milling around at the northern end of this crescent. Evidently Beauregard had some confidence in Wigfall's military acumen because the general looked upon Morris Island as one of his most important positions, and he anticipated a Federal attempt to land troops there. Wigfall was at Morris Island when the Confederate shelling of Fort Sumter began, about 4:30 on the morning of April 12.[4] Charlotte Wigfall, with the wife of South Carolina Senator James Chesnut, joined the other observers on rooftops to watch the administration of "anti-abolition pills" upon the Federals.

For two days the fort took a severe beating while failing to dent the Confederate installations. The safest of the Confederate positions was Morris Island, out of reach of Sumter's guns and not the object of a Federal invasion. The Federal relief expedition merely watched the burning fort continue to battle hopelessly. When Confederate officers on the island noticed that Anderson's flag had been shot away, they discussed what should be done to induce Anderson to give up the useless fight. Evidently convinced that there was nothing for either side to gain by continuing what was obvious carnage, and seeing a heroic role for himself, Wigfall decided to bring a dramatic finish to the battle. Accompanied by a Palmetto State private, he commandeered a small boat and two black oarsmen and set out for the fort, either ignoring or not hearing the warnings of danger and shouts for them to return. When he continued, the Morris Island guns were stilled, but those of all the other Confederate batteries and those of Sumter continued blazing. One shell burst directly over the boat, showering iron fragments around it. Upon landing, Wigfall walked around the breakwater until he found

4 Whiting to Beauregard, April 11, 1861, *Official Records*, I, 302, also 292–93, 299, 302–303; Wigfall to his wife, April 12, 1861, and Wigfall to Louly, April 11, 1861, Wigfall Papers; Charlotte Wigfall to Louly, April 12, 1861, in Wright, *Southern Girl*, 38–39; Chesnut, *Diary*, 35–36.

a gun casement to crawl through. With a white handkerchief tied to the point of his upraised sword, he confronted the astonished Federal gunner and asked for a parley with Major Anderson. After some confusion among the Federals, Anderson appeared. Wigfall pointed out the futility of continuing the battle and asked for the surrender of the fort, and, though he had no authority to do so, he assured Anderson that Beauregard would allow the same terms he had offered when he had ordered the evacuation of the fort. Anderson's men would be allowed to salute their flag and board the Federal ships that were waiting outside the harbor. Anderson consented and ordered a white flag to be shown from the top of the ramparts. The firing stopped immediately, and as Wigfall started back to Morris Island he was met by a boat carrying other aides with the official surrender terms from Beauregard. These were similar enough to those proposed by Wigfall that no complications were encountered in the final settlement.[5]

As he had undoubtedly hoped, Wigfall became the Confederate man of the hour and was accorded another hero's welcome by

[5] James Chester, "Inside Fort Sumter in '61," in *Battles and Leaders of the Civil War*, I, 50–74; Stephen D. Lee, "The First Step in the War," in *ibid.*, 74–81; A. R. Chisolm, "Notes on the Surrender of Fort Sumter," in *ibid.*, 82–83; Ferguson Memoirs, IV, 9–10; Charleston *Daily Courier*, April 15, 1861; Charlotte Wigfall to Halsey, April 15, 1861; Chesnut, *Diary*, 39, 45. Wigfall's account is in Wigfall to Major D. R. Jones, April 15, 1861, Wigfall Papers, and *Official Records*, I, 66; Samuel Wylie Chapman, *The Genesis of the Civil War: The Story of Sumter, 1860–1861* (New York, 1887). Most of the southern accounts were similar to that in the Savannah, Georgia, *Republican* as quoted in the *Texas Republican*, May 4, 1861, recounting the "Recklessness and Gallantry of Sen. Wigfall"; his exploits were "as gallant and chivalrous as any deed of modern time." Charlotte Wigfall was surprised that the New York *Times* published a letter which did justice to Wigfall; Charlotte Wigfall to Halsey, May 8, 1861, Wigfall Papers. In 1864 Horace Greeley, editor of the New York *Tribune*, credited Wigfall's action as due to one of the virtues of his caste, "repugnance to witnessing a conflict between parties too palpably ill-matched," in Horace Greeley, *American Conflict* (2 vols.; Hartford, 1864), I, 448. But most northern accounts were more like that of John G. Nicolay, *The Outbreak of War* (New York, n.d.), 68; when he referred to the "eccentric Senator Wigfall" at Fort Sumter, who acted with "more grandiloquence than authority" and "more enthusiasm than memory" when he reported an unconditional surrender; see also Abner Doubleday, *Reminiscences of Forts Sumter and Moultrie in 1860–1861* (New York, 1876), 162–65; and *Harper's Pictorial History*, I, 60–61, concerning Wigfall's "ludicrous visit" to Fort Sumter.

the people of Charleston. From his home state came assurances
from Democratic leaders that he could, without opposition, become the next governor of Texas. But Wigfall expressed disinter-
est in that office as well as a seat in the Permanent Congress. He
had found a more glorious way to serve. There seemed to be no
end of listeners to hear Wigfall's own account of his deed, nor
did Wigfall tire of telling it. Especially was he eager to relate
his exploit to the London newspaperman William H. Russell.
Russell, with Major Whiting, was visiting Sumter three days
after the surrender when he met Wigfall returning from a revisit.
Wigfall recognized someone in the other boat and jumped in,
almost upsetting them. It appeared to Russell that Wigfall had
been "paying his respects to Bacchus or Bourbon," for he was
decidedly unsteady in his gait, "but his head was quite clear,"
and he was determined that Russell should know all about his
exploit, which he related, using "strong illustrations and strange
expletives." [6]

Most northerners took an altogether different view of the affair. Louly, in Massachusetts, reported to her father that the
"miserable Boston papers" were telling as many lies as ever, saying "you had stuck yourself where you had no business," and
were not wanted. To her brother she wrote that Boston was the
scene of great excitement; "all the military were getting ready
(wretches!), and every one is on the lookout for war in earnest."
After she had seen the crowd of Bostonians volunteering for the
army, fourteen-year-old Louly assessed the situation more as-
tutely than many of the southern adults. She knew that the North
was not ready to give up the fight and that now the South had
either to conquer or be conquered. But like most southerners,
she hoped that "our brave men will fight till every drop of blood
is shed before they submit to the rule of Black Republicanism." [7]

The "tug" had come, and none too soon for Wigfall. His

[6] Chisolm, "Surrender of Fort Sumter," 82–83; Charleston *Daily Courier*, April
15, 1861; Charlotte Wigfall to Halsey, April 20, 25, 1861, Wigfall Papers; Russell,
Diary, 62–63.

[7] Louly to Wigfall, April 20, 1861, and Louly to Halsey, April 16, 1861, both in
Wigfall Papers.

prediction that a vigorous policy toward the fort would induce Virginia to join the Confederacy seemed about to be realized. Ex-Secretary of War John Floyd wrote from Virginia that he was certain they would soon secede. The future for the Confederacy and for Louis Wigfall looked bright as he and his wife departed Charleston for Montgomery, Alabama, the capital of "Secessia," where he would finally take his seat in the Confederate Provisional Congress.[8]

Their journey by rail was arduous but filled with plaudits for the senator. At every depot he was called upon for a speech, and as their route took them deeper into the South, their reception became warmer. When they arrived in Montgomery, they were besieged with admiring crowds, and a local paper lauded him as an unsurpassed laborer "in the vineyard of southern rights." Charlotte Wigfall, though extremely fatigued, was affected by the high spirits of the Montgomery populace, even catching some of their optimism that the issue might be settled without bloodshed or that the South would win in less than three months. The senator, however, was convinced that war was coming and, perhaps impressed by northern reaction to their loss of Sumter, he intimated that it would be a lengthy one. But he remained certain that cotton was king, so the South would ultimately win.[9]

It seemed to Wigfall that most of the men in Montgomery wanted to be in the war as officers. He was, said his wife, made perfectly unhappy by demands to help obtain appointments, mostly army commissions. For the duration of his stay, applicants for office barred his path and lay in wait for him outside his hotel room. This was only one of a number of problems the Wigfalls faced in Montgomery. Hotel accommodations were so poor as

[8] Floyd to Wigfall, July 3, 1861, and Charlotte Wigfall to Halsey, April 19, 1861, both in *ibid.* It was not until after Lincoln called for 500,000 troops to put down the southern rebellion that Virginia and other border states joined the Confederacy, in May, 1861.

[9] Immediately after leaving Charleston, the Wigfalls had a two-day rest and visit with Louis' brother, the Reverend Arthur Wigfall, in Grahamsville, South Carolina. Charlotte Wigfall to Halsey, April 24, 25, with a clipping from a Montgomery newspaper April 23, 1861, May 6, 8, 1861; Charlotte Wigfall to Louly, April 26, 1861, *ibid.*

to increase sentiment among Confederate congressmen to move the capital. The two Montgomery hostelries were like the Raven of Zurich—known not only for uncleanliness of nest but also for size of "bill." This pointed up another of Wigfall's chronic problems, lack of funds. Provisional congressmen received only eight dollars a day, and that did not begin for the Wigfalls until he took his legislative seat late in April. Charlotte Wigfall was sure that it would be impossible for the family to live on such a pittance and hoped that more satisfactory arrangements would be made soon. If not, she was certain that her husband's position in the government would "certainly enable him to fall upon some plan for an adequate support of his family." In the meantime the children, especially Halsey, were warned to economize.[10]

Sixteen-year-old Halsey was a cause of major concern for his parents for more than financial reasons. Two days before Fort Sumter was fired upon, he had written from his private school in Belmont, Virginia, that if everything went smoothly, he would enter the University of Virginia the next year and intended to earn a master's degree before he was twenty-one. A few days after the shelling of Sumter, however, he reported there was a company of his classmates volunteering for the Virginia forces. Halsey was disenchanted with what he called the Old Dominion's disgraceful failure to join the Confederacy, but he hoped to get enough money to allow him to go south to join.[11]

His parents anticipated this and wrote that same day for him to make up his mind to devote himself to his books. His mother desired that he be prepared to enter the ministry, whether he did so or not. Wigfall sent his son a telegram and a long letter urging him to stay in school. The fiery senator expressed surprise that sixteen-year-old boys were leaving school for the army. At any rate, he said, he was unwilling that his son should begin the serious business of life without education.[12]

10 Charlotte Wigfall to Halsey, April 19, 25, May 6, 8, 13, 1861, *ibid*; see also Russell, *Diary*, 88–89; and T. C. DeLeon, *Four Years in Rebel Capitals* (Mobile, Alabama, 1890), 24.
11 Halsey to Louly, April 10, 25, 1861, Wigfall Papers.
12 Charlotte Wigfall to Halsey, April 25, May 6, 1861, and Wigfall to Halsey, May 1, 1861, both in *ibid*.

Halsey was not convinced. Within three weeks after Fort Sumter, thirty boys had left his school for the army, and more were going daily. Louly begged him to stay; after all, she said, their father would be the last one to advise anything that was unworthy of the son of Louis T. Wigfall. Perhaps that was the reason their father was weakening in his determination for Halsey to stay out of the army; other boys were going, how could the son of Lou Wigfall stay behind? Through his wife he sent word to Halsey that if he *were* to go into the army, he should go to Texas and join up with Ben McCulloch. Charlotte Wigfall maintained that a sixteen-year-old was too young for military life, but "if you and your Father both will have it, I should of course give up." [13]

The Wigfalls were also worried, unnecessarily, about their daughters. Charlotte Wigfall's mother, who was caring for the girls in a suburb of Boston, was decidedly southern in her sentiments, but she reported that they were surrounded by Yankees who opened their lips only to revile and threaten the South. Louly "dared not walk out alone," and eight-year-old Fanny had already had some skirmishes with neighbor girls over politics. [14] The Wigfalls had schooled their children well.

The senator, always the political animal, labored constantly for what he thought was the best interests of the South. Perhaps it was to help persuade England to recognize the Confederate States of America that he strove so diligently to impress the London *Times*'s Russell of the justice of the southern cause. While the correspondent was in Montgomery in early May, Wigfall was his nearly constant companion. He arranged meetings and dinners for himself and Russell with Davis and other Confederate dignitaries (who did not impress the Englishman a great deal) and tried to explain to him just what the southern ethos was all about. Before arising in the mornings, Russell usually found Wigfall at his bedside. On one particular May morning Russell marveled at Wigfall as the senator passed his hands through his locks

[13] Halsey to Louly, May 7, 19, 1861; Louly to Halsey, May 11, 1861; and Charlotte Wigfall to Halsey, May 13, 23, 1861, all in *ibid.*
[14] T. L. to Charty [Charlotte Wigfall's mother to Charlotte], May 13, 1861, *ibid.*

and poured out his ideas "with wonderful lucidity and of affecta-
tion of logic" all his own:

> We are a peculiar people, sir! You don't understand us, and you
> can't understand us, because we are known to you only by Northern
> writers and Northern papers. . . . We are an agricultural people;
> we are a primitive but a civilised people. We have no cities—we
> don't want them. We have no literature—we don't need any yet. . . .
> We do not require a press, because we go out and discuss all public
> questions from the stump with our people. We have no commercial
> marine—no navy—we don't want them. . . . Your ships carry our
> produce, and you can protect your own vessels. We want no manu-
> factures: we desire no trading, no mechanical or manufacturing
> classes. As long as we have our rice, our sugar, our tobacco, and our
> cotton, we can command wealth to purchase all we want from those
> nations with which we are in amity, and to lay up money besides.
> But with the Yankees we will never trade—never.[15]

Other Confederate congressmen were taking up a good deal of
legislative time saying essentially the same things but doing little.
The second session of the Confederate Provisional Congress had
been called by President Davis for April 29. It was then that
Wigfall took his seat for the first time, having missed the first
session while he was still in the United States Senate. There was
widespread criticism of many of the members as crude political
hacks. Except for Wigfall, the seven-man Texas delegation was
considered rough and conceited.[16]

Wigfall was probably planning to absent himself from the Congress and politics altogether—at least temporarily. He had refused
an offer of the governorship of Texas; elections for the Permanent Congress were coming soon, and he had expressed his dis-
inclination for a seat there. Wigfall contemplated a military

15 Charlotte Wigfall to Halsey, May 6, 8, 1861, *ibid.*; Russell, *Diary*, 92–93, 99,
102.
16 On February 4, 1861, John H. Reagan and Wigfall had been elected deputies
by acclamation in the Texas Secession Convention. Reagan asked that his election
be reconsidered, and someone else did the same for Wigfall's. In the ensuing election, Wigfall was the only delegate selected with a majority on the first ballot. It
took five ballots to complete the seven-man slate. *Journal of the Secession of
Texas*, 73–80. Wigfall was appointed to the Committee on Foreign Affairs; *Journal of the Provisional Congress, Confederate States of America*, 2nd Sess., 159, 169.
Wilfred Buck Yearns, *The Confederate Congress* (Athens, Georgia, 1960) , 19;
DeLeon, *Rebel Capitals*, 24, 31–32.

career. He thrived upon strife with a well-defined foe, and there were no such foes in the Confederate Congress. Further, the most ambitious men were "seeking the bubble reputation in the cannon's mouth" rather than in Congress. Wigfall still savored the lingering taste of martial glory from Fort Sumter, with its instantaneous fame. It is likely that he would have become the commander of the First Texas Brigade if it had been mustered into the Confederate army when the brigade was formed. But the government refused the offer of the Texans' services because it was not known if they would be needed. Wigfall thus had to content himself with military junkets, as when he and Davis inspected the artillery at Pensacola, Florida, in mid-May, and with concentrating upon military legislation. His first bill, introduced on his first day in the Provisional Congress and subsequently passed, was for increasing the size of the army. His martial fervor was so well known in Montgomery that his return from Pensacola naturally created the impression that no immediate hostility was anticipated there. Although Davis and Wigfall traveled together, the return of Davis caused no such response.[17]

The relationship between Wigfall and Davis could have been mutually beneficial. Whether Wigfall remained in the legislature or went into the army, presidential favor could be most helpful to him. On the other hand, Davis, who wanted to keep Congress and the country pliable to his will, could increase his influence through the popular Wigfall. The President was already experiencing minor opposition from some southern leaders and did not want it to grow. Further, Wigfall evidently respected and admired Davis, having helped make him President of the Confederacy when most fire-eaters had wanted Barnwell Rhett. In fact, Wigfall had helped persuade Rhett to support Davis. These factors could account for Wigfall's early influence with the President. It was largely upon the recommendation of Wigfall and his

[17] Charlotte Wigfall to Halsey, April 25, 1861, Wigfall Papers; Chesnut, *Diary*, 112; George T. Todd, *Sketch of the History of the First Texas Regiment . . .* (n.p., n.d.), 2; Russell, *Diary*, 119; *Texas Republican*, June 1, 1861; *Journal of the Provisional Congress*, 2nd Sess., 170, 195, 198–99, 203, 216–17.

friend C. C. Clay that Davis appointed L. P. Walker, an Alabama fire-eater, as the Confederacy's first Secretary of War.[18]

The Davises and Wigfalls were together a great deal during May, the last month the Congress was in Montgomery. There was even then, however, a note of discord in the Wigfall-Davis relationship; from the start, Charlotte Wigfall had reservations about the plumply attractive and younger Varina Davis. She confided to her daughter Louly that she had not yet made up her mind whether she would like the President's wife—"Queen Varina," as some of her friends called her—and would not decide before seeing more of her.[19] Rather than the two becoming closer, their initial coolness developed into overt enmity. This and the complications which soon developed between the senator and the President evolved into a quarrel of such magnitude that the Confederate cause was harmed.

Their relationship during the spring of 1861 was excellent. When the Congress adjourned on May 21, to convene the next month in the new Confederate capital of Richmond, the Wigfalls were planning to spend the interim in Texas. At the request of the President, their plans were abruptly changed. According to Charlotte Wigfall, Davis begged the senator to serve on the President's staff. Wigfall accepted with alacrity. It was proof, she said, of what she had thought for some time: Davis was truly fond of her husband and relied greatly on his judgment. The Wigfalls did not mind changing their destination in order to accompany the President to the new capital.[20]

During the six-day trip to Richmond, his mother wrote Halsey that the President was received everywhere with "the most rapturous enthusiasm and your Father has had his part." She proudly

---

18 DeLeon, *Rebel Capitals*, 39; Chesnut, *Diary*, 5, 9; Yearns, *Confederate Congress*, 145; R. B. Rhett to Wigfall, April 15, 1864, Wigfall Papers; see also Ben McCulloch to Wigfall, April 2, 1861, Wigfall Papers, for a statement about Wigfall's "great influence with the President . . . ."

19 Charlotte Wigfall to Louly, April 29, 1861, Wigfall Papers; Russell *Diary*, 97.

20 Charlotte Wigfall to Halsey, May 23, 30, 1861, and Charlotte Wigfall to Louly, May 30, 1861, both in Wigfall Papers.

reported that the southern people admired him and that his position on the President's staff and "the terms of intimacy they are known to be on gives them additional confidence in him." When the party arrived in Richmond early in the morning of May 29, one local paper described their coming as the event of the age. The Richmond population, swelled in preceding weeks by an influx of Confederate officials, soldiers, and their families, turned out with the armory band and cannon salutes to welcome the President and his staff. Wigfall rode with President Davis and Governor John Letcher in a splendid open carriage. All along the route to the temporary "White House" at the Spotswood Hotel, the distinguished guests were showered with bouquets by wildly cheering crowds numbering in the thousands. The cheers continued after the party had reached the hotel and until Davis, Wigfall, and others appeared on a balcony to speak.[21]

That afternoon Wigfall accepted his accolades as a hero, making four speeches and leading the President and other dignitaries to review the First Texas Regiment camped near town. The next day he inspected Tennessee troops and, his wife boasted, "had his hands full of all sorts of business." Charlotte was sure that, with the exception of only the President, her husband was the most popular man in the South. With wishful thinking which revealed the romanticism of the southern mind and, in the light of later developments, an amusing touch of irony, she expressed her certainty that the two heroes would take the field to direct the Confederate military efforts which were expected soon.[22]

Although he was still Davis' aide, Wigfall spent the next several days with the Texas troops, giving them little-needed morale-building speeches, and much-needed training. There were as yet not enough of them to make up a brigade, the commander of

---

[21] Charlotte Wigfall to Halsey, May 30, 1861, *ibid*; Richmond *Daily Express*, May 30, 1861; DeLeon, *Rebel Capitals*, 86.

[22] Charlotte Wigfall to Halsey, May 30, 1861, Wigfall Papers; Dallas *Herald*, June 12, 1861. The two were also the object of attention in the North. It was rumored that a New York sculptor offered to make a marble statue of the soldier who would "bag" Wigfall or Davis. Dallas *Herald*, May 29, 1861.

which would be a brigadier general, and Wigfall "had to fight hard" to get the Confederate government to pay the expenses to ship more Texans to Virginia.[23]

A few days afterward, on June 29, 1861, came what was evidently the first indication of a possible rift between Davis and Wigfall. In the presence of Wigfall and Mary Chesnut, H. P. Brewster, a Texan who served on General John B. Hood's staff, was "chafing at Wigfall's anomalous position." Wigfall's outward reaction convinced Mary Chesnut that he was "calm and full of common sense; a brave man" who saw no need to display his temper. She said he told Brewster that until the Confederacy was stronger, "it would be disastrous for us, the head men, to engage in a row among ourselves." To this Brewster replied that he thought the new country already strong enough to bear "a rupture between Mr. Davis and Mr. Wigfall." [24]

If Wigfall had any differences with the President, he was keeping them to himself; this was not so with Charlotte Wigfall in her relationship with Varina Davis. Earlier that month she had written to Louly that the President's wife did not improve much on acquaintance; she had some good qualities, "but very many very objectionable ones." Still, Charlotte added that she and the first lady got along very well. But there was a hint of envy when she wrote that while she and Louis could not afford to continue living at the Spotswood at five dollars a day, the Davises were moving into their handsome home, and Varina Davis was driving about with horses and carriage, all provided by the government. Further, Charlotte undoubtedly resented being referred to as one of "Mrs. Davis' Ladies," as her group was commonly called. After considering the displays of petty enmity between Charlotte and Varina, Mary Chesnut concluded that "Mr. Davis and Wigfall would be friends" if their wives would not interfere.[25] Thus, the men were evidently not friends and the women may have been partially to blame.

23 Charlotte Wigfall to Halsey, June 5, 1861, and Charlotte Wigfall to Louly, June 20, 1861, both in Wigfall Papers; *Texas Republican*, June 22, 1861.
24 Chesnut, *Diary*, 71.
25 Charlotte Wigfall to Louly, June 11, 1861, and Charlotte Wigfall to Halsey,

Perhaps Wigfall was tiring of his "anomalous" position; he was spending less and less time with the man he was supposed to be "aiding." However, there existed no visible split between them. General Beauregard, then in command of Confederate troops at Manassas, wrote to Wigfall on July 8, 1861, in order to get certain grievances "properly presented" to the President. But on that same day, Wigfall's position was made even more "anomalous" when he became commander of the Texas troops, now called a battalion. Since his command was no larger, his appointment carried with it only a lieutenant-colonelcy. But the battalion was being mustered into Confederate service, and Wigfall could wait no longer. Thereafter, he stayed at the camp at the New Fair Grounds near Richmond, coming into town only to see his wife and to sit occasionally with Congress.[26]

When Wigfall accepted the aideship, Charlotte was sure that it was to last at least until Congress reconvened on July 20, and later, even after he became commander of the Texans, she hoped that he would continue as Davis' aide.[27] Thus Wigfall was not only a member of the Provisional Congress, he was commander of the First Texas Battalion and officially, but not practically, aide to the President. By being so close to Richmond, Wigfall did find time to attend Congress once in awhile, even after the first battle of Manassas.

When Davis went to Manassas, ninety miles north of Richmond, on July 19, in anticipation of the coming battle and did not bother to tell Wigfall that he was going, Mary Chesnut thought that ended Wigfall's aideship. Wigfall was evidently

---

June 14, 1861, both in Wigfall Papers; Eron Rowland, *Varina Howell, Wife of Jefferson Davis* (2 vols.; New York, 1931), II, 146–48; Robert F. W. Allston to Adele Pettigru Allston, July 15, 1861, in J. H. Easterby (ed.), *The South Carolina Rice Plantation; as Revealed in the Papers of Robert F. W. Allston* (Chicago, 1945), 178; Chesnut, *Diary*, 96.

26 Beauregard to Wigfall, July 8, 1861, and Charlotte Wigfall to Halsey, July 8–9, 1861, both in Wigfall Papers; Todd, *First Texas Regiment*, 2; Staff Officer's File. About the same time, however, Wigfall was being removed from one position, that of United States Senator. On July 10 and 11, he was finally expelled by the northern senators; *Congressional Globe*, 37th Cong., 1st Sess., 40, 60–62.

27 Charlotte Wigfall to Halsey, May 23, 1861, Wigfall Papers.

miffed at this, but not even Varina Davis knew the President was going until he had gone,[28] and perhaps Davis thought Wigfall's place was with his troops.

The "Stormy Petrel's" luck did not hold for the first battle of Manassas; he was not there. The Texas Battalion started to the battle during the first day, but their train crashed into a washed-out culvert and forty of Wigfall's men were killed or crippled. The remainder did not reach Manassas until the next morning, after the battle was over. It was consoling to Charlotte Wigfall, and probably to her husband as well, that Davis also did not get there until soon after the battle was over. Still Charlotte hoped that her husband would remain the President's aide unless he could command a brigade, and she added, still more hopefully, that more troops had been added to the Texas Battalion the same day and that Robert Toombs, who had been Davis' secretary of state, had been made a brigadier general.[29]

It was in the midst of wild celebration after the news of the Confederate victory at Manassas that the third session of the Confederate Provisional Congress convened. Three days after it opened and two days after the battle of Manassas, Wigfall "visited" Congress and told his wife that he would be able to stay in Richmond most of the time.[30] President Davis was also back to address Congress.

Wigfall asked to have five thousand copies of the President's message printed to be sent out to constituents, thus the break between the two was not complete. But in the presence of a few people, Wigfall criticized the Confederate failure to march into Washington from Manassas. Indeed, there was little to stop the rebels, except that their own armies were as disorganized by victory as the Federals were by defeat. Nevertheless, Davis' critics continued to blame him for missing the chance to end the war at that point. Mary Chesnut does not say whom Wigfall blamed, but it appears to have been Davis and his commissary general,

28 Chesnut, *Diary*, 85–86.
29 Todd, *First Texas Regiment*, 2–3; Ferguson Memoirs, IV, 8; Charlotte Wigfall to Halsey, July 23, 1861, Wigfall Papers; Chesnut, *Diary*, 86.
30 Charlotte Wigfall to Halsey, July 21, 23, 1861, Wigfall Papers.

Lucius B. Northrop. One reason that General Joseph E. Johnston gave for his army's inability to press the attack was the shortage of necessary food supplies because of Northrop's insistance that all subsistence had to come from Richmond. Johnston and several other generals quarreled with Northrop about the most expeditious manner of supplying food to the army, and Wigfall took the side of his friend Johnston. Davis felt that criticism of one of his appointees was criticism of himself.[31]

Wigfall also took Johnston's side in a far more serious controversy, one which helped to split the Confederacy—the quarrel over the general's rank. When the rebel Congress formulated the basic laws for their armies, they made a pledge to officers who resigned their commissions in the United States Army. These officers were told that the relative rank of officers of each grade would be determined by their former commissions. An amendment provided for five full generals. Johnston, who was the highest ranking general to leave the United States Army, naturally assumed that he was the ranking general in the Confederate States Army, but there was no general order issued to clear up the confusion of rank during the period of flux when southern states and the Confederacy were raising armies independent of one another.[32]

Three days after Manassas the controversy over rank ignited. General Robert E. Lee, serving as military advisor to the President, ordered a new adjutant general into Johnston's headquarters. Johnston, certain that he outranked Lee, was outraged. He protested repeatedly to the War Department, but evidently the only attention his letters received was Davis' marking them "Insubordinate." Neither Davis nor anyone else in his administration bothered to explain how the generals ranked or that Lee had been appointed military advisor to the President. Even Lee was uncertain of his rank and position.[33] Wigfall, already slighted

31 Dallas *Herald*, August 7, 1861; Chesnut, *Diary*, 74, 91, 99, 114, 205. Russell, in his *Diary*, 100, said that Wigfall, on May 8, 1861, had opposed an attack on Washington, or any offensive movement; Alvy L. King, "The Relationship Between Joseph E. Johnston and Jefferson Davis During the Civil War," (M. A. Thesis, West Texas State University, 1960), 28, 34.

32 *Official Records*, I, 127–31, 163–64, 326–27.

33 D. H. Maury, *Recollections of a Virginian in the Mexican and Civil Wars*

by Davis, was quite willing to take the side of his good friend Johnston.

The females contributed greatly to the quarrel. On the same day that Wigfall was criticizing Davis for not following up the victory at Manassas, Mary Chesnut noted that after some "little unpleasantness" there was a complete reconciliation between the wives of the two men. But a few days later, word spread that Charlotte Wigfall was describing Varina Davis as "a coarse western woman." Furthermore, though Lydia Johnston had referred earlier to the first lady as a "western belle," when the quarrel between her husband and the President broke out, she took back the "belle" and substituted "woman." When Charlotte Wigfall announced triumphantly in public that several prominent politicians were in a coalition against Jeff Davis, her husband stroked his beard and said nothing. Mary Chesnut was convinced that he had too much common sense not to see how quarreling among themselves must end. Five days later she was happy to record the Davises' reconciliation with the Wigfalls, who dined with the President. The little Wigfall girls even stayed the night at the executive mansion.[34]

Wigfall's daughters had arrived in Richmond in early August, but the family was not reunited. Halsey was in military school at the University of Virginia while he awaited a commission in the Confederate Army. Charlotte Wigfall would stay with all the children for a short while in Richmond, but Wigfall went to join his troops at Manassas to withdraw them to Dumfries, about seventy-five miles north of Richmond.[35]

While spending most of his time away from Richmond, Wigfall moved up in rank, but Davis held his ascendency to a slower pace than Wigfall desired. Two of his prominent Texas friends called on Davis about mid-August to recommend Wigfall for promotion to brigadier general. But Davis nominated him for only a one-

---

(New York, 1894), 144–45; Johnston to Samuel Cooper, June 24, 29, 1861, and Lee to R. S. Garnett, July 1, 1861, both in *Official Records*, II, 239, 1007.

[34] Chesnut, *Diary*, 92, 107, 109, 106.

[35] Charlotte Wigfall to Halsey, June 5, August 6, 1861; Louly to Halsey, August 2, 1861; and Halsey to his mother, September 12, 1861, all in Wigfall Papers.

step rise to colonel. It was confirmed by Congress on the day it was requested, August 28, 1861. Wigfall did little if anything to earn a promotion during the fall of 1861. He was evidently able to train and, to some extent, discipline his troops, but though there were repeated false alarms, his Texans saw no action. Charlotte and the Wigfall girls joined him at Dumfries where they spent "some happy weeks going out every afternoon to see the dress parade of the Regiments." The number of Wigfall's troops was increasing to brigade level, however, and on November 21, Davis nominated him for a brigadier-generalcy. But the nomination was not confirmed by Congress until December 13.[36]

Perhaps his confirmation was delayed because, five days before his nomination, Wigfall had already been elected to a Senate seat in the Permanent Congress which was to be organized the following February. The Texas legislature had anticipated his nomination to brigadier general, and since they were sure he would render valuable service in either position, they said he should have his choice. But the Confederate Congress was reluctant to give him such a choice. No sooner was his commission finally confirmed than Wigfall made up his mind that he would resign it as soon as the permanent legislature convened in February. During that six weeks he was again alternating between the camp and Congress. As usual, he was trying to get his fellow solons to pass what he considered "very important military legislation," especially the raising of more troops. But he was ready to become a full-time congressman again.[37]

36 W. P. Ballinger Diary, August 19, 1861, W. P. Ballinger Collection, University of Texas Archives, Austin, Texas; *Journal of the Provisional Congress*, 3rd Sess., I, 433–38; Major W. H. Whiting to Wigfall, November 16, 1861; Charlotte Wigfall to Halsey, November 18, 1861, Wigfall Papers; Wright, *Southern Girl*, 74–75. Wigfall's commission was to date from October 21, 1861. *Journal of the Provisional Congress*, 5th Sess., I, 473–74, 568, 596.

37 *Journal of the Senate of Texas, Ninth Legislature,* November 16, 1861, pp. 22–23; B. T. Selman to Wigfall, November 21, 1861, Staff Officer's File; Louly to Halsey, December 27, 1861. About the time that Wigfall decided he would resign his commission as a brigadier general, his son was receiving his as a lieutenant and joined an artillery unit stationed near Centerville, Virginia. Halsey to his mother, September 12, December 17, 1861; Charlotte Wigfall to Halsey, January 4, 1861, Wigfall Papers; *Journal of the Confederate Congress*, 1st Cong., 1st Sess., I, 630–31, 637–39, 667, 676.

Chapter VI

A Tyrant of Wonderful Ability

THE PERIOD of the first three sessions of the First Permanent Congress, February, 1862, through May, 1863, was a time of great optimism for Wigfall and the Confederacy. Legislators debated a great many important topics but, evidently feeling secure, took little action upon them. Most of the congressional agenda was filled with military legislation, and in proposing, debating, and voting on martial matters, Wigfall proved a militarist. During this period, he was proadministration, backing almost all of the legislation that Davis favored and introducing several administration bills. But the President and the senator soon differed over strategy and their quarrel became public knowledge. Like the Confederacy, the Wigfall's enjoyment of a period of high hopes faded half-way through the war.

In early 1862 the Wigfalls were pleasantly situated in a private home on Franklin Street in Richmond. The daughters enrolled in private schools for girls of elite families. Louly's classes were held next door at the famous Miss Pegram's, where she thrived and was considered by many to be one of the most beautiful in a school noted for its lovely students. The proximity of such a center of learning gave Halsey a special incentive to come home whenever he could. His visits were infrequent, however, even though during much of 1862 his regiment was in bivouac at Orange Courthouse and Fredericksburg, Virginia. All of the family were well and in good spirits except Charlotte Wigfall. She had a depressing winter, worrying about Halsey, going out little, and having few visitors. Nor was she evidently cheered much when on February 18 her husband became senator in the first Permanent Confederate Congress.[1]

Wigfall's first debate in this session centered upon the minor issue of a resolution committing the Confederacy to war until Union forces were pushed off the last foot of southern soil. The "man of action" as usual, he denounced paper resolves in favor of one or two well-fought battles. Wigfall reflected the general southern attitude that the Confederacy had beaten the Yankees at Manassas and could beat them again. But to do so there would have to be an effective army in the field. The enlistment rate had gone down, and many a farmer-soldier had gone home to plant a crop and had not come back.[2] Conscription seemed to be the only solution.

On April 1, 1862, Wigfall surprised many of his colleagues by proposing to establish the first conscription system in American history. He introduced the administration's bill to conscript all Confederate men age eighteen through thirty-five for three years of service. Condemning volunteering as a "broken reed," the Texan called on Congress to cease the child's play. Was conscription constitutional? He declared in Falstaffian vein that he would let anyone "spit in his face and call him a horse" if it were not.[3]

1 Charlotte Wigfall to Halsey, January 4, February 8, October 9, 1862; Louly to Halsey, February 1, 1862; Halsey to his mother, March 24, 1862; Charlotte Wigfall to Halsey, February 8, 1862, all in Wigfall Papers. Wigfall drew a four-year term; his colleague W. S. Oldham, six years. *Journal of Congress*, 1st Cong., 1st Sess., 6, 10–13.

2 "Proceedings of the Confederate Congress," 1st Cong., 1st Sess., in *Southern Historical Society Papers*, XLIV, 63–64; Chesnut, *Diary*, 204. The Confederate Congress kept no daily record of debates such as the *Congressional Globe* for the United States Congress. The nearest thing to it is the accounts of the congressional sessions by newspaper reporters, mostly from the Richmond *Examiner*, compiled by the Southern Historical Society and published in its *Papers* in volumes XLIV–LII (1923–1959). Yearns, *Confederate Congress*, 274, says that very little that was said in the Confederate Congress is omitted from the "Proceedings," which are cited hereinafter as "Proceedings of Confederate Congress" with the appropriate volume and page numbers.

3 "Proceedings of Confederate Congress," 1st Cong., 1st Sess., XLV, 26–28; Yearns,

Wigfall was one of the few strong states' rightists to back the measure. His doing so did not signify his conversion to any Confederate nationalism, though in arguing for conscription, he "could not admit that the Southern States were joined in a 'loose league.' " Wigfall was a militarist, espousing the predominance of the army and exalting military virtues and ideals, as well as urging military preparedness.[4] To many Confederate congressmen, however, the Confederacy *was* a loose league, and they were unwilling to give the central government the power to draft their state's citizens. Among the staunch opposition were most of Wigfall's Texas colleagues, who were convinced that by objecting to conscription as being unwise and unconstitutional, they were reflecting the attitudes of their constituents. Nevertheless, the first conscription law in American history was passed, 19–5, on April 16, 1862, just fifteen days after Wigfall had introduced it.[5]

Zealously Wigfall sought to implement his interpretation of the intent of the act, even pushing for conscription of aliens and citizens whether they lived in their home state or another. His effort to draft aliens went down in unceremonious 2–1 defeat in April, 1863. Wigfall undoubtedly could not understand why his colleagues would not take appropriate action to meet the danger confronting the country. There was a significant threat. In April, 1862, Union General George McClellan and 135,000 Federals landed on the tip of the peninsula between the James and York rivers about seventy-five miles from Richmond. By May 1, McClellan's army advanced twenty miles to Yorktown where Johnston had only 53,000 men (including Halsey Wigfall) .[6]

Confederate Congress, 64–65; also *Journal of Congress*, 1st Cong., 1st Sess., 753. Wigfall's argument on the constitutional issue is continued in "Proceedings of Confederate Congress," 1st Cong., 2nd Sess., XLVI, 44–46, 76–77.

4 "Proceedings of Confederate Congress," 1st Cong., 1st Sess., XLV, 27; Charleston *Mercury*, April 2, 1862; Albert Burton Moore, *Conscription and Conflict in the Confederacy* (New York, 1924), 25. *Cf.* Alfred Vagts, *A History of Militarism, Civilian and Military* (New York, 1959), 13–18, 156–57.

5 Yearns, *Confederate Congress*, 68–70; Moore, *Conscription and Conflict*, 137; *Journal of Congress*, 1st Cong., 1st Sess., 139–42, 145–49, 153–54, 767. The North passed a similar law a year later.

6 *Journal of Congress*, 1st Cong., 3rd Sess., 340; Halsey to Louly, April 30, 1862, Wigfall Papers.

Senator Wigfall had more time than usual to devote to this emergency since Congress was recessed during the months of May through July, 1862. The result was more of his advice to generals and criticism of the President. For one thing, he blamed Davis for not relieving pressure from Virginia by invading Maryland. Contemptuously he reported to Clay that instead of taking the needed action, Davis was probably off somewhere engaged in prayer. Wigfall regretted ever having attempted to move "such a dish of skimmed milk to an honorable action." [7] Richmond could be defended from houses and streets by the people *if* they had a leader, said the short-tempered Texan; as it was, Johnston's army was the country's only salvation.

Wigfall's respect for the President as a leader was greatly diminished if it had not disappeared altogether. It was a mutual loss of regard. Guy M. Bryan, a Texan who had visited Davis in May, reported that the President had talked freely with him and had told him that the presidential confidence in Wigfall had been withdrawn first, because of his drunkeness and then, his making speeches at the hotels against him. There was talk around the capitol about Wigfall's drinking, and he was critical of the President's strategy of meeting McClellan on the peninsula. After Davis refused to order an invasion of Maryland, Wigfall had tried to persuade him to abandon Virginia coastal positions in order to concentrate troops to meet McClellan near Richmond. This was in perfect accord with General Johnston's proposed course of action. They probably arrived at their conclusions independently, both realizing that Johnston was outgunned and outmanned and both fearing that McClellan could use his boats on the rivers to land troops behind the Confederates, trapping them on the peninsula.[8]

[7] Chesnut, *Diary*, 218. Four months later, the Army of Northern Virginia did invade Maryland unsuccessfully, being driven off after the costly battle of Antietam; Wigfall to Clay, May 16, 1862, Clay Papers.

[8] W. P. Ballinger Diary, June 22, 1862. There was, said Bryan, already great opposition to the President. Chesnut, *Diary*, 194; Wigfall to Johnston, May [2?], 1862, Johnston Papers. A copy, undated, of Wigfall's letter to Johnston is also found in Wigfall Papers.

For the time being, however, McClellan prepared to use his artillery to pound Johnston's men at Yorktown who had no comparable guns and could not reach the Federals. Despairing of vain efforts to "infuse red blood into [the] inanimate body of a government," Wigfall suggested that Johnston disobey Davis' orders: "If McClellan could wake up some morning and find your camp evacuated it would disturb him more than the arrival of fifty thousand fresh [Confederate] troops." That is exactly what Johnston did, on the day Wigfall wrote. With masterful timing, Johnston covertly withdrew just a few hours before the Federal barrage was due to open and a few days before the expected Federal flanking action occurred. By May 17, Johnston's army, virtually untouched, was camped three miles from Richmond.[9]

Although Davis was extremely concerned and critical, the tactics followed by Johnston and agreed to by Wigfall were probably the wisest. Had the Confederates remained in Yorktown, it is likely that little could have been gained except one or two day's time, and that at a high price. Johnston moved to catch McClellan's forces which were divided by the flooded Chickahominy River and weakened by a month in the swamp. Thus the battle of Seven Pines (May 31–June 1) was joined, the battle that Johnston hoped would end the campaign and perhaps the war. The campaign would probably have been ended with great loss to the Federals had not Johnston been wounded the first day and had he not given verbal orders which were misunderstood by his tactical commander General James Longstreet.[10]

Wigfall joined the fray the second day as an aide to Longstreet, remaining with him from June 1–7, but he evidently did

9 Wigfall to Johnston, May [2?], 1862, Wigfall Papers. Johnston to Lee, April 27, 1862, *Official Records*, XI, Pt. 3, pp. 469–70; Joseph E. Johnston, *Narrative of Military Operations* . . . (Bloomington, Indiana, 1959), 111–16; Joseph E. Johnston, "Manassas to Seven Pines," in *Battles and Leaders of the Civil War*, II, 202–203; Jefferson Davis, *Rise and Fall of the Confederacy* (New York, 1958), II, 86–87; King, "Relationship Between Johnston and Davis," 66–71.

10 King, "Relationship Between Johnston and Davis," 69, 75; Wigfall to Johnston, undated, but after the war, copy in Wigfall Papers. The fact that Davis appointed Robert E. Lee to replace the wounded Johnston as commander of the Army of Northern Virginia may have helped promote the quarrel developing between the President and Wigfall.

nothing more than care for the wounded.[11] While Lee assumed command of Johnston's Army of Northern Virginia and took stock of the situation through June and July, Wigfall continued as Longstreet's aide, visiting his headquarters daily and becoming good friends with him. When Lee took the offensive, the Texan had foreknowledge of the Confederate tactics which pushed the Federals back down the peninsula during the Seven Days' Battle (June 26–July 2, 1862). Wigfall accompanied the Confederate forces throughout the campaign.[12] Again his role was that of locating and caring for wounded Texans.

To his wife he reported that "the slaughter has been terrible— but our success glorious." Confederate success would have been more glorious had they been able to close the trap, but McClellan removed most of his troops from the peninsula. His invasion had been repulsed, however, with heavy Federal losses. Charlotte Wigfall, who was reluctant for her husband to be in the fight *unless* he had a command, expressed great relief that he and Halsey were safe. Louly was "very glad" that her sixteen-year-old brother had been in a fight, hoping that he had killed some "Yankees," and that he would be in more battles. Charlotte Wigfall was evidently concerned also about her husband's political career. She wrote to Louly who was visiting in North Carolina (probably because of possible danger to Richmond), warning her against repeating gossip about the Davises. Louly replied that she had been careful not "to compromise Papa as regards Mr. D." [13]

Although Wigfall-Davis quarrel would yet grow in intensity, it was already serious at this point. Basically it was over military strategy. Each of the two strong-willed "military experts" was sure he knew best. Davis, a graduate of West Point, had led with distinction a regiment in the Mexican War before he became a

---

11 Charlotte Wigfall to Louly, June 8, 1862, Wigfall Papers. Wigfall's wife, like many other Richmond women, helped care for the wounded when they reached the city's hospitals.

12 Wigfall told his wife the detailed plans; she immediately put them into a letter to Louly but did not mail it till after the batle had begun. *Ibid.*, June 25–28, 1862.

13 *Ibid.*, June 11, 29, 1862, July 11, 1862; Louly to her mother, May 29, June 2, 1862, *ibid.*

United States senator. Whether he really meant what he said
when he expressed his preference to be a commanding general
rather than commander-in-chief [14] (he had harbored ambitions
for the presidency while in the Senate), Davis certainly resented
Wigfall's criticism of his military policies. Still, the breach was
not complete; their differences were not public and there were
many subjects upon which they could agree, such as widespread
conscription.

Wigfall's efforts to conscript persons subject to military duty
whenever found precipitated discordant debate. Some border-
state senators objected on the grounds that their states were occupied by Federal troops and since Confederate armies were not
protecting their state, their men should not be conscripted. Wigfall insisted that the draft act applied to every white man in the
Confederacy between the ages of eighteen and thirty-five. Senator
John B. Clark of Missouri expressed concern for citizens of Kentucky and Missouri who, having fled from the enemy, were in the
Confederacy looking for homes for their families. Clark asked
Wigfall if it were his design to catch these men and put them into
the army? Wigfall declared that that "was exactly his design." [15]

Some Confederates and students of southern history have said
that conscription saved the Confederacy for the time. But the
Confederacy needed saving often, and four months later Wigfall
was asking for an extension of conscription, raising the age limit
from thirty-five to forty-five. This met greater opposition than the
original bill had met, and Wigfall spoke more vehemently for it
on and off the Senate floor than he had for the first bill. His loud
nocturnal nagging at visitors to his room often kept his hotel
neighbors awake.[16]

Several of his compatriots argued that if there were to be any

14 Reagan, *Memoirs*, 109; Chesnut, *Diary*, 20.
15 "Proceedings of Confederate Congress," 1st Cong., 2nd Sess., XLV, 221–22.
16 See Moore, *Conscription and Conflict*, 335–56; and Archer Jones, *Confederate
Strategy from Shiloh to Vicksburg* (Baton Rouge, 1961), 47–48; Mary S. Estill (ed.),
"Diary of a Confederate Congressman [F. B. Sexton of Texas], 1862–1863," *Southwestern Historical Quarterly*, XXXVIII (April, 1935), 281.

conscription at all, then the militia, which was needed to protect each state, should be exempted. Senator W. S. Oldham spoke for many of his fellow Texans when he dared the government to try to conscript the Texas troops who had volunteered to defend their state's borders against Indians and Jayhawkers. Wigfall abruptly criticized such an attitude as being short-sighted and vigorously defended the Davis administration for its conscription policy.[17]

It was over Wigfall's protest that a compromise was reached in a bill to muster into the Provisional Army a regiment of Texas volunteers who would remain upon and protect their frontier. He steadfastly maintained that the South's only hope of success was in having but one Confederate army under the command of Confederate generals. He did not believe in partisan rangers, he said, expressing the belief that they did more harm to their own country than to the enemy.[18]

Wigfall also opposed Yancey's plan to allow the discharge of soldiers if they reached the age of forty-five before their three-year enlistment was over. Yancey's proposal was defeated, but the fiery Texan was so perturbed over the timidity of some of his colleagues that he berated them day and night. For several nights Congressman F. B. Sexton of Texas heard Wigfall's scathing denunciations which penetrated the partition between their hotel rooms. One can picture the timorous Sexton shaking his head sadly as he confided to his diary what he thought of Wigfall: "He is a desperate man—a tyrant at heart, yet a man of wonderful ability. Strange that such a mind should be combined with such a heart." By January of the next year, Sexton had concluded that Wigfall was a "very bad man." At about the same time, other Texans were evaluating their senator a little more cautiously. W. P. Ballinger said that some of his friends had remarked about

17 Charleston *Mercury*, August 30, 1862; Moore, *Conscription and Conflict*, 137.
18 *Journal of Congress*, 1st Cong., 1st Sess., 771; "Proceedings of Confederate Congress," 1st Cong., 2nd Sess., XLV, 27–28, 221–22, 253. A personal appeal from Governor Francis Lubbock did not alter Wigfall's position. Lubbock to Wigfall, October 27, 1862, "Executive Records," III, No. 281, pp. 393–95, Texas Archives.

Wigfall's ability, but that they looked upon him as a ruthless man.[19]

By 1863 many Texans were dissatisfied with the policies of Wigfall and the administration. The Texans' major grievance stemmed from their belief that their soldiers were being sent across the Mississippi River and sacrificed by an administration of easterners. Sexton wrote to a friend that his hotel neighbor had temporarily, in mid-1863, "stifled his jalousies [sic]" and "complained of no one," in an effort to soothe the feelings of some Texans. Still, half of the Texas delegation opposed the administration and their senator on conscripting Texans.[20]

Wigfall did draw the line before conscripting state and local officials. While subscribing to the principle that every citizen owed military service to the Confederacy, he denied that that government had the right to exact such service as would destroy the state governments. Senator Benjamin H. Hill of Georgia disagreed; supposing that the enemy could be repelled only by calling out *all* leaders, he asked, would not the central government have the power to call out state officials? Certainly not, replied Wigfall, evidently referring to the states' rights basis of the Confederacy, "Perish the Republic, but call not upon us to commit perjury." [21] This second draft bill, passed September 27, 1862, exempted most state and local officials.[22]

The lists of exemptions on both bills, however, were too long to suit Wigfall, who worked to reduce them by removing some of the exempt teachers, ministers, druggists, and others. Significantly, Wigfall favored the most unpopular exemption of all— that of planters and overseers in charge of at least twenty slaves— as authorized by an act of October 11, 1862. According to its stated purpose, the act was to make sure that the slaves were kept under control. Wigfall said he supported it because planters and

19 *Journal of Congress*, 1st Cong., 2nd Sess., 260–62; Estill, "Diary of a Confederate Congressman," 283; Ballinger Diary, November 17, 19, 1862.
20 Francis B. Sexton to James H. Starr, August 30, 1863, James H. Starr Papers, University of Texas Archives, as cited in Yearns, *Confederate Congress*, 56.
21 "Proceedings of Confederate Congress," 1st Cong., 2nd Sess., XLVI, 31.
22 *Ibid.*, 32–36; *Journal of Congress*, 1st Cong., 2nd Sess., 319–21, 335–36, 368.

overseers were the only ones who could make the Negroes work. It was, nevertheless, one more indication of his low regard for democracy and his determination to sustain the planter aristocracy. Whatever its purpose, to many poor southern whites the act was proof that it was "a rich man's war and a poor man's fight." [23] Many more were convinced of this unfairness by the law which allowed a draftee to avoid military service by hiring a substitute.

Wigfall criticized substitution on the basis of military expediency, pointing out that the system had produced dissatisfaction and lowered morale in the army. Furthermore, he said, every man (except planters who owned twenty slaves or more) was needed in December of 1863; so the substitutes and the men who had hired them would have to go into the army. After all, said Wigfall, Congress was actually doing the "substitute men" a favor by forcing them to do their duty; for if there was anything which would damn a man in the estimation of his countrymen, it would be to have shirked his duty and furnished a substitute.[24] Militarily, substitution was a poor policy, and other Confederate officials worked to overturn it. After it had been in operation a year and a half, the secretary of war asked Congress to repeal it because substitutes were poor fighters and active deserters, hiring themselves for the army only to desert as soon as possible and then repeat the process. Finally, a law of December 28, 1863, prohibited any further use of substitutes.[25]

By late 1863 the need for still further extension of conscription was generally realized by Confederate legislators; thus, the major question was how far to extend it. A number of congressmen were eager to take the lead this time, but Wigfall seized the initi-

23 *Journal of Congress*, 1st Cong., 1st Sess., 203–204; 1st Cong., 2nd Sess., 285–87, 310–12; 1st Cong. 3rd Sess., 305–308; "Proceedings of Confederate Congress," 1st Cong., 2nd Sess., XLVI, 190–93; XLVIII, 104–109, 147–48, 195–97, 212; XLIX, 152–55.
24 "Proceedings of Confederate Congress," 1st Cong., 2nd Sess., XLV, 273; 1st Cong., 4th Sess., L, 26, 119–21, 150–58, 200–201; *Journal of Congress*, 1st Cong., 3rd Sess., 455, 497–99; New York *Times*, January 24, 1864. "Subscription men" were stigmatized in Confederate society; see Chesnut, *Diary*, 367.
25 *Report of the Secretary of War*, November 26, 1863, cited in Yearns, *Confederate Congress*, 76–77; *Journal of Congress*, 1st Cong., 3rd Sess., 457.

ative by proposing age limits of sixteen through sixty, as usual more extreme than most were willing to accept. Furthermore, the length of service would be decided by the President and exemptions would be pared greatly. On February 17, 1864, after two months of controversy, both houses passed Wigfall's basic bill after lowering the upper age limit to fifty and specifying that the oldest and youngest conscriptees would constitute a home guard for detail duty and emergency use in their own states.[26]

In the meantime, thousands of able-bodied southern men defied the conscription laws with impunity. Draft delinquents who were arrested by Confederate authorities were often released by state judges who issued writs of habeas corpus to almost everyone who applied. Thus, another serious question of states' rights and military strength arose. Davis asked Congress to do something about this serious problem by authorizing him to suspend the writ where necessary. Wigfall agreed that some suspension of the writ was needed and on February 20, 1862, introduced a bill to grant the President's request. Admitting that it was a broad power to give any one man, he pointed out that Davis had promised to apply the law sparingly and only in those areas where absolutely necessary. Predictably, there were voices raised in fear for individual liberties and states' rights, but an act granting broad powers of suspension was passed by both houses on February 27, 1862.[27]

Although Davis did use the power sparingly at first, applying it only to the area around Norfolk, there was widespread criticism of the suspension. Opposition became greater when on March 1, 1862, Davis extended the suspension of the writ to Richmond itself. Wigfall belittled the matter, saying that he did not think it was as important as others did, but Congress decided that a reevaluation of the power was in order. On April 19 it passed an act which restricted the President's power in two significant respects, limiting suspension of the writ to offenses against the

26 *Journal of Congress*, 1st Cong., 3rd Sess., 446, 546–47, 554–55, 572, 573, 580–82, 594, 765–69.

27 *Ibid.*, 150; 1st Cong., 1st Sess., 28, "Proceedings of Confederate Congress," 1st Cong., 1st Sess., XLIV, 65.

Confederacy and limiting the duration of the act to thirty days after the next meeting of Congress. Suspension of the writ did remedy the problem, for it meant that the state courts could not free a man held by the Confederate enrolling authorities. Its effectiveness had antithetical results: encouraging the administration to seek an extension of the act's duration, and making critics even more determined to restore the writ.[28]

By early 1864 the matter of manpower was a crucial one, and Davis urged Congress to enhance his power to suspend the writ. Once more the Texas senators were on opposing sides. Oldham, again reflecting sentiment in Texas, led the Senate opposition to any suspension. Wigfall continued to strive for broadly circumscribed presidential authority to suspend the writ.[29]

Concerned about the way that states' rights were hampering military power, Wigfall introduced a resolution on May 5, 1864, which sought to define Confederate and state jurisdictions over civil rights. In a speech supporting his resolution, Wigfall attempted to unravel the intricate constitutional knots of a dual system. While upholding the compact theory and the right of states to interpret the constitution, Wigfall contended that Congress had the undoubted right to suspend the privilege of the writ of habeas corpus and defined a *federal* rather than a confederate system of government: "the State and Confederate governments are separate . . . governments; . . . each . . . is a perfect government in itself; . . . neither can inquire into the legality . . . of the arrests of persons in custody under . . . the authority of the other, or afford such persons any relief." Furthermore, as to the citizens of each state, "the Constitution of the Confederate States . . . is equally supreme and binding over them as their State constitution is and . . . the [Confederate] Government . . . to the extent of its delegated powers, . . . is as fully empowered to act for them as their State government; and when it does so

28 "Proceedings of Confederate Congress," 1st Cong., 2nd Sess., XLVI, 246; Yearns, *Confederate Congress*, 151.
29 Yearns, *Confederate Congress*, 152; *Texas State Gazette*, July 14, 1863; *Journal of Congress*, 2nd Cong., 1st Sess., 692–93, 703–704, 708–12.

act, their State government, having no supremacy over the Confederate Government, can not release them from their obligation to obey." [30]

Thus, in strengthening the military efforts by denying state courts the right to free violators of the Confederate conscription act, Wigfall defined a central government at least strong enough to sustain itself.

Despite rebuttals by members of both houses who held strict states' rights views on the issue, Wigfall's pleas evidently impressed many southerners and helped to head off the attempt to curtail the duration of the act authorizing suspension. And the House of Representatives finally complied with the President's request to *extend* the suspension act which was to expire in July, 1864, but neither Davis, Lee, nor Wigfall could persuade the Senate to go along.[31] Once again Wigfall had demonstrated that he would compromise his states' rights beliefs when he felt that by doing so he could strengthen the army significantly.

In a closely related problem, but one of less importance militarily, Wigfall resumed his strict interpretation of the constitution. He maintained that the Confederate courts had no right to override state court decisions. The question was a divisive one. Under the authority of the Confederate Constitution, the Provisional Congress passed the Judiciary Act of March 16, 1861, organizing each state as a federal judicial district and providing for a supreme court, which was given appellate jurisdiction over state courts. Extreme states' rightists insisted that the high court should have no jurisdiction over any case that had been ruled upon by a state court. There was so much controversy over the issue that the supreme court was suspended until it could be or-

30 *Journal of Congress*, 2nd Cong., 1st Sess., 22–24, 30; "Proceedings of Confederate Congress," 2nd Cong., 1st Sess., LI, 36–37, 55–56.
31 "Proceedings of Confederate Congress," 2nd Cong., 1st Sess., LI, 98–99; 101–104, 133; Chapman, *Edgefield*, 503; Ballinger Diary, September 19, 1864; Yearns, *Confederate Congress*, 157–58; Dallas *Herald*, September 3, November 5, 1864; Houston *Daily Telegraph*, September 21, 23, October 10, 1864; Galveston *News*, September 21, 1864. In all, Congress suspended the writ of habeas corpus for sixteen months during four years of war; *Journal of Congress*, 2nd Cong., 1st Sess.; Yearns, *Confederate Congress*, 159–60.

ganized under the permanent congress. Except for some weak attempts which came to naught, the question lay dormant until September, 1862, when Senator Benjamin Hill of Georgia decided that the time had come for the establishment of a strong Confederate court. Wigfall, who had not been in the Confederate Congress during the earlier debates, agreed with Hill, saying that there should be some tribunal to decide questions between the states and the Confederacy.[32]

He did not agree with the Georgia senator on the relative importance of the state and Confederate courts. Hill proposed that the judges of the Confederate courts be paid more than state court judges so that the Confederate courts would attract the more capable jurists. Wigfall contended that it was for that very reason that the *state* judges should be paid more; the supreme court, one of inferior dignity and circumscribed jurisdiction as compared with the state courts, should not offer a higher salary and attract the more capable state judges to it. It was not at all desirable, the Texan said, to have the finest talent on the supreme court. From his viewpoint the greatest misfortune that ever befell the country was that a man of John Marshall's high character and intellect should have remained upon the Supreme Court of the United States for as long as he did, strengthening that court and the central government so much that it destroyed the Union.[33] Perhaps further reflection on these dangers was the reason Wigfall changed his mind in the next four months, persuaded that there should be no supreme court at all for the Confederacy.

The legislative showdown came when Senator Clay of Alabama proposed to repeal those sections in the Judiciary Act of March, 1861, which conferred appellate jurisdiction over state courts upon the supreme court. This time Wigfall aligned himself against the nationalists. Senator Hill, speaking in support of a strong Confederate judiciary, disparaged Wigfall's attack upon John Marshall and the Supreme Court of the United States. In a refreshingly frank appraisal, Hill described "the gentleman from

32 "Proceedings of Confederate Congress," 1st Cong., 2nd Sess., XLVI, 245–46.
33 *Ibid.*, 207–209.

Texas" as "an able man; he grows upon you as you know him. I
think a great deal more of him than I used to do when I heard of
him through the newspapers, in the United States Senate. But he
can . . . sometimes fly . . . faster on a tangent at a right angle from
the truth than any other man, as he has done in this question."
As he was doing more and more often, Wigfall ignored the personal remarks, responding simply with a lengthy exposition upon
the unconstitutionality of appellate jurisdiction over the state
courts.[34]

As the debates became more heated, the legislators' compo-
sures ravelled, but it was not Wigfall who lost his self-control.
It was Hill who threw the ink bottle at Yancey, grazing his
skull.[35] Wigfall met all proposals for a strong court by repeating
his earlier arguments of unconstitutionality. After more than
two months of debate, he helped throttle the issue by belittling
it, expressing anxiety that the Senate should dispose of matters
of "pressing importance," such as his bill for the organization of
a corp of engineers, because spring was at hand and trestles, pon-
toons, and such needed to be built. Consideration of the establishment of the court waited while the Senate passed Wigfall's
bill to organize a company of engineers for each infantry division
in the army. When the vote on Clay's proposal to abolish the
supreme court's appellate jurisdiction over state courts was called
for, it passed the Senate by a large majority.[36] The House never
got around to voting on it.

Undoubtedly Wigfall was more concerned with engineer com-
panies than in supreme courts, more with military might than in
state or individual rights. In a further effort to strengthen the
Confederate military effort, he was already involved in another
controversy—confiscation for the army. There was general real-

34 *Ibid.*, 210, 224–25; New York *Times*, February 2, 1863.
35 Wigfall was on the special committee which investigated and condemned this
"violation of dignity to the Senate." *Journal of Congress*, 1st Cong., 3rd Sess., 48.
Evidently Wigfall was not considered a brawler or he would not have been appointed to this committee.
36 "Proceedings of Confederate Congress," 1st Cong., 3rd Sess., XLVIII, 2–4, 26–
27, 53–54, 60–61, 76, 214–17, 316–17; Moore, *Conscription and Conflict*, 84–87, 165;
Yearns, *Confederate Congress*, 38; New York *Times*, February 2, 1863.

ization in Congress that some sort of impressment was needed, and was indeed already being done by commanders. The problem was to regulate the practice with safeguards for the civilians and, at the same time, supply the army as efficiently as possible. A number of proposals were advanced. Wigfall's would allow impressment agents to take property, including slaves and produce needed by the farmer, for military use. Despite a vague provision calling for the dismissal from the service of any officer who should "wantonly or oppressively impress or take any property of a citizen," Wigfall was clearly more interested in supplying the army than he was in providing safeguards for citizens. The government could impress such private property as was needed, paying what it considered was a fair price, he insisted. Numerous critics favored more restrictive bills such as those offered by Yancey or Landon C. Haynes (of Tennessee) who provided explicit safeguards for property.[37]

Despite an adverse report from the military committee, Wigfall defended his bill, pronouncing all others as simply impractical, warning that an army would starve to death before it could be fed under the conditions laid down by Yancey and others. In reply to those who deprecated the taking of produce from farmers, the Texan stated his belief that there were occasions when it might be necessary to take the last pint of meal from a family or the last horse from the lone widow. There was, he averred, no antagonism between the army and the people, for the army was the people. Although the military committee reported adversely on a compromise bill, largely Wigfall's, it was passed by both houses in March, 1863. Undoubtedly more persuasive to critics than the fire-eater's oratory was his acceptance of a provision which allowed a property owner to appeal to an arbitration board of distinguished persons from his vicinity and then to the courts if he disputed the price set by the impressment officer. In the meantime, the army would have the use of the goods. But Wigfall continued to oppose arbitration and vicinage appraise-

37 "Proceedings of Confederate Congress," 1st Cong., 3rd Sess., XLVII, 148–49; XLVIII, 51–53, 173, 242–44, 252–53; *Texas Republican,* March 26, 1863.

ment, and a month later he proposed to abolish them in order to facilitate the military effort. His proposal failed; too many legislators agreed with Sexton that it was a "radical amendment." [38]

Wigfall was successful, however, in using military necessity to pass a bill that he had worked for unsuccessfully in the United States Senate. By the fall of 1861 the Davis administration had realized the need for additional railroads to fill voids in the transportation system from Richmond to key positions in the South and West. In February, 1862, the Confederate Congress, over determined opposition, had appropriated a million dollars for such a connection between Virginia and North Carolina. In March a Texan congressman, C. C. Herbert, introduced a bill for a similar grant for a Louisiana-Texas rail connection. Wigfall supported it avidly in the Senate. Again he was on an opposing side from the more consistent states' righter Oldham, who declared that he had been elected on the principle of opposition to such a measure and though favoring the building of a railroad, he thought that the states of Texas and Louisiana should build it. Evidently a majority of the Senate agreed, for the bill failed. But Davis asked for its reconsideration. Wigfall so moved, speaking for the bill on the basis of military necessity. This time the Senate passed it, 12–9. The act, similar to others which dealt with Confederate railroads, provided for $1,500,000 in Confederate bonds for the construction of a line from New Iberia, Louisiana, to Orange, Texas.[39] Again, Wigfall had departed from states' rights principles.

In spite of the question of states' rights, such a railroad was a necessity to the Confederacy. Texas would have played a greater role in the war effort had it not been so remote by land and cut off from the sea by the Federal blockade. Ten days after Davis signed the bill, however, New Orleans was captured, separating

---

[38] *Journal of Congress*, 1st Cong., 3rd Sess., 320, 327–28, 747–48; "Proceedings of Confederate Congress," 1st Cong. 3rd Sess., XLVIII, 51–53, 240–47, 252–56, 262–64, 272–73, 276–79; XLIX, 189ff.; Yearns, *Confederate Congress*, 118–19; Estill, "Diary of a Confederate Congressman," 59.

[39] "Proceedings of Confederate Congress," 1st Cong., 1st Sess., XLV, 158–60; *Journal of Congress*, 1st Cong., 1st Sess., 197–98, 220, 305; Robert C. Black, *The Railroads of the Confederacy* (Chapel Hill, 1952), 158–60; Yearns, *Confederate Congress*, 129.

Texas even more effectively from the rest of the Confederacy, and the railroad project was dropped by the war department.[40]

Although Wigfall failed to obtain the Confederate-built railroad, the next year he helped establish Confederate control over the privately built ones. He pronounced the "rascally railroads" so inconsiderate of the public welfare that they had to be coerced into giving priority to military needs. Thus he supported the bill to give the secretary of war the authority to commandeer the roads he needed in any emergency, and if they were uncooperative he could impress them for the government. On May 1, 1863, the bill became law. One year later Wigfall tried unsuccessfully to have all the railroads put under government control. Had it been passed then, the law might have served the purpose hoped for in February, 1865, when the railroads were taken over by the Confederate government.[41] By that time it was too late.

It is understandable why military men looked at Wigfall as their congressional champion. When Robert E. Lee was lamenting the large number of exemptions allowed by Congress, he queried his son General Custis Lee: "Cannot Genl Wigfall do something for us with Congress?" General Longstreet flattered his Texas friend by pointing out his importance to the armies, "all of our hopes rest upon you." But an even greater compliment was paid Wigfall by his closest confidant during the war years, General Joseph E. Johnston, who discussed all of his problems of command with him because Wigfall had "a head to comprehend grand war & a heart to sympathize" with his friends. Generals often wrote directly to the Texan with specific requests for legislation, as Longstreet did in August of 1863, asking for laws concerning provost marshals, draft violators, substitutes, and appointment of officers.[42]

Early in his senatorial career, Wigfall made it clear that on a

40 Black, *Railroads*, 161.

41 "Proceedings of Confederate Congress," 1st Cong., 3rd Sess., XLVII, 174–77; *ibid.*, 2nd Cong. 1st Sess., LI, 237–38; Yearns, *Confederate Congress*, 130–31.

42 Lee to his son Custis, February 13, 1863, in Clifford Dowdey and Louis H. Manarin (eds.), *The Wartime Papers of R. E. Lee* (Boston, 1961), 410–12. Already, in the fall of 1862, Lee had turned to Wigfall for aid in getting additional Texas troops; Robert E. Lee to Wigfall, September 21, 1862, in Wigfall Papers; also in Wright, *Southern Girl*, 94; and a copy in Guy M. Bryan Papers, University of

number of subjects he preferred to have sound army regulation rather than poor congressional legislation. Thus he showed again his militarism, ranking military institutions and ways above the prevailing attitudes of civilian life. Wigfall assured those who feared excess militarism that there was no danger of military despotism. Even when General Braxton Bragg was criticized by many congressmen who felt he was guilty of summary execution of his troops for slight offenses, Wigfall came to the defense of the general, citing a "common law" of the army which gave the commander the power of life and death over his troops.[43]

Paying less attention to the needs of enlisted men than to those of generals gave Wigfall a reputation for "living too high up in his ballroom." [44] He did point out to Secretary of War James Seddon the importance of recognizing and promoting enlisted men as well as officers for skill and valor. This would stimulate their ambition and provide better leaders, Wigfall advised. He was more liberal with recognition for soldiers than with money for them, opposing most bills for pay increases for enlisted men. One reason he opposed pay raises for them, he explained, was because they were fighting for their country, not for money. Further, he said he was opposed to inflating the currency by increasing the soldiers' pay; such increase would not benefit the soldiers, but rather the sutlers. Instead he favored giving the soldiers tobacco and introduced a bill for that purpose. Yet he seemed not to have been greatly interested in the bill; one year later he asked what had happened to it. Subsequently it was passed. Wigfall could "see no equity" in a bill for the government to pay for volunteers' travel expenses to their camp, however, and helped to defeat that proposal.[45]

The Texas senator was zealous, however, in obtaining for the

Texas Archives. James Longstreet to Wigfall, November 7, 1862; August 17, 1863; J. E. Johnston to Wigfall, December 2, 1862, all in Wigfall Papers.

43 "Proceedings of Confederate Congress," 1st Cong., 1st Sess., XLV, 57–58, 113–19; Vagts, *History of Militarism*, 13–18, 156–57.

44 Chesnut, *Diary*, 235.

45 Wigfall to Seddon, December 5, 1862, Wigfall Papers; *Journal of Congress*, 1st Cong., 2nd Sess., 428–29; "Proceedings of Confederate Congress," 1st Cong., 1st Sess., XLV, 76; 1st Cong., 3rd Sess., XLVIII, 41–42; XLIX, 10, 64; 1st Cong., 4th Sess., L, 71, 395–96.

soldiers all that had been promised to them. For several months before the collapse of the Confederacy, the government had not met the army and navy payrolls. One month before the government fell, Wigfall helped to win these back-payments. The previous month he had supported a bill to require the payment of wages to Confederate enlisted men held as prisoners of war.[46]

Wounded veterans received less consideration from Wigfall. Caustically he demeaned a bill to give civilian job preferences to veterans who had been discharged from the army because of wounds or loss of health in battle. Even though the bill expressly stated that such preference would be given only when the qualifications of candidates were equal, Wigfall maintained that "the general tone" of the bill was to "make clerks out of wounded ploughmen," and Wigfall said he did not believe that the government was ever intended to be an eleemosynary institution. If a hospital were to be built for crippled soldiers, he said, he might support it.[47] One may wonder how he came to be a vice-president of the Association for the Relief of Maimed Soldiers.

Wigfall's interest in hospitals seemed to extend little further than in providing guards for the patients to keep them from "straggling off and poisoning themselves at whiskey shops." [48] There was another evil in the army hospitals as demoralizing as whiskey, he said, and that was army doctors, who, "having nothing to do at home, attached themselves to the army." [49] He seemed

[46] "Proceedings of Confederate Congress," 2nd Cong., 2nd Sess., LII 475; *Journal of Congress*, 2nd Cong., 2nd Sess., 595, 688.

[47] "Proceedings of Confederate Congress," 1st Cong., 1st Sess., XLV, 62–65; 1st Cong., 2nd Sess., XLVII, 101–104. The Association for the Relief of Maimed Soldiers was established in January, 1864. Its stated objectives included that of supplying artificial limbs for army and navy men who were maimed while in the service of their country. Confederate legislation to aid the association was not enacted until March 11, 1865 (Wigfall voting for it), providing for free transportation to and from artificial limb factories, for purchase of materials at cost from the government, and for other such services. Evidently some work was accomplished by the association. By October 10, 1864, the association had placed orders for 499 artificial limbs, and H. H. Cunningham said it is likely that these and others were eventually provided for men who needed them. See Cunningham, *Doctors in Gray: The Confederate Military Service* (Baton Rouge, 1958), 91, 144–45. It is doubtful that Wigfall was active in promoting the efforts of the association. Other prominent vice-presidents of the association included George A. Trenholm of South Carolina and Pierre Soulé of Louisiana.

[48] "Proceedings of Confederate Congress," 1st Cong., 3rd Sess., XLVII, 225.

[49] *Ibid.*, 1st Cong., 1st Sess., XLV, 145.

most perturbed that the physicians held commissions as officers. Striving to keep the army aristocracy pure, Wigfall worked to restrict the doctors' authority to purely medical matters and keep their ranks as low as possible.[50]

Wigfall was extremely concerned about who was commissioned, how they were commissioned, and how highly they ranked.[51] He was especially upset by the provision of the law of April 16, 1862, which allowed enlisted men to elect their own company and regimental officers. To induce men to reenlist for the war, Congress allowed them to choose their own captains. This was a poor policy because such officers had to court the favor of the men in order to keep their positions; they were not likely to elect an officer who would discipline them. The President, the secretary of war, General Lee, and most other senior officers were appalled at such a system and said so vociferously. But Wigfall found little support in Congress for his efforts to have the President make all appointments, with the Senate having the power of confirming the senior officers.[52]

Thus, despite the personal differences and conflicts over military strategy between Wigfall and Davis, the Texan remained a supporter of the President's legislative program, particularly those measures which would strengthen the army. Even Wigfall's states' rights principles were expendable for the army, as shown by his advocacy of a federally financed railroad and denial of the state court's jurisdiction over conscription cases. Always the aristocratic militarist, he was without the slightest identification with ideas of liberty and equality. His avid support of the exemption of the large-scale planter class from conscription, of suspension of the writ of habeas corpus, and of the arbitrary confiscation of property by the army marked Louis Wigfall as a selfish man, certain that only his ideal of rule by aristocracy was important.

50 *Ibid.*, 1st Cong. 2nd Sess., XLVI, 39; 1st Cong. 3rd Sess., XLIX, 128, 240–41; *Journal of Congress*, 1st Cong., 3rd Sess., 371; Cunningham, *Doctors in Gray*, 40.

51 *Journal of Congress*, 1st Cong., 1st Sess., 394–96, 443–44; "Proceedings of Confederate Congress," 1st Cong., 1st Sess., XLV, 47.

52 Chesnut, *Diary*, 249–50; "Proceedings of Confederate Congress," 1st Cong., 2nd Sess., XLV, 42, 202–205, 215–16, 247–48; *Journal of Congress*, 1st Cong., 2nd Sess., 315–16; Yearns, *Confederate Congress*, 61, 63, 65, 104–105.

Chapter VII

What Hope for a Reasonable Man?

TO WIGFALL, only he and a few select friends had enough sense and ability to keep the Confederate ship of state afloat. Launched in a rough sea, the Confederacy in 1863 was headed for the rocks of economic, political, and military failure. The administration and Congress proved unable to cooperate in their futile efforts to deal with the serious problem of finance, inflation, and transportation. Prices for poorer and poorer fare and for more and more crowded quarters climbed ever higher. By July, 1863, the relentless pressure from the North added to rebel frustration. Charleston was attacked again by the Federal fleet; Vicksburg fell, allowing the Union forces to sever the Trans-Mississippi West from the rest of the Confederacy; Lee's invasion of the North was repulsed with heavy losses at Gettysburg. Threats to the Confederacy bred more frustration than cooperation, and Davis quarreled more and more with Congress, his generals, and state leaders.

Some of Davis' detractors, such as Congressman Henry S. Foote of Tennessee and Senator Oldham of Texas, had been consistent Davis critics from the origin of the Confederacy. A large number of others, such as Postmaster General John H. Reagan of Texas, recognized Davis' faults but remained loyal to their leader. Wigfall and a few others began as supporters but became increasingly disenchanted with the Chief Executive. Although he had criticized Davis privately, and Davis had said that he had withdrawn his confidence from Wigfall because of his drinking, the senator continued to be the champion of the administration's proposed legislation until October of 1862 when his design for a general staff came before Davis.

To aid in developing plans and in coordinating movements, the Provisional Congress had enacted the Staff Act of February 26, 1861, giving each general of an army a staff of quartermaster, engineer, ordnance, adjutants, and aides-de-camp. These officers were selected and assigned by President Davis. Compared to the Union army staffs, those of the Confederacy were extremely small, inexperienced, and low in rank. Most of the Union staff officers were generals while those of the Confederacy were below the rank of colonel. Thus the southern generals were often overworked because of a lack of experienced and authoritative staffs to help them in planning battles and in operating their armies.[1]

In September, 1862, Wigfall introduced a bill to remedy this situation. He proposed to allow each general of an army to select his own staff, the more important members, such as quartermasters, to have the rank of brigadier or above. As the editors of the "Proceedings of the Confederate Congress" have observed, the bill was one of the most important considered by the rebel legislature. Many generals, the Senate Military Committee, and both houses endorsed the bill, but Davis vetoed it. Wigfall's bill was unacceptable, said Davis, because the staffs provided would be large and unwieldy, taking men needed on the battlefield, and it would not allow the President a voice in the selection and assignment of officers.[2] Davis was not going to give up any military authority that easily.

Perhaps to soften the blow, Davis asked Wigfall, along with Oldham, to confer with him the day before the veto. Neverthe-

[1] Eaton, *A History of the Confederacy*, 120; Bell Irvin Wiley, *The Road to Appomattox* (Memphis, 1956), 94–102, Frank E. Vandiver, *Rebel Brass* (Baton Rouge, 1956), 18, 21–22.

[2] *Journal of Congress*, 1st Cong., 2nd Sess., 444–45, 481, 485, 486; "Proceedings of Confederate Congress," 1st Cong., 2nd Sess., XLVI, 9, 110; Wigfall to Joseph E. Johnston, undated, Wigfall Papers.

less, Davis' refusal to accept Wigfall's staff plan contributed greatly to their quarrel, and their differences came into the open for the first time. Soon after, Mary Chesnut was appalled by the "republican independence" of both of the Wigfalls, who turned their backs upon the President and first lady, actually snubbing them at a Richmond party.[3]

Wigfall had been definitely pro-administration, as demonstrated by his voting to confirm presidential appointments, but with the veto came a change. Within five days after the presidential negation of the staff bill, he voted against the confirmation of Davis' appointments of William J. Hardee and John C. Pemberton as lieutenant generals. During the same time, Wigfall opposed a measure to allow the President the authority to appoint officers during the coming recess of Congress, even if the appointment then should be subject to Senate confirmation at its next session.[4]

Davis still had too much influence with Congress for Wigfall to block confirmation of the President's appointments or of granting presidential power to make temporary appointments without Senate confirmation. But Davis' tender feelings were no doubt bruised. He struck back quickly. On October 11 he wrote Wigfall: "It has been suggested to me that you thought [General T. H.] Holmes had failed in his duty at Malvern Hill [in the Peninsular campaign], by being too slow in getting into position, and in that connection I wish to say to you that he was ordered . . . " and there followed a lengthy defense of Holmes, one of his favorites.[5]

As far as defending his generals from criticism which he felt was unjust, Davis was within his province. He was convinced that

[3] Davis to Wigfall and Oldham, October 7, 1862, Wigfall Papers; Chesnut, *Diary*, 282. For fourteen months Mary Chesnut kept no daily journal, but in October, 1863, she wrote of that period from memory.

[4] *Journal of Congress*, 1st Cong., 2nd Sess., 470, 488; "Proceedings of Confederate Congress," 1st Cong., 2nd Sess., XLVI, 98. The northern-born Pemberton was suspect to many southerners, but Hardee was generally respected, having authored a military tactics book in the "old army." Chesnut, *Diary*, 217.

[5] Davis to Wigfall, October 11, 1862, Wigfall Papers, and Wright, *Southern Girl*, 88–89.

it was absolutely necessary that a general obtain and preserve his popularity and influence with his men.[6] Perhaps Davis had just learned of the criticism which had passed four months before; at any rate, the timing and tone of his letter were hardly calculated to assuage the fiery Wigfall.

General Longstreet was aware of the consequences that a Wigfall-Davis quarrel might have. Alarmed at a report that Wigfall and the President had had "an unpleasant interview," Longstreet wrote to the Texas senator on November 7, 1862, begging him not to allow anything to bring about such a feud. The army rested its hopes upon Wigfall, said Longstreet, and the hopes of the country rested upon the army. The general warned Wigfall that he would readily perceive the weight he had to carry.[7]

By the time Longstreet's entreaty reached Wigfall, Davis had found another way to slight the Texan. On November 14, George W. Randolph resigned his position as secretary of state because he disagreed with Davis' reliance upon the secretary as merely a clerk to carry out the orders of the President without taking any initiative. To replace him, Davis appointed James A. Seddon. The following day, Wigfall called upon Davis and discussed the matter of replacing Randolph. Wigfall agreed with Davis that either Seddon, General Joseph E. Johnston, or General G. W. Smith could fill the position and preferred them, as Davis did, in that order. Wigfall was not told that the President had already appointed Seddon. The senator found out about it the next day. According to John H. Reagan, "Matters connected with the appointment of Mr. Seddon . . . caused Senator Wigfall, who had been an ardent supporter of the Administration, to become a violent opponent of the President, and to join with . . . Foote of Tennessee and other malcontents, in giving [Davis] what trouble they could." The day that Wigfall learned of this presidential duplicity, Davis called Reagan into his office and asked him what

6 J. A. L. Fremantle, *The Fremantle Diary* . . . , edited by Walter Lord (Boston, 1954), 168–69.

7 Longstreet to Wigfall, November 7, 1862, Wigfall Papers.

was wrong with Wigfall. Why was the senator denouncing the administration in the Senate? [8]

Not only did Wigfall resent the manner in which Seddon was selected, he also regretted the loss of Randolph from the War Department; they had agreed upon the policy of concentrating troops in the West. Randolph had issued orders to General Theophilus H. Holmes to move his 30,000 troops from their unthreatened position in Arkansas to join General J. C. Pemberton in Mississippi, bringing 70,000 Confederate troops against 45,000 for the Federals in that area. Davis disagreed and countermanded the order, prompting Randolph's resignation. This affair probably increased Wigfall's anxiety about the fate of Texas and the entire West. He decided that the Confederacy's most able general—Joe Johnston, in Wigfall's estimation—was needed there. According to the analysis of his daughter, Wigfall's persistent advocacy of putting Johnston in command of *all* Confederate troops in the West led to the "severance of friendly relations" between the President and himself.[9]

In November, 1862, Johnston was still recovering from his Peninsular campaign wounds, but true to Wigfall's expectations, Davis appointed the general to command the "western department." Contrary to the wishes of Johnston and Wigfall, however, the department was made up of the states of Tennessee and Mississippi. From the outset, Johnston was sure that a "great mistake" had been made in the arrangement of his command because Mississippi and Arkansas should have been united, not Tennessee and Mississippi. Wigfall, far more ambitious for Johnston than the general was for himself, wanted his authority to include Texas, as well as Tennessee, Mississippi, *and* Arkansas.[10]

Shortly after Johnston arrived in the West, he and Davis dis-

[8] Reagan, *Memoirs*, 161.

[9] *Ibid.*; Davis to Randolph, November 12, 1862, *Official Records*, XIII, 914–15; Wright, *Southern Girl*, 159–60.

[10] Louly to Halsey, November 14, 1862; Charlotte Wigfall to Halsey, November 26, 1862; Johnston to Wigfall, December 2, 1862, Wigfall Papers; Wigfall to Clay, December 11, 1862, Clay Papers.

agreed over policy. Johnston's most pressing problem was to save Vicksburg from General U. S. Grant's force of Federals, which far outnumbered the Confederates there under Pemberton. Johnston's proposed solution was the same as Randolph's, that Holmes be ordered to bring his troops from Arkansas to reinforce Pemberton, giving him a force superior to Grant's. Davis was still not receptive to the plan. But Wigfall was still convinced that such a concentration of troops was necessary. He urged Johnston to state his views fully and frankly to the War Department; if nothing else, this would give a written record which would protect him. Wigfall promised to do what he could to have the general's proposals carried out. To do this, the senator hoped for much from Secretary of War Seddon.[11]

Wigfall told his friend C. C. Clay that they were fortunate to have a man of Seddon's character with whom they could "be on terms." Wigfall's appreciation of Seddon was enhanced by two things. The secretary's gracious reception of Wigfall's suggestion was one factor. After receiving one of Wigfall's letters, Seddon expressed his appreciation for the advice and added that he would always be grateful for any suggestions from Wigfall's "fuller knowledge and riper experiences." Also, the senator was convinced that Seddon agreed with him that all of the Confederate armies in the Mississippi Valley should be under the command of Johnston. No wonder Wigfall pronounced Seddon a "gentleman *and* a man of sense." [12]

Wigfall kept his promise to Johnston and accepted Seddon's invitation for advice by writing to the secretary to urge that Holmes's entire force be ordered to Vicksburg. This would save the port city and allow the destruction of first Grant's army and then the Federals in Tennessee. Political considerations should not interfere, said Wigfall; they "should weigh nothing in the movement of troops." When Oldham and other Texans were

11 Johnston to Wigfall, December 2, 1862, Wigfall Papers; Wigfall to Johnston, December —, 1862, copy in *ibid.*
12 Wigfall to Clay, December 11, 1862, Clay Papers; Seddon to Wigfall, December —, 1862, Wigfall Papers.

pressing Wigfall to join them in insisting that all the troops from west of the Mississippi be returned from the east, Wigfall told them publicly that if he had control of the army, every soldier from Arkansas and Texas would be united with Confederate troops under one commander on the eastern side. This was the policy to follow, Wigfall urged Seddon; on whichever side of the Mississippi the enemy appeared, he should be met with the entire western force and crushed. If he appeared on both sides, concentrate on one, defeat him there, then cross the river and defeat him again.[13]

Repeated warnings by Wigfall, Johnston, and others who said that the West was in danger, brought Davis to the area in December to look the situation over for himself. During this tour the President decided that reinforcements for Mississippi should come from General Braxton Bragg in Tennessee instead of from Arkansas as Wigfall, Johnston, Bragg, and Adjutant General Samuel Cooper advised.[14] Wigfall had told Clay that Davis would not realize the wisdom of a unified command because he was trying to do the impossible, attend to the civil duties of his office and command the army at the same time; even "Napoleon had never attempted such a thing." [15] Complicating the problem was Johnston's insistence that he could not exercise any general control over both Tennessee and Mississippi and his conclusion, communicated to both Davis and Wigfall, that his command was only a nominal one and he should be given some other position.[16]

[13] Wigfall to Seddon, December 8, 1862, in Wright, *Southern Girl,* 100–103.
[14] Davis to Samuel Cooper, November 29, 1862; Johnston to Cooper, November 24, December 4, 6, 1862; Davis to Seddon, December 15, 1862, *Official Records,* XVII, Pt. 2, pp. 758, 765–68, 777, 780–81; XX, Pt. 2, pp. 435–38, 449–50; Johnston to Wigfall, December 15, 1862, in Wright, *Southern Girl,* 104–10.
[15] Wigfall to Clay, December 11, 1862, Clay Papers. Wigfall's preoccupation with military matters continued as the third session of the first permanent Confederate Congress convened on January 12, 1863. The letters of Charlotte Wigfall and Louly during this period show the anxiety over high rent, smallpox, and scarlet fever, as well as Halsey's welfare on the front lines. But Wigfall concentrated on martial problems, leaving Oldham almost the entire task of dealing with resolutions from the Texas Legislature and inquiries from individual Texans. Louly to Halsey, January 17, 31, 1863; Charlotte Wigfall to Halsey, January 17, February 12, 1863, Wigfall Papers.
[16] Johnston to Davis, January 2, 6, 1863, *Official Records,* XVII, Pt. 2, p. 823;

Johnston had the sympathy of Wigfall and many military men. Even though Seddon seemed convinced that the President intended the western command to be a significant one, Davis' brother-in-law General Richard Taylor, who regarded both Davis and Johnston highly, observed that Johnston actually "commanded nobody." The major cause of Johnston's dissatisfaction was not the absence of an actual command in the West, but rather, as he revealed to Wigfall, his own absence from the Army of Northern Virginia. He pleaded with the senator to help him return to command in Virginia, but he doubted that Wigfall could help, because the task would require "diplomacy and cunning." And the general said he thought his friend lacked *the latter*.[17]

Johnston probably doubted also that Wigfall had enough influence with the President. Some others, however, still thought that Wigfall could move Davis. Congressman Lawrence M. Keitt, an old South Carolina acquaintance in search of a commission as brigadier general, asked the senator to see the President "and give me your influence." Wigfall was "seeing" Davis socially as the two still went through the motion of cordial relations. On the last day of January, Wigfall joined others in dining with the President, but before going took the precaution of eating a good dinner, and fortifying his nerve by a pipe and a nap. Charlotte Wigfall was surprised that her husband was treated "with civility" by Varina Davis that night. Possibly, Charlotte wrote to her son, the Davises deemed it "inexpedient to quarrel." [18]

Nevertheless, Wigfall did not have the influence to persuade Davis to replace Lee with Johnston as commander of the Army of Northern Virginia. There was another possibility which would

Johnston to Wigfall, January 8, 1862, Wigfall Papers. See also Joseph E. Johnston, "Jefferson Davis and the Mississippi Campaign," in Johnson and Buell (eds.), *Battles and Leaders of the Civil War*, III, 472–82; and Gilbert E. Govan and James W. Livingood, *A Different Valor: The Story of General Joseph E. Johnston, C.S.A.* (New York, 1956), 166–74.

17 Seddon to Johnston, February 5, 1863, *Official Records*, XVIII, Pt. 2, pp. 626–27; Richard Taylor, *Destruction and Reconstruction* (New York, 1955), 207; Johnston to Wigfall, January 26, 1863, in Wright, *Southern Girl*, 121–23.

18 Lawrence Keitt to Wigfall, January 16, 1863; Louly to Halsey, January 31, 1863; Charlotte Wigfall to Halsey, February 1, 1863, all in Wigfall Papers.

allow Johnston to have direct command of an army. That was for him to replace Bragg as head of the Army of Tennessee. Several members of Congress had been critical of Bragg for lack of accomplishments and for what some thought was unjustifiably harsh punishment inflicted upon his troops. After Bragg's disappointing campaign in Kentucky in the fall of 1862 and his attempts to blame his failures upon his subordinates, Wigfall joined the swelling ranks of the anti-Bragg group; however, he thought that Bragg was such a favorite of Davis that nothing could be done about it. But criticism of Bragg reached such proportions that Davis reluctantly asked Johnston to investigate conditions within the Army of Tennessee. Johnston's report upheld Davis' faith in Bragg, recommending that he remain in command. Johnston closed with a suggestion to the President that should it appear necessary to remove Bragg, "no one . . . engaged in this investigation ought to be his successor." [19]

It would thus seem that it should have been clear to all concerned that Johnston did not want command of the Army of Tennessee. On several occasions he had written to Wigfall, praising Bragg for his accomplishments and remarking that it would do no good to replace him. With chagrin, Wigfall notified Johnston that Seddon had concluded that Johnston did not desire the command of Bragg's army. The senator had drawn a different conclusion—that his proud friend wanted the command but did not want to appear to want it. If this were the case, Wigfall wrote the general, just write that "you understand me." "It is not easy for me to say," replied Johnston. The existing arrangement in the West was unworkable, he admitted, but he said he could not ask the removal of a brother officer and then be his successor.[20]

Without waiting for the reply, Wigfall informed Johnston: "I

[19] Yearns, *Confederate Congress*, 148; Senator G. A. Henry to Wigfall, October 25, 1863, and Johnston to Wigfall, January 8, 1863, Wigfall Papers; Wigfall to Clay, December 11, 1862, Clay Papers; *Journal of Congress*, 1st Cong., 3rd Sess., 337; Johnston to Davis, February 23, 1863, *Official Records*, XXII, Pt. 2, pp. 624, 757–61.

[20] Johnston to Wigfall, December 2, 1862, January 8, 26, 1863, March 4, 8, 1863, Wigfall Papers; Wigfall to Johnston, February 27, 1863, Johnston Papers.

have been pressing Seddon to remove Bragg." He was sure, the Texan said, that Johnston could have either Bragg's or Pemberton's army. Wigfall's choice for his friend was obvious. *If* Johnston took the Army of Tennessee, he should not keep Bragg as second in command, the senator advised. Wigfall reasoned that Bragg was hated by his men, his officers, and the people of Tennessee, and if he stayed, he would transfer that hate to Johnston. Wigfall's assessment of Bragg's unpopularity was correct. In March, the Tennessee delegation asked the President to take Bragg out of their state, for his presence depressed the entire population there. Johnston was the officer most requested as his successor.[21]

One of Davis' strongest characteristics was his loyalty to those generals with whom he was on good terms, but he reluctantly agreed with Seddon that for the sake of harmony and morale Johnston should replace Bragg. Johnston was just as reluctant to comply. Contrary to Wigfall's advice, the general requested Bragg's continued presence.[22] Nevertheless, the Texan had achieved what he had set out to do—replace an ineffectual commander with a friend whom he considered to be a great general. The senator must have realized that it was not his efforts alone which brought it about; what influence he had exercised had been devious, applied indirectly through Seddon.

Indeed, few if any congressmen had any direct influence upon Davis. Even his legislative supporters were embarrassed by his lack of communication with them individually or collectively. In January, 1863, Wigfall proposed to take a step which should have facilitated understanding and cooperation between Congress and the executive branch. He introduced a bill to grant cabinet members a seat upon the floor of the Senate. There were

21 Wigfall to Johnston, February 28, 1863, Johnston Papers; G. A. Henry to Wigfall, October 25, 1862, and (General) Leonidas Polk to Wigfall, March 2, 1863, Wigfall Papers; Polk to Davis, March 30, 1863, *Official Records*, XXIII, Pt. 2, p. 745; Yearns, *Confederate Congress*, 148; King, "Relationship Between Johnston and Davis," 87; Govan and Livingood, *Johnston*, 182.

22 Bragg's presence was necessary, said Johnston, because he was suffering from his war wounds. Johnston to Davis, April 10, 1863, *Official Records*, XXIII, Pt. 2, pp. 745–46.

constitutional provision and practical precedence for this "British system" in the Confederacy. Four members of the Provisional Congress had served concurrently as cabinet members, and this had proved so satisfactory that specific allowance for the practice was included in the permanent constitution. Soon after, however, a bill introduced to put the system into operation failed to pass either house. A year later, Wigfall introduced his proposal: "That the principal officer in each of the executive departments of the Confederate Government shall be entitled to a seat upon the floor of the Senate; . . . with the privilege of discussing any measures appertaining to his department." [23]

There were two major benefits which would accrue from adopting his bill, Wigfall told the Senate. For one thing, if the cabinet members were present in the Congress, they could offer valuable advice which would facilitate wise legislation, and they would in turn receive many "edifying suggestions." From an interchange of opinions, reasoned Wigfall the statesman, the government would be made more efficient. In the second place, said Wigfall the snide critic, if cabinet members would take a seat in the Senate, "we would have no more inefficient men in any of the offices. No man would be appointed by the President who could not comprehend and understand the policy and views of the Executive." [24]

Senator Benjamin Hill spoke in favor of Wigfall's bill, saying that the system had worked well in the Provisional Congress, where more information could be gained in fifteen minutes than could be had in a month in their present Congress. But a number feared, as Yancey said he did, that such a measure would seriously affect the independence of the Senate. Senator Landon Haynes moved to amend the bill by striking out the proposed privilege of cabinet members to discuss any measures pertaining to their departments. Wigfall replied that this provision was a transcript of the constitution and that its deletion would amount to the

23 "Proceedings of Confederate Congress," 1st Cong., 3rd Sess., XLVII, 24; XLVIII, 287; *Journal of Congress*, 1st Cong., 3rd Sess., 153; see also Yearns, *Confederate Congress*, 220, 228.
24 "Proceedings of Confederate Congress," 1st Cong., 3rd Sess., XLVIII, 288.

destruction of the bill. Haynes's emasculating amendment was passed 14–8, nevertheless, and, as this virtually defeated the bill, Wigfall consented to an indefinite postponement of the matter. It was never revived. Thus an imaginative experiment which might have proved its worth in American government was laid to rest. Even as his cabinet proposal failed, Wigfall reintroduced his general staff arrangement, expressing confidence that it would be passed—over Davis' veto if necessary. This time Wigfall divided his plan into three different bills submitted at the same time. The bills ran into trouble, however, as administration supporters in the House added amendments unsatisfactory to Wigfall, forcing committee conferences and long delays. His persistence was undoubtedly bolstered by a letter from General Leonidas Polk who said that additional staff officers for commanders were indispensable. Although Wigfall helped keep Congress in session for a month longer than many wanted to stay, it adjourned on May 1, 1863, without having reached a final decision on the staff bills.[25]

The Wigfalls had planned to take a trip to Texas at the close of the session, but General Grant and Admiral Andrew Foote interfered. As a part of Grant's attack upon Vicksburg, Foote had run his Union gunboats past the city's artillery, making it hazardous and expensive for Confederates to cross the river. In late April, a Dr. Levi Jones told the Wigfalls that he had just arrived in Richmond from Texas and the trip had cost him $300. The price would be higher, Wigfall was sure, since the gunboats were now a threat. Rather than go far into debt and risk capture, the senator and his family gave up the trip. Merely living in Richmond was putting the Wigfalls into debt. In April, 1863, their board was raised to $240 per month, so they decided to find some place in the country for the summer, some place near enough to Richmond to hear its news every day.[26]

[25] Wigfall to Clay, April 12, 1863, Clay Papers; Wigfall to Johnston, undated, Johnston Papers; Polk to Wigfall, March 21, 1863, Wigfall Papers; *Journal of Congress*, 1st Cong., 3rd Sess., 145, 153, 176, 221–22, 374; "Proceedings of Confederate Congress," 1st Cong., 3rd Sess., XLVIII, 236–37, 275–76, 287–89; XLIX, 1–2, 540.

[26] Louly to Halsey, November 14, 1862, in Wright, *Southern Girl*, 91–92, 129; Charlotte Wigfall to Halsey, April 20, 1863, Wigfall Papers.

By June 5, the Wigfalls were comfortably settled at Orange Courthouse, closer to the Army of Northern Virginia than to Richmond. They were eighty miles northeast of the capital, while parts of the Army of Northern Virginia were virtually in their front yard. Chancellorsville was only twenty-five miles to the east. It was here less than a month earlier that the Confederacy sustained a costly victory—losing Stonewall Jackson. Charlotte Wigfall's reaction to the death of Jackson, "a hero and a favorite" of hers, was typical of many southerners; it was an irreparable loss. May, 1863, found her more disheartened about the war than she had ever been. She added prophetically that it was going to be a "dreadfully anxious summer for us." [27]

In Wigfall's analysis, the battle of Chancellorsville was "a double blunder." Lee should not have come out of his trenches; he should have forced General Joseph Hooker to fight him there or retire across the river. Or, the Texan continued, having come out, Lee should not have broken off the fight when Hooker was beaten but should have crushed him.[28]

Most of Wigfall's summer in Virginia was spent in visiting and corresponding with a number of generals. All of them seemed to be aware of the probability of Pemberton's losing Vicksburg to Grant.[29] The threat became so grave that in May, Davis had Johnston return to Mississippi to command the forces there. Johnston reported that he could do nothing against Grant without more men and asked that troops be sent from the East. From his talks with eastern-front generals, Wigfall learned that rather

27 Charlotte Wigfall to Louly, June 5, 1863, and Charlotte Wigfall to Halsey, May 11–12, 20, 1863, both in Wigfall Papers; Wright *Southern Girl,* 136.

28 Wigfall to Johnston, June 15, 1863, Johnston Papers. The Texan's bias against Lee, fostered perhaps by Lee's holding the command desired by Johnston, was showing. Lee had had to come out of his trenches or be surrounded and crushed by two Union armies, each larger than his own. Lee's victory might have been complete, had Jackson lived to push his troops to cut off Hooker's only escape route. But after Stonewall's death, Lee would probably have been beaten had it not been for Hooker's timidity. See Allan Nevins, *The War for the Union* (2 vols.; New York, 1960), II, 441–53.

29 Wigfall to Clay, June 12, 1863, Clay Papers; Wigfall to Johnston, June 15, 1863, Johnston Papers; and Charlotte Wigfall to Halsey, May 17, 18, June 14, 16, 23, 1863; Halsey to his mother, June 18, 1863; Halsey to Louly, June 13, 14, 23, 1863; Beauregard to Wigfall, May 16, 1863; Longstreet to Wigfall, May 23, 1863, all in Wigfall Papers.

than send men to the West, Davis had decided to adopt Lee's plan for an invasion of the North, hoping to relieve both Virginia and the West. Wigfall agreed that it might work if the government did not interfere with Lee. The senator requested Clay to ask Seddon to try to "induce Davis for once to let a general dispose of his troops in his own way." Wigfall probably had little hope of this. He was no doubt aware of the situation described that week by Confederate Secretary of State Judah P. Benjamin, when he explained to a British observer that "Davis' military instincts still prevailed" and that Benjamin felt that Davis would rather be a general than President.[30]

Reports coming from the West were discouraging, but Wigfall seemed optimistic about Vicksburg. Despite his belief that Davis had committed an act of "stupendous wickedness" by entrusting so vital a position as Vicksburg to such an untried and unpopular man as Pemberton, Wigfall expressed great confidence in Johnston and did not fear the result where he was concerned.[31] As it turned out, however, Davis meddled far more with Johnston at Vicksburg than he did with Lee at Gettysburg.

Wigfall was personally concerned with both campaigns, with his close friend Johnston at Vicksburg, and his son Halsey at Gettysburg. Since February, Halsey had been in several cavalry operations in Virginia as a member of Jeb Stuart's horse-drawn artillery. In violation of Lee's orders, Stuart had accomplished one of his dramatic but costly "rides around the enemy." Thus the horse artillery, including Halsey, was not engaged at Gettysburg until the last day, and then at long range. For this and other reasons, Lee suffered a costly defeat in Pennsylvania, July 1–3, 1863. On July 8, Charlotte Wigfall wrote to Louly in Charlottesville that they had read of "another battle," but the senator doubted that Halsey was in it. It was not until July 7 that Halsey had an opportunity to write his parents about his adventures.

[30] Wigfall to Johnston, June 15, 1863, Johnston Papers; King, "Relationship Between Johnston and Davis," 88–93; Govan and Livingood, *Johnston*, 197–98; Wigfall to Clay, June 12, 1863, Clay Papers; Fremantle, *Diary*, 169.

[31] General Johnston's wife to Charlotte Wigfall, May 19, June 14, 1863, Wigfall Papers; Wigfall to Clay, June 12, 1863, Clay Papers.

News of Pemberton's surrender of Vicksburg reached Wigfall before the news of Lee's defeat at Gettysburg.[32]

The militaristic senator must have been frustrated in having so little knowledge of army affairs. After Gettysburg he wrote to Stuart asking if Halsey could not come home for a while since things were quiet on the front. Stuart replied that he regretted that the actual state of affairs was so different from what Wigfall supposed; Halsey's unit was seeing action almost every day.[33]

The Wigfalls evidently felt no compunction about writing to their son's commander for favors, since they considered Stuart a friend of the family. Charlotte Wigfall even wrote to remind him that fulfillment of his promise to help obtain Halsey's commission as first lieutenant was overdue. Further, she had talked with another friend, Halsey's division commander John Bell Hood, about a staff position for her son. Hood agreed, she said, that this would give Halsey better opportunities to study and learn about such things as strategy, the movement of troops, and to become familiar with the duties of the adjutant general's office. The ambitious mother told her son that it was time for him to think over these matters and be prepared to talk about them when they met next time. Four months later Halsey became an aide on Hood's staff. Major General Hood figured in another of Charlotte Wigfall's ambitions. It would be nice to have a major general for a son-in-law, she told her daughter Louly. Although many considered the fifteen-year-old Louly to be a beautiful girl, and Richmond rumors had her and Hood engaged, Louly thought her chances with the handsome general were not good.[34]

Wigfall thought highly of Hood. From him, Halsey, Hampton, and Longstreet, the senator slowly gathered reports of the fiasco at Gettysburg and again came to the conclusion that Lee had

32 Halsey to Wigfall, February 6, 1863; Charlotte Wigfall to Louly, July 8, 1863; Halsey to Wigfall, July 7, 1863, and Charlotte Wigfall to Halsey, July 16, 1863, all in Wigfall Papers; Douglas S. Freeman, *Lee's Lieutenants: A Study in Command* (3 vols.; New York, 1944), III, 147–50.
33 Stuart to Wigfall, undated, quoted in Charlotte Wigfall to Halsey, August 11, 1863, Wigfall Papers; and in Wright, *Southern Girl*, 147–48.
34 Charlotte Wigfall to Halsey, August 26, 1863, and Louly to Halsey, August 11, 1863, both in Wigfall Papers; Chesnut, *Diary*, 37.

erred gravely. In response to Clay's query whether Lee had resigned, Wigfall expressed strong regrets that he had not. Rather,
raged Wigfall, Lee's "blunder at Gettysburg, . . . his utter want
of generalship" had only increased Davis' admiration of him.
Wigfall was usually more sound in his judgment of military affairs, and perhaps he would not have denounced Lee so emphatically had it not been for Davis' partiality for the Virginian, a
sharp contrast to the presidential attitude toward Wigfall's friend
Johnston. According to the Texan's report to Clay, Davis avidly
defended Lee's conduct while denouncing Johnston in the most
violent manner, attributing the fall of Vicksburg to him alone,
regretting that he had been sent to the West, and accusing himself of weakness for yielding to outside pressure, saying that he
had always known of Johnston's lack of ability. Wigfall asked
Clay if it had ever occurred to him that Davis' mind was becoming unsettled, concluding that no sane man could act the way the
President was doing.[35]

As soon as Johnston was sent back to Mississippi from Tennessee, three weeks before the fall of Vicksburg, Wigfall prophesied
to Clay that "should disaster befall our armies there, I have no
doubt the attempt will be made to throw the responsibility on
Johnston." A few days before that, the senator sent a similarly
worded warning directly to Johnston. Even in December of 1862,
Wigfall had advised the general to record all of his plans, suggestions, and correspondence with the War Department so he would
be protected. In mid-June, 1863, the Texan urged the general to
send copies of all these records to him for use as he saw fit.[36]

Johnston was reluctant to believe that there was such a threat;
he did not send the records Wigfall requested until two months
later, five weeks after the fall of Vicksburg. By then he realized

[35] Halsey to his father, July 7, 1863; Hampton to Wigfall, July 15, 1863; Halsey
to Louly, July 18, 1863; Longstreet to Wigfall, August 2, 1863; Halsey to his
mother, August 13, 1863; and Wigfall to Halsey, August 16, 1863, all in Wigfall
Papers; Wigfall to Clay, August 13, 1863, Clay Papers. For a defense of Lee's actions at Gettysburg, see Douglas S. Freeman, *R. E. Lee: A Biography* (4 vols.; 1935),
III.

[36] Wigfall to Clay, June 12, 1863, Clay Papers; Wigfall to Johnston, June 15,
1863, Johnston Papers.

that his friend had been correct about Davis. In alarm Johnston wrote that the whole power of the government was preparing to overwhelm him.[37]

By that time Wigfall had marshaled imposing support for the general. In June the senator assured Johnston that he had friends who would stand by him in his hour of trial and fortunately they were not without power. For the next two months Wigfall evidently did everything he could to see that justice was done for Johnston. Among staunch Davis supporters there was talk that Johnston should be removed from command, but the Wigfalls were convinced that the public would sustain him. There already existed strong antiadministration and anti-Pemberton sentiment for various reasons, and Johnston had his loyal following. Wigfall's function was to coordinate the opposition to Davis while generating still more support for the general. Capitalizing upon the recent military reverses and the existing animosity toward Davis, Wigfall used Johnston's letters effectively. Even Senators Thomas J. Semmes of Louisiana and Henry C. Burnett of Kentucky, who were proadministration throughout the war, promised Wigfall that they would allow no injustice to be done to Johnston. After two months of sub rosa persuading, Wigfall assured Johnston that all of the worthy opinions in Richmond were with him.[38]

Convinced from the outset that his and Johnston's strategy of concentrating troops should have been followed, Wigfall was outraged at what he considered the unnecessary loss of Vicksburg and the severance of the West. Even in May, 1863, when he was returned to Mississippi from Tennessee, Johnston's tactics for combating Grant were not followed because of direct interference by Davis. As the commanding general in the department, Johnston sent an order to Pemberton to leave Vicksburg and attack the Federals at Clinton, thirty miles to the east. Johnston planned to

[37] Johnston to Wigfall, August 12, 1863, Wigfall Papers.
[38] Wigfall to Johnston, June 15, August 9, 1863, Johnston Papers; Charlotte Wigfall to Halsey, July 16, 22, 1863; Charlotte Wigfall to Louly, July 22, 1863; and Governor Francis W. Pickens to Wigfall, July 28, 1863, all in Wigfall Papers; Yearns, *Confederate Congress*, 238, 243.

attack from the opposite side at the same time; then they would combine to meet any counterattack. Six days earlier Pemberton had received orders from Davis saying that it was necessary to hold onto Vicksburg. The President had all along insisted that this direct communication with lower officers was essential in order to save time, but it frequently meant that the commanding general did not know what his subordinate officers were doing.[39]

A majority of Pemberton's officers advised him to execute Johnston's order, but he refused. Instead he attempted an attack upon Grant's supply line. But Grant, unlike Pemberton, was willing to operate without a base; he had no supply line. Pemberton was trapped near Edward's Station, about fifteen miles east of Vicksburg, and lost over three thousand men and much artillery. The Confederates retreated to Vicksburg where they were surrounded by sixty thousand Federals, with more arriving by the hour.[40]

Johnston considered his force of 23,000 too small to attack Grant, so he asked Davis for more troops. Grant said later that Johnston's decision was a wise one, as an attack with that small a force would only have caused losses on both sides without hope of altering the result. Instead of ordering men to Johnston, Davis decided to adopt Lee's plan which led to Gettysburg. Wigfall was in agreement with Confederate General D. H. Hill when he said that one corps sent to Johnston would have enabled him to crush Grant.[41]

[39] Johnston to Pemberton, May 13, 1863; Pemberton to Johnston, May 14, 1863, *Official Records*, XXIV, Pt. 3, pp. 870–77, 249–95, 322–25; Taylor, *Destruction*, 207; Thomas L. Snead, "With Price East of the Mississippi," in Johnson and Buell (eds.), *Battles and Leaders of the Civil War*, II, 730.

[40] Pemberton's Report, *Official Records*, XXIV, Pt. 3, pp. 249–95; Govan and Livingood, *Johnston*, 201–203; King, "Relationship Between Johnston and Davis," 91–92.

[41] Johnston to Seddon, May 16, 17, June 2, 4, 5, 1863; Johnston to Davis May 21, 23, June 1, 1863; Seddon to Johnston, May 12, 18, 23, June 3, 5, 1863; Johnston to Cooper, May 16, 18, 25, 1863; Davis to Johnston, May 18, 21, 24, 28, 30, 1863, all in *Official Records*, XXIV, Pt. 3, pp. 190–95, 214–20, 223; Ulysses S. Grant, "The Vicksburg Campaign," in Johnson and Buell (eds.), *Battles and Leaders*, III, 493–539; D. H. Hill, "Chickamauga—The Great Battle of the West," in Johnson and Buell (eds.) *Battles and Leaders*, III, 638–39; King, "Relationship Between Johnston and Davis," 90–94; Govan and Livingood, *Johnston*, 209–20.

The northern strategy of forcing dispersal of Confederate forces by attacks at widely scattered points was successful; Davis was firmly committed to a policy of holding territory. A possible justification for this policy in the earliest stages of the war was the southern emphasis upon localism. It had been suggested that southerners would not have supported the war effort had not significant forces been maintained in the various states. But it has also been pointed out that later in the war, when this "bugaboo" was dispelled, Davis' general policy still included the holding of territory at all costs.[42]

The Confederate States of America was involved in a new kind of war, modern war, requiring closely coordinated, large scale activity and expert administration. The Confederacy under Davis could not break from previous patterns of localism. The President organized the South into military departments, placing a general in command of all troops in each department. Scholars in military history have pointed out that such a policy is fatal in time of war. Most Confederate military men saw this.[43] Johnston, Beauregard, Wigfall, and others favored concentration of troops, with emphasis upon maneuverability, surprise, and attack of enemy armies at their weak points, rather than spreading Confederate forces thin to hold territory and await an attack. The Confederate victory of First Bull Run was won by the junction of Johnston's and Beauregard's troops.

Many inside and outside of the War Department agreed with Robert Kean, head of the Bureau of War, who said that Davis had no policy at all, "either of finance, supply, or strategy." Once when Secretary of War Seddon was asked if the President had a plan for meeting impending emergencies, he replied that Davis had none, and that "he never *had had* any." [44]

---

42 Jones, *Confederate Strategy*, 19–22.

43 Wiley, *Road to Appomattox*, 78–90; Sir Frederick Maurice, quoted in Henry Steele Commager (ed.), *The Defeat of the Confederacy* (New York, 1964), 43.

44 Robert Garlick Hill Kean, *Inside the Confederate Government: The Diary of Robert Garlick Hill Kean, Head of the Bureau of War*, ed. by Edward Younger (New York, 1957), 72, 80, 100, 101, 167, 187; Seddon's emphasis, as quoted in Jones, *Confederate Strategy*, 26.

In Wigfall's analysis, the loss of Vicksburg was entirely the responsibility of Davis. He agreed with the Richmond *Whig* when
it said that there were three causes for the fall of Vicksburg—
the scattering of the forces, the prejudices against men of proven
ability, and Davis' partiality for an incapable commander. But
Wigfall went further, telling Seddon that it was the President's
"pig-headedness & perverseness" which had brought that disaster
upon the country. In addition, Wigfall was then certain that
Davis and Pemberton were trying to blame Johnston for it. In
his determination that that would not happen, Wigfall devoted
still more of his time, almost all of his waking hours, to military
affairs. Louly said that he lived on army matters, and that she was
sick of the sound of them, though she admitted that it was well
that someone thought about them for everything seemed to be
going to ruin as fast as possible.[45]

Pessimism pervaded the Wigfall household that week; two
days after Louly's lament, the senator revealed his despondency
to C. C. Clay. Wigfall was convinced that Davis was *non compos
mentis*, that Johnston could do nothing with the administration
against him, and that Lee was a blunderer. The southern people
had nothing to look to except Congress, Wigfall moaned, won-
dering "what hope can any reasonable man draw from that
source?" Agreeing with Clay that the Confederate currency was
in a deplorable condition, Wigfall said there was no hope there
either, not as long as Christopher G. Memminger headed the
Treasury Department. Cynically, Wigfall suggested the abolition
of the Treasury Department and the hiring of a public printer
to issue money as wanted; this would at least save paying Memminger's salary.[46]

Wigfall unloaded his despair upon Clay, saying that he was
the only one to whom he could open his heart fully. But Clay had
serious problems which gained Wigfall's sympathy. The Alabama
senator's home had been lost to the Federals, his relatives were in

[45] Richmond *Whig*, July 9, 1863; Wigfall to Johnston, August 9, 1863, Johnston
Papers; Louly to Halsey, August 11, 1863, Wigfall Papers.
[46] Wigfall to Clay, August 13, 1863, Clay Papers; Clay to Wigfall, August 5,
1863, Wigfall Papers.

the hands of the enemy, he was racked with a variety of physical ailments, and he feared the coming election. Although Clay was a good friend of Wigfall and was critical of the President's personality and methods, he was considered by the public and by the newspapers to be "one of Davis' men," and they were becoming more and more unpopular. Evidently Wigfall could do no more than offer sympathy. Clay was defeated in the November elections.[47]

On another occasion Wigfall demonstrated his willingness to give more than sympathy—to a man who apparently was unknown to him beforehand. Wigfall took the time and effort to go from Orange Courthouse to Richmond, evidently in the interest of a John B. Lincoln. According to Charlotte Wigfall, Lincoln was just back from "Yankeeland" after having walked 140 miles in search of his son, probably a Confederate soldier who was lost during Lee's invasion, without finding him. Wigfall went with Lincoln to Richmond to see if they could learn anything there. The senator returned the next day, evidently without having located Lincoln's son.[48]

Wigfall also tried to help Quartermaster General Abraham C. Myers, even though he opposed the senator's plan for government operation of the railroads. Myers was criticized by many for this, but the probable reason Davis disliked him, as explained by Wigfall and others usually knowledgeable in these matters, was because Myers' wife called the dark-skinned Varina Davis "an old squaw." Myers, however, was popular with Congress, which, in keeping with a part of Wigfall's staff plan, passed an act declaring that the Quartermaster office should carry with it the rank and pay of a brigadier general. Davis, with what has been described as "sardonic cleverness," interpreted this to mean that Congress wished to remove Myers since he was only a colonel. Although Congress devoted part of its attention during the win-

---

47 Wigfall to Clay, August 13, 1863, Clay Papers; Clay to Wigfall, August 5, September 11, November 15, 1863, in Wigfall Papers; Montgomery *Advertiser*, August 26, 1863, clipping sent to Wigfall by Clay, September 11, 1863, Wigfall Papers; Yearns, *Confederate Congress*, 56.

48 Charlotte Wigfall to Halsey, July 16, 1863, Wigfall Papers.

ter of 1862 to "a hand-to-hand fight with Mr. Davis on account of . . . Myers," Wigfall seems not to have become upset about the affair until August of 1863, when the President replaced Myers with General A. R. Lawton. This was Davis' latest act of "petty tyranny & reckless disregard of law & contemptuous treatment of Congress," railed Wigfall. After sketching Myers' military background and personal sacrifices for the Confederacy to show that he was deserving, the senator contrasted his treatment with that of Davis' "pet" Lucius B. Northrop, who, as commissary general, received full rank and pay.[49] Northrop continued to serve despite vituperative criticism from Lee, Johnston, Beauregard, Wigfall, and many other state and Confederate officials who said his incompetent supply system had lost the South several battles.

Wigfall said he had never known such an outrage as in the Myers case and vowed "for once I will not submit in silence." From Attorney General Thomas Watts, the senator extracted a decision that Myers held the post and rank as bestowed by Congress. Seddon proved less cooperative. The fiery Texan saw the secretary of war several times and wrote him twice, imploring him to interpose and prevent Davis from making any more issues with Congress and asking how, in this, their day of darkness, Davis could find time to "cultivate & nurture his . . . malignancy toward individuals." In this account he gave Clay, Wigfall said he asked Seddon how the President could not rise to the height of great issues which were occupying the thoughts of everyone else. When Myers was not reappointed and Seddon did not even answer Wigfall's letters, the senator concluded that the secretary had been subjugated and had lost his manhood. The Texan averred that the "squaw quarrel" was not finished; Myers had many strong friends in Congress who would not yield quietly.[50]

49 Wigfall to Clay, August 13, 1863, Clay Papers; Robert Garlick Hill Kean, Diary, August 13, 1863, quoted in Eaton, Southern Confederacy, 138; Chesnut. Diary, 285, 330, 352; James L. Orr to James H. Hammond, January 3, 1864, Hammond Papers. See also E. Merton Coulter, The Confederate States of America (Baton Rouge, 1950), 380, Vol. VII of Wendell Holmes Stephenson and E. Merton Coulter (eds.), A History of the South (10 vols.; Baton Rouge, 1949-).
50 Wigfall to Clay, August 13, 1863, Clay Papers. Three days after he had writ-

Concern for Myers did not diminish Wigfall's anxiety over the threat to Johnston's prestige and military effectiveness. While the senator was gathering material to defend Johnston, Davis was collecting records to indict him. The use of the legal term seems justified inasmuch as the President planned a court of inquiry to determine responsibility for the loss of Vicksburg. Neither Wigfall nor Johnston knew of the court until two days after it was supposed to have convened on August 15. Apparently Davis had received his materials on July 15, for on that date he wrote the general a fifteen-page letter with selections from various orders and letters to indicate how Johnston had made a grave error by interpreting his orders of May 9, 1863, sending him back to Mississippi, to have removed him from the responsibility of command in Tennessee. Johnston's temperate reply asked for a reconsideration of the charge that his misapprehension was a serious military offense, pointing out that it had not affected his actions because while commanding in Mississippi he could not have directed Bragg's operations in Tennessee. Copies of both of these letters were included in the records Johnston sent to Wigfall.[51]

The senator had already heard that Davis was preparing the letter to Johnston—and Wigfall had other disturbing news for the general. For one thing, such proadministration newspapers as the Richmond *Sentinel* were trying to fasten responsibility for Vicksburg upon Johnston. Also, Wigfall learned from Seddon that Pemberton had written Davis that the disastrous attack upon Edward's Station was made against his own judgment and under positive orders from Johnston. Wigfall had, he reported to his friend, gone immediately to see Davis and Seddon to warn them that he had proof that the fault was not Johnston's. Deeming Pemberton's letter "a piece of unmitigated meanness," Wigfall warned Johnston not to assume any responsibility that was not his own, as he had done with Bragg. In protecting Bragg, Wigfall

ten to Clay, Wigfall was visited in Charlottesville by Myers to talk of his affairs. Wigfall to Halsey, August 16, 1863, Wigfall Papers.

51 Davis to Johnston, July 15, 1863; Johnston to Davis, August 8, 1863, quoted in Johnston, *Narrative of Military Operations*, 230–41, 244–52; Johnston to Wigfall, August 12, 1863, Wigfall Papers.

pointed out, Johnston had protected the President; and Davis would sustain Pemberton at Johnston's expense if he could. But, Johnston was assured, he had at least one friend who would see that justice was done.[52]

In the next day or two Wigfall learned that Pemberton had submitted his official report to the War Department, and the senator was sure that some of the information appearing in the pro-Davis newspapers was coming directly from that office. When he tried to see Pemberton's report, he was told that all of the papers relating to the Vicksburg campaign had been taken out by the President. Apparently Seddon had been influenced by Pemberton's report; Wigfall said that the secretary was disposed to blame Johnston for the loss of Vicksburg. According to the senator, he reminded Seddon of Johnston's proposals and how they should have been followed, and warned him that if a "war" was begun on Johnston, all correspondence would be published, showing the wisdom of his views and exposing the "stupidity of Davis." Further, Wigfall warned that he would carry his defense of Johnston to the floor of the Senate where he would be heard throughout the Confederacy. Wigfall expressed his assurance that after he had had several such conversations with Seddon, instead of prancing on a very high horse, the secretary "was quietly ambling on a gentle & rather diminutive pony." [53]

Both Johnston and Wigfall seem to have wanted to play down the affair and keep it quiet at least temporarily, but Davis made an issue of it and it was soon in the public eye. He ordered a court of inquiry convened; its purpose, he told Pemberton, would be to "develop the real causes of events and give to the public the means of doing justice to the actor." [54] Although the orders called for the inquiry to begin on August 15, Johnston was not notified

52 Wigfall to Johnston, August 8, 9, 1863, Johnston Papers.

53 Wigfall to Johnston, August 11, 1863, *ibid.*

54 Colonel E. J. Harvie (Johnston's aide) to Joe Davis (the President's brother), August 12, 1863, and Davis to Pemberton, August 9, 1863, both in *Official Records*, XXX, Pt. 4, pp. 490–91; LII, Pt. 2, p. 515; King, "Relationship Between Johnston and Davis," 101–102.

until August 17. The court had been delayed, however, and the War Department, after conceding Johnston's right to be present in his own defense, rescheduled the hearing for September 9. When Johnston and the other witnesses arrived in Atlanta for the inquiry, they were told to return to their stations since the court had been postponed.[55]

No reason for the suspension was given. Perhaps the critical military situation in Tennessee, where General William S. Rose-crans was pushing Bragg out of the state, had something to do with it. But since Bragg had already been flanked before the end of August, and the state was in jeopardy even before Johnston left the West to come to the inquiry, there may have been other factors. Wigfall said he was not surprised that the court was post-poned indefinitely, telling Johnston that he had probably ex-plained too clearly the strength of his case and the weakness of the case of Pemberton and Davis. Wigfalls' intervention was probably a factor; his threat to Seddon and Davis to take John-ston's case to the Confederacy from the Senate floor may have caused reconsideration by the administration. Plans for the in-quiry were evidently laid at about the same time Wigfall was issuing his warnings.[56] Thus he may have helped cause cancella-tion of plans for the court after they were put into motion but before they were put into effect.

Once it had been set, Wigfall and Johnston were disappointed that the inquiry was postponed. The general said he was anxious to show how completely his military opinions regarding his own department were disregarded. He was particularly eager to pub-licize the letters Davis had sent to him. Wigfall promised that a congressional committee would bring out all of the facts if Davis did not reconvene the court before Congress met in December.

[55] Johnston to Cooper, August 17, 1863; Cooper to Johnston, August 20, 1863, Johnston to Davis, September 8, 1863, *Official Records*, LII, Pt. 2, 1058; XXX, Pt. 4, p. 625; Johnston, *Narrative*, 253, 255.
[56] Govan and Livingood, *Johnston*, 231; Hill, "Chickamauga," 640–41; Wigfall to Johnston, August 11, October 6, 1863, Johnston Papers; Davis to Pemberton, August 9, 1863, *Official Records*, LII, Pt. 2, p. 515.

In the meantime the Texan kept the case up to date, quizzing Johnston on details of disputed stories and analyzing the general's official report.[57]

In addition to the case against Pemberton and the President, Wigfall was incidentally compiling a dossier against Davis and Bragg—mostly letters from worried generals. Longstreet regretted that he was going west to serve under Bragg and asserted that he would fight against it if he had any hope of getting anyone but himself to replace Bragg. Longstreet doubted that Johnston would be appointed. Promising to keep Wigfall posted, the "Stolid Dutchman" closed with an almost tender admonition to Wigfall: "Do not forget me because I have gone so far away from you." Wade Hampton, one of the most respected men in the South, also had kind words for Wigfall, thanking the senator for sundry acts of charity in his behalf. For Bragg in particular and the administration in general, Hampton had only disparagement. While recuperating from his Gettysburg wounds, Hampton had time to reflect upon a question to Wigfall, a question more and more people were asking: "Is there no way to get Johnston into the field?" Hampton doubted it; the Confederacy was "too slow." Wigfall hardly knew how to answer; even Johnston was not sure of his status. If he had been a commander without an army before, he was now—in the fall of 1863, at Meridian, Mississippi—far removed from any action. Even though Davis was so concerned about the West that he made a tour there, Wigfall said he feared that Bragg would be kept in command until the Army of Tennessee was destroyed.[58]

Davis' dictum that commanders had to have the respect of their

[57] Johnston to Wigfall, September 15, (referring especially to Davis' letters of July 15 and September 14, 1863), November 12, 26, 1863; Johnston to Cooper (Report of Operations in the Department of Mississippi and Eastern Louisiana), November 1, 1863, in Wigfall Papers; Wigfall to Johnston, October 6, 1863, Johnston Papers; see also "Davis-Johnston Correspondence, together with that of the Secretary of War and the Adjutant and Inspector General, during the Months of May, June, and July, 1863," *Confederate State Papers* (1863–64).

[58] Longstreet to Wigfall, September 12, 1863; Hampton to Wigfall, October 2, 1863, Johnston to Wigfall, November 12, 1863; Wigfall to Halsey, November 2, 1863, Wigfall Papers; Wigfall to Johnston, October 6, 1863, Johnston Papers.

subordinates was redounding against sustaining Bragg. Wigfall's old friend John Manning, who had recently been made a major general in the West, wrote that the dissatisfaction with Bragg and a general desire to be commanded by Johnston were universal in the Western Army. Even after Bragg had defeated Rosecrans in a gory battle at Chickamauga, the criticism continued. Bragg had failed to push his advantage, giving Rosecrans time to bring up mass reinforcements. Soon after, Bragg's chief of staff, General W. W. Mackall, confided to his wife that Johnston's presence would be worth ten thousand men to this army, but even with the happiness of the whole people at stake, Davis would indulge his prejudices "like a spoiled child." [59]

Like Mackall and the others who wanted Johnston for the Army of Tennessee, Wigfall doubted that the proud general would ever again command an army. Apparently he had read in the newspapers that James Chesnut, then serving as aide to Davis, had endorsed Bragg as being popular with his army. "So the world goes," Wigfall sighed pessimistically. In fact, however, Chesnut, who upon Davis' orders inspected the Army of Tennessee twice in the fall of 1863, had joined the throng of Bragg's critics and reported to the President what he must not have wanted to hear. Davis was told by Chesnut that "every honest man he saw out west thought well of Joe Johnston." Colonel Chesnut and his wife were loyal to the President, but Mary Chesnut observed that Bragg had a way of earning everybody's detestation.[60] Though even his friends and advisers wanted him to replace Bragg with Johnston, Davis refused.

Wigfall was no doubt frustrated and embittered, but he did not carry his bitterness to the public. In a number of speeches he made during the fall in the Richmond area, he had numerous opportunities to attack Davis' policies. Instead he urged Confederates to support the administration.[61] In one interview he

---

[59] Wigfall to Halsey, November 21, 1863; Mackall to his wife, September 27, 29, October 5, 9, 10, 12, 1863, quoted in Govan and Livingood, *Johnston,* 233.

[60] Wigfall to Halsey, November 2, 21, 1863, Wigfall Papers; Chesnut, *Diary,* 317, 321, 328.

[61] In speeches at Louisa Courthouse, Charlottesville, Orange Courthouse, Staun-

reminded southerners that their interests were identical with those of the government.[62]

The origin of the quarrel between Davis and Wigfall was rooted in a major difference of opinion about proper military policy and organization for the Confederacy. Both men took such differences personally. Davis misused two southern generals of great ability—Johnston and Beauregard. It is extremely significant that both of these generals agreed with Wigfall as to the appropriate military strategy for the Confederacy and that beginning in early 1863, he defended them in the Senate. Wigfall was particularly outraged at the President's treatment of Johnston, who was not only the senator's friend but was considered by him to be the most able general in the South.

The Wigfall-Davis quarrel had not reached public proportions by the end of 1863. It is not unlikely that even many high civilian officials still believed as Governor Pickens of South Carolina did in July, 1863, when he expressed his faith in Wigfall's "well known intimacy with the President." This was well after the controversy over Vicksburg was raging. Wigfall was working behind the scenes, however, to disaffect influential leaders in Richmond. By September he had helped to make Johnston the "polar star" of those leaders, especially dissatisfied congressmen, who found it easy "to cuss Jeff Davis." [63] But it was only to those people and friends that Wigfall expressed such wishes as his desire "to hang Jeff Davis." Mary Chesnut was less impressed with such "virulent nonsense" about her close friend the President than she was with Wigfall's "usual strong common sense." [64]

Wigfall did show some good sense in military strategy and in legislative proposals. But partly because of his own faults he kept his sound ideas from reaching fruition. The fate of his proposal

---

ton, Harrisonburg, and other places; Charlotte Wigfall to Halsey, September 16, October 25, 1863; Hampton to Wigfall, October 2, 1863, Wigfall Papers; New York *Times*, October 13, 1863.

[62] *Record of News, History, and Literature*, I (Richmond, October 15, 1863), 165, quoted in Coulter, *The Confederate States of America*, 165.

[63] Francis W. Pickens to Wigfall, July 28, 1863, Wigfall Papers; Mary Chesnut to Varina Davis, September —, 1863, quoted in Chesnut, *Diary*, 343.

[64] Chesnut, *Diary*, 329.

to seat cabinet members in Congress is symbolic of his problem. It was a worthwhile plan but he could not get an unbiased hearing for it because he could not resist using it as a means of criticizing Davis. Wigfall could also have helped his cause militarily much more than he did. At the beginning of the war while he was aide to Davis, he had the opportunity to coax the President toward the wiser course of concentrating troops to meet the Union armies. But the senator's churlishness, his lack of tact, and his tendency to fix blame irritated Davis' hypersensitivity to criticism, aggravated the President's frustrated military instincts, and excited his pettiness when he thought his presidential authority was being usurped in the slightest degree. Thus the senator and the President both hurt the cause to which they were devoted. Therein lay one of the tragedies for the Confederacy.

Chapter VIII

To Hang Jeff Davis

THE CONFEDERACY had suffered serious losses in 1863, but southerners did not despair. They still had armies in the field and
hopes that the North would relent. As late as September, 1864,
President Lincoln expressed his fear that the northern people
would elect a "peace candidate" as President and let the Union
be divided. But the South was in a bad situation. The currency
was so depreciated, Louly Wigfall remembered later, that with
cornmeal at $50 a bushel and bacon at $8 a pound, it was almost
impossible to procure the necessities of life in Richmond. Even
when Wigfall stayed by himself in the capital, the cost of his
room, board, gas, and coal exceeded his senator's pay by $10 per
month. Halsey said that the finances of the country were the primary subject of discussion even with soldiers. To his father he
expressed the hope that Congress could do something to alleviate
inflation which seemed to him the greatest evil confronting the
Confederacy. Even so, Louly said she never heard the eventual
success of their cause questioned during that "winter of suffering
and anxiety." [1]

But during the last two years of the war most southerners lost
their will to continue the struggle. Inflation and military reverses
were only two of the reasons. As Confederate leaders seemed

[1] Wright, *Southern Girl*, 165–66; C. C. Clay to his wife, December 9, 1863, Clay
Papers; Halsey to Wigfall, December 20, 1863, Wigfall Papers.

powerless to solve these problems, they tried to fix the blame upon one another. This dissension was as large a factor as any in vitiating the southern war effort. In the fourth session of the First Confederate Congress, the Wigfall-Davis quarrel became public knowledge. Three days before Congress convened, Wigfall told the Chesnuts of his desire "to hang Jeff Davis," [2] and before the session was over the Texan had laid the ground work for what he hoped would be the President's political demise and the establishment of a senatorial hegemony.

One South Carolinian who visited the Confederate Congress early in this session and wrote of his impressions to James Hammond thought it was the weakest legislative body he had ever seen. Wigfall was the only legislator the observer referred to specifically in his comment to Hammond: "Wigfall is strong as you know, but erratic . . . , when he gets a thing in his head, he pursues that alone, to the neglect of everything else, no matter how important. He can't control [himself]." [3]

With near singularity of purpose, Wigfall attacked Davis. From the beginning of the new session the senator indicated his general course. During the first week, R. W. Johnson of Arkansas introduced to the Senate a plan that he and Wigfall had devised to limit the tenure of cabinet members to two years. The plan would make it necessary to send new nominations to every new Congress, giving the upper house a fresh chance to overhaul the administration. It was, as Robert Kean, head of the War Bureau, said, a direct attack upon the President, "so intended and regarded." Wigfall bragged to Kean that it would produce a radical change in government. Another insider, War Clerk John B. Jones, analyzed the cabinet plan as a declaration of war by the Senate upon the President. But not all the Senate was for the bill. [4] It was debated for two months, and even though the judiciary committee approved it, the plan never came to a vote.

In the meantime Wigfall sought with whatever political weap-

2 Chesnut, *Diary*, 329.

3 A. P. Aldrich to Hammond, February 15, 1864, Hammond Papers.

4 Kean, *Diary*, 126; Jones, *Rebel War Clerk*, cited in Yearns, *Confederate Congress*, 232.

ons that were available to undermine the influence of Davis. During January and February of 1864 he repeatedly voted against confirmation of the President's appointments of officers and to override his vetoes, failing in every instance.[5]

The main bone of contention between Davis and Wigfall continued to be the Joseph E. Johnston affair, even after Davis asked the general to assume command of the Army of Tennessee. Increasing public pressure had caused Bragg to resign the command in November, 1863. Although Davis' obeisance to public opinion was extremely infrequent, and although he had said earlier that he regretted bowing to public demand and putting Johnston in command in Mississippi, the President yielded again. But Johnston was virtually a last resort for the President. He had first tendered the post to Hardee and then to Lee, but both declined, and other generals supported Johnston. Lydia Johnston thanked Wigfall as one of the general's friends who had "untied his hands." But Wigfall, with uncharacteristic modesty, declined credit, telling Johnston that it had been Lee who had had the most to do with it.[6]

Wigfall had worked assiduously for Johnston. Two days after the appointment he wrote to the general: "I have received all your letters and they . . . have done us much good." At one meeting with Seddon and others in the secretary's room, an appeal was made to have Johnston sent immediately to Tennessee. Wigfall's friends were certainly aware of his sentiments on the matter; thus, when his opinion was asked, he could resort to sarcasm without being misunderstood. He said he did not approve of Johnston's being sent unless they wished disaster. Caustically Wigfall suggested that it might be better to send Pemberton who, despite

[5] *Journal of Congress*, 1st Cong., 4th Sess., 544, 549, 586, 674–75, 808.

[6] Kean, *Diary*, 127; William Hardee to Samuel Cooper, November 30, 1863; and Lee to Jefferson Davis, December 7, 1863, both in *Official Records*, XXXI, Pt. 3, pp. 764, 792; Ishbel Ross, *First Lady of the South: The Life of Mrs. Jefferson Davis* (New York, 1958), 187; Lydia Johnston to Charlotte Wigfall, December 18, 1863, Wigfall Papers; Wigfall to Johnston, March 17, 1864, Johnston Papers. Mary Chesnut thought that Lee had restored Johnston to the command. Chesnut, *Diary*, 335. Seddon said nothing of Lee's part in it. Govan and Livingood, *Johnston*, 238.

his incompetency, would be supported by the President and might not prevent a victory. He was satisfied, the Texan said, that if Johnston were sent, every effort would be made to produce his defeat. In seriousness he wrote to Johnston that that was true—but there was a point beyond which Davis dared not venture in contriving defeat for the general. Wigfall was "all anxiety," he wrote his friend, to know that he had accepted the command. The senator thought that Bragg's failures had reduced the administration to a low state; thus Davis would have to give Johnston some support.[7]

One might have expected the quarrel to abate at least temporarily after the new appointment, but it continued without surcease from either side. Varina Davis took pains to have it widely known that Johnston was not the first choice. Wigfall and Johnston continued to prepare their counterattack against the pro-administration newspapers. The senator was especially outraged at Davis' publication of correspondence which he had "mutilated" to show only his side of the story.[8]

Wigfall was at the same time attacking the President from yet another direction. While a Confederate district court issued a mandamus on Davis' appointee Lawton to pay Myers as quartermaster general, Wigfall was engineering a resolution of inquiry as to whether Myers was discharging the duties of the office and if he was not, then who was? Typically the President showed his disdain for the Senate by referring the matter to Seddon for a reply. Seddon's explanation that Lawton was the only quartermaster general was of course unsatisfactory to Wigfall.[9] The Texan maintained that Lawton's appointment was not legitimate and that the Senate "had been cheated." On January 26 he introduced and obtained passage of a more pointed resolution: "That A. R. Lawton is not authorized to discharge the duties of said

7 Wigfall to Johnston, December 18, 1863, Johnston Papers.

8 Ross, *First Lady of the South*, 187; Wigfall to Johnston, December 18, 1863, Johnston Papers; see also Johnston to Wigfall, December 16, 27, 31, 1863, Wigfall Papers.

9 "Proceedings of Confederate Congress," 1st Cong., 4th Sess., L, 109–10. Seddon privately termed it a "curious" resolution. Kean, *Diary*, 126.

office," and on February 12 still another, asking whether Lawton was drawing the pay and allowances of a brigadier general, and if so, under what law. Despite these and a letter to the same effect signed by seventy-six members of the House of Representatives, Davis remained adamant, Lawton remained quartermaster general, and the Senate eventually confirmed him. Wigfall's boast to censure Davis on the Myers affairs proved empty, but the President was losing friends and had few left.[10]

Wigfall also failed during the same time to obtain censure of the President on "irregular" appointments in general. Senator James L. Orr of South Carolina called the attention of the Senate to the fact that by law all officers appointed under the Provisional Congress should be renominated to the Senate of the Permanent Congress. Pointing out that the President had not done that, Orr proposed to amend an appropriations bill with a proviso that none of the money be used for salaries to those officers. As early as January 15, Wigfall had secured passage of a resolution asking the President to tell the Senate how many such officers had been appointed. In supporting the Orr amendment in his resolution, Wigfall took the opportunity to castigate Davis. While voicing his reluctance to vote for a resolution expressing "want of confidence" in the President, Wigfall said he could not keep quiet when incompetent officers held their commands illegally. "Battles had been lost and widows and orphans made" in consequence of the President's illegal action, Wigfall argued. Johnson of Arkansas prevailed upon Orr to withdraw his amendment, however, saying that he thought Wigfall's "expression given in debate" should have the desired effect upon the President.[11]

Wigfall was not at all satisfied. A week later he resumed the issue, saying that while he did not doubt the President's sincerity, he did doubt his judgment. If Davis' judgment had been as good as his, Wigfall maintained matter-of-factly, the South would not

[10] "Proceedings of Confederate Congress," 1st Cong., 4th Sess., L, 108–12, 307–309, 422; *Journal of Congress*, 1st Cong., 4th Sess., 622–23, 718; Kean, *Diary*, 126, 127, 130.

[11] "Proceedings of Confederate Congress," 1st Cong., 4th Sess., L, 373–75; *Journal of Congress*, 1st Cong., 4th Sess., 574.

have lost one army surrendered at Vicksburg (by Pemberton) and another routed at Missionary Ridge (under Bragg). Without giving up on other curbs upon the President, during the summer of 1864, Wigfall contrived to hammer at Davis' irregular appointment of officers.[12]

Confidence in Davis' judgment to appoint officers was undermined. Whether this was because of the President's own actions, as in sustaining Bragg and Pemberton, or because of Wigfall's denunciation, is difficult to assess. Wigfall probably did help in defeating a bill to allow the President the authority to reassign commanders without the consent of the Senate. Speaking at great length, the senator quoted Marshall Ney (after Quatre Bras) and Napoleon to show that "nothing was so disastrous" to any army as the irresponsible changing of officers. The bill lost by a tie vote.[13]

Wigfall would deny the President even the authority to select his own military advisor—because he selected Bragg. Speaking on a bill to provide a staff and pay for Bragg in his new job, Wigfall pronounced him incompetent for commanding more than a training camp where he would be kept from tyrannizing his subordinates. The senator said he had been restrained frequently from expressing his opinions by the remark that it would not do to break down confidence in the President, but he asked why the Senate should go on voting confidence in Davis when they felt none. Even after the bill passed, Wigfall and others continued to snipe at the President and Bragg.[14]

Wigfall's opposition to Davis' appointments was a part of his four-faceted onslaught against the President. This attack was necessary, the senator wrote to Johnston, because it was the opinion of "the leading men that Davis' bad judgment of men & bad temper together will ruin the country unless he can be controlled." The President had to be made to conciliate with the Senate, said Wigfall; this could be done with a threat to his power

12 "Proceedings of Confederate Congress," L, 443; LI, 197–98, 207–208; *Journal of Congress*, 2nd Cong., 1st Sess., 165–66, 203–204.

13 "Proceedings of Confederate Congress," 2nd Cong., 1st Sess., LI, 235–36.

14 *Ibid.*, 141–42, 191, 238–39; *Journal of Congress*, 2nd Cong., 1st Sess., 29, 220.

and popularity. In rambling letters to friends during March and April of 1864, Wigfall sketched four ways to accomplish this control. First, to curb Davis' power, the Senate had to reject his unwise appointments. Second, to threaten Davis' popularity, the responsibility for military losses had to be fixed where it belonged—upon the President. Third, Congress, the Senate especially, had to compel Davis' observance of the constitution and hem him in with additional restrictions. Fourth, and "above all," Davis' general responsibility to the country had to be established through public debates. To Wigfall this last part meant destroying confidence in the President by belittling him in public.[15]

The Texan may have begun preparation for the third part of his plan—constitutional curbs upon the President—as early as November of 1863, when Charlotte Wigfall noted that her husband was "reading and writing" in preparation for going to Richmond.[16] Wade Hampton asked Wigfall in December how he was getting along with his "plans," but until April of 1864, there is nothing definite in his correspondence about constitutional changes. That month he wrote to Hammond for "advice." Hammond evidently thought of Davis as a tyrant and possible dictator, and before coming to his point, Wigfall offered his most penetrating analysis of Davis so that Hammond would understand him.

> The liberties of our country are in no danger from him . . . . If [the sceptre] were offered, his trembling hand could not hold it. The captain who pipes his crew to prayers & not to the pumps when his ship springs a leak will never sail under a black flag. . . . The last thing a Caesar, Cromwell or Napoleon would have thought of when the gunboats were in the river would have been—joining the Church. . . . His vanity is excessive & craves above all things military reputation. As to military matters, he is a mere superficialist. . . . Yet he undertakes to direct all the military movements of the war. . . . Now this is the very point on which I want your opinion.[17]

15 Wigfall to Johnston, March 19, 1864, Johnston Papers; Wigfall to James H. Hammond, April —, 1864, Hammond Papers; R. B. Rhett to Wigfall, April 15, 1864, Wigfall Papers.
16 Charlotte Wigfall to Halsey, November 25, 1863, Wigfall Papers.
17 Wigfall to Hammond, April —, 1864, Hammond Papers.

Davis and Lincoln were the first Presidents who "supposed they were actually & not potentially" commanders-in-chief, and Wigfall doubted the wisdom of such a policy. He cited Macaulay as saying that a king of England could not constitutionally command his army but acted only through responsible agents. Wigfall wondered if this was not the intention of the founding fathers in drafting the Constitution. Why should there not be a commander-in-chief appointed by the President with the advice and consent of the Senate and removable through the same process. A man would then be selected for his military ability, Wigfall pointed out. He suggested, "Suppose the Congress advises the calling [of] a convention to make such an alteration." [18]

In reply, Hammond was even more vituperative than Wigfall in denouncing Davis but had nothing to say about the senator's proposals for constitutional reins for the President. Barnwell Rhett's reply showed more thought. Evidently Wigfall had written essentially the same letter to him as he had to Hammond. Rhett advised the Texan against any attempts to change the constitution during the war. The country was in too bad a condition for people to give a hearing to such proposals, Rhett warned. Further, the President had too much influence over military leaders, voters (most of whom were in the army), and Congress for any changes to be effected until after the war. The only thing constructive Rhett could advise was for Congress to compel the President to observe the laws.[19] Wigfall was already trying that without much success.

The South would win its independence, he was sure, but it would have to be in spite of the "terrible incompetency" of the executive; so Wigfall could not wait. According to Beauregard, at the same time the senator was planning constitutional reforms, he was also carrying on a protracted correspondence in preparation for a move to censure Davis for not seizing opportunities to invade the North during the fall of 1861. Beauregard, who was in

[18] *Ibid.*
[19] Hammond to Wigfall, April 15, 1864; Rhett to Wigfall, April 15, 1864, Wigfall Papers.

sympathy with the plan, urged General G. W. Smith to send relevant information to Wigfall but to keep quiet about it so that Davis would commit himself and then they could "fasten on him the lie." [20]

C. C. Clay tried to dissuade Wigfall from his ruinous course. After talking with the President, Clay wrote that Davis was genuinely interested in making up with the senator. According to Clay, the President said he was sure that Wigfall would not have become inimical to him if the Texan had aired his grievances to him and heard his defense. Clay, who had just been selected by Davis to spy in Canada for the Confederacy, implored his Texas friend to keep the peace, for it was important that they should at least seem to the enemy to be united. In truth, the Confederacy was greatly disunited. And as the public debate over the responsibility for Vicksburg warmed, General Johnston became a storm center of the South, with pro- and anti-Davis southerners aligning as anti- or pro-Johnston.[21]

Wigfall was the most ardent defender of the general, but Johnston evidently thought that the senator was not doing enough to vindicate him. In fact, there was nearly a rift between the two. The more Johnston saw of the attacks upon himself in the newspapers, the more he was convinced that Davis was supplying selected parts of official information. The general urged Wigfall to have the full record published immediately. But Wigfall, probably hoping to get more congressional support, insisted upon waiting until the new Congress met in May, 1864. A month before Congress convened the general said peevishly that publication was already so late that he was somewhat indifferent on the subject.[22]

The senator and the general had other differences, too. Wig-

20 Wigfall to Johnston, March 19, 1864, Johnston Papers; Beauregard to Smith, March 31, 1864, *Official Records*, LI, Pt. 2, p. 844.

21 Clay to Wigfall, April 29, 1864, Wigfall Papers; Alfred P. James, "General Joseph Eggleston Johnston, Storm Center of the Confederate Army," *Mississippi Valley Historical Review*, XIV (December, 1927), 342–59.

22 Joseph E. Johnston to his brother Beverly Johnston, February 14, 1863; and Wigfall to Johnston, March 17, 1864, both in Johnston Papers; Johnston to Wigfall, April 1, 1864, Wigfall Papers.

fall was irritated at Johnston's insistence upon defending Bragg. And Johnston resented Wigfall's criticism of one of the general's staff as not "occupying the social position" to merit such a job. This brought a curt reply from Johnston that he had not considered that qualification as necessary for a commissary general. It was the proud Virginian who smoothed matters by writing that he expected Wigfall to criticize him when necessary. Then, as he had said he would, Wigfall obtained a congressional order for the publication of Johnston's side of the Vicksburg story.[23]

The second Congress had scarcely convened when Grant, by then general-in-chief of the Union armies, began his multipronged offensive against the South. The two major threats were posed by General W. T. Sherman facing Johnston in the West, and Grant and Meade facing Lee in Virginia. Both Johnston and Lee were greatly outnumbered, and there seemed to be little that Congress could do about it. Indeed, one senator said it was the President's opinion that Congress might as well have stayed home. This brought Wigfall to his feet for a lengthy lecture on the fallacy and danger of such an attitude, regardless of what the President thought. But once he was up, he could suggest nothing more than feeding the officers better, and he introduced a bill to allow junior officers two rations and higher officers three.[24]

It was fitting that the second Confederate Congress begin with such legislation. Despite Wigfall's criticism of his colleagues for failing to pass corrective currency legislation and other such constructive bills,[25] Congress concentrated mostly upon extremely minor military matters in 1864 and 1865. Perhaps they had little choice; the military situation was grave. In Virginia, Grant stead-

---

[23] Wigfall to Johnston, March 18, 1864, Johnston Papers; Johnston to Wigfall, April 1, 5, 23, 1864, Wigfall Papers; *Report of General Joseph E. Johnston of his Operations in the Departments of Mississippi and East Louisiana . . . Published by Order of Congress* (Richmond, 1864).

[24] "Proceedings of Confederate Congress," 2nd Cong., 1st Sess., LI, 22–25, 58. This was evidently in response to Halsey's message to his father that the army was "very much 'down on' Congress" for small rations. According to Lieutenant Wigfall, they were barely managing to exist on a third of a pound of bacon. Halsey to his mother, April 9, 1864, Wigfall Papers.

[25] "Proceedings of Confederate Congress," 2nd Cong., 1st Sess., LI, 24–25.

ily pushed Lee toward Richmond. In the West, Johnston slowly gave ground as Sherman backed him toward Atlanta. Refusing to attack a superior force unless conditions were virtually perfect, Johnston conducted a masterful retreat, offering resistance but falling back repeatedly just as he was about to be flanked. Three times Sherman launched full scale attacks against Johnston, and each time the Federals suffered heavy losses.

Just after one of these battles, Johnston received a welcome visitor with unwelcome news. Senator and Mrs. Wigfall, on their way to Texas after the close of Congress, had come through Atlanta to leave Louly and Fanny with Lydia Johnston, and for the senator to have a talk with the general. Wigfall brought Johnston a disquieting but reliable report that Davis intended to remove him from command on the pretext that the people of Georgia had lost confidence in him. The senator had told influential Confederates in Richmond that there had been no such loss of confidence, and then he had come to Atlanta to see for himself. After talking with various Georgia leaders, he concluded that his first impression was correct. Undoubtedly, Johnston was still highly respected and trusted by people of the state. Halsey, as a member of Hood's staff, had been with Johnston since the beginning of the campaign and still looked upon him as the greatest soldier on the continent.[26]

Johnston told Wigfall that he could help most by convincing the administration that the best chance of defeating Sherman lay in additional cavalry for attacks against his railroad communications. Johnston had asked for this repeatedly, but Davis replied that the general would have to do with what he had.[27] Instead of approaching the President directly, Wigfall went to

26 Wigfall to Johnston, no date (probably a copy of a memorandum written later to aid Johnston in describing the events); Halsey to Wigfall, May 30, 1864, Wigfall Papers. After talking with Georgia citizens and Johnston's soldiers, Senator Richard Walker of Alabama concluded that confidence in the general seemed unlimited. Walker to Assistant Secretary of War John Cambell, July 4, 1864, *Official Records*, LII, Pt. 2, pp. 685–86; *cf.* Yearns, *Confederate Congress*, 142.

27 Johnston to Bragg, June 12, 13, 16, 26, 27, July 16, 1864; and Bragg to Johnston, June 27, 1864, all in *Official Records*, XXXVIII, Pt. 4, pp. 750, 770, 772, 777, 792, 796.

those Georgians whom he hoped Davis would heed: Governor Joseph E. Brown; General Howell Cobb, one of the most respected men in the South; Benjamin H. Hill, a Davis spokesman in the Senate; and others. After Wigfall talked with them, each agreed that cavalry was needed and that they would urge the President to send it. Brown and Cobb wrote urgent letters to that effect. Hill thought the situation so desperate that he visited Johnston and then went directly to Richmond with his request.[28] Davis was unmoved and continued to express his belief that Johnston could do the job with the troops he had.[29] Thus, as the Wigfalls made their hazardous way to Texas, Johnston was being pushed perilously close to Atlanta.

Since their Texas trip had been cancelled in 1863, the Wigfalls thought it was imperative that they go in 1864. They did so not only at their own risk, but with some peril to their daughters also. Before Atlanta had been placed in jeopardy, Lydia Johnston had invited the girls to stay with her, but by June 28 the general feared for their safety. "You expose your children to risk," he warned Wigfall, imploring him not to leave them in Atlanta while its fate was uncertain. Nevertheless, the girls were left there. A letter dated July 29, from Jackson, Mississippi, was the last one they received from their parents for four months.[30]

"You must come to Texas this summer. *Don't Fail*," General John A. Wharton, a friend from Texas, had exhorted Wigfall. Wharton evidently thought it of major importance that the senator come; he offered to lend him three thousand dollars to finance the trip. The general, who had been promoted to brigadier general with Wigfall's help and had then taken a brigade of Texas Rangers to war, may have been Wigfall's most enthusiastic admirer. To Wharton, Wigfall was the only civilian "developed

28 Wigfall to Johnston, undated memorandum, Wigfall Papers; Brown to Davis, June 28, July 5, 1864; Cobb to Seddon, July 1, 1864; Seddon to Hill, July 13, 1864; and Hill to Seddon, July 14, 1864, all in *Official Records*, XXXIX, Pt. 2, pp. 680, 688; XXXVIII, Pt. 5, 858; LII, Pt. 2, pp. 693–95, 704–707. See also Govan and Livingood, *Johnston*, 297–300.
29 Davis to Brown, July 5, 1864, *Official Records*, LII, Pt. 2, p. 681.
30 Johnston to Wigfall, June 28, 1864, Wigfall Papers; Wright, *Southern Girl*, 177–81.

by the Revolution," who deserved a place in history. Thanking him for securing staff officers for the Ranger brigade, Wharton said that without them the Federals under N. P. Banks could not have been stopped in Louisiana. Since Texas was then safe for many months, the general said, he was urging acceptance of Wigfall's idea to unite Texas troops with Johnston in Georgia.[31]

If Wharton wanted Wigfall to come to Texas to plead for troops for Johnston, everyone concerned was disappointed. On the way to Texas, probably at Mobile about July 25, Wigfall got word that Davis had replaced Johnston with Hood as commander of the Army of Tennessee. Johnston received the order on July 17, just as he was completing preparations for an attempt to trap the Federals. While in Georgia, Wigfall had talked with Johnston about these plans to catch Sherman's army divided at Peach Tree Creek and with its back to the Chattahootchee River. Johnston also explained the plans to his successor, but the pugnacious Hood did not wait. Davis wanted an aggressive general, and Hood was that. Sherman and Grant were both pleased by the change. When Grant heard of it, he predicted rash and ill-advised attacks. There was as much apprehension among Confederates as there was joy in the Union camp. General E. Kirby Smith said that Johnston would have beaten Sherman; but, speaking for many of his fellow officers, Kirby Smith predicted: "Sherman will destroy Hood." [32] He did. The cavalry which Johnston had requested was sent to Hood in September, too late to be effective. Soon only pitiful remnants were left of the Army of Tennessee, and Sherman had razed Atlanta and made his "March through Georgia," separating another section of the South; all of this before the Wigfalls returned from Texas.

[31] Wharton to Wigfall, July 20, 1864, July 21, 1862, Wigfall Papers. Wigfall had already left for Texas and had not acknowledged Wharton's offer by September 1. Wharton to Wigfall, September 1, 1864, Wigfall Papers.

[32] Wigfall to Halsey, July 25, 1864. This letter was not found, but is described in one which Halsey sent to his mother, August 7, 1864; Halsey to Wigfall, July 31, 1864; and Wigfall to Johnston, undated memorandum, all in *ibid.*; Horace Porter, *Campaigning with Grant* (New York, 1897), 244; also W. T. Sherman, "The Grand Strategy of the Last Year of the War," in Johnson and Buell (eds.), *Battles and Leaders*, IV, 247–59; E. K. Smith to his mother, August 17, 1864, in Joseph Howard Parks, *General Edmund Kirby Smith, C.S.A.* (Baton Rouge, 1954), 428–29.

Wigfall's evident purpose for going to Texas was to explain his unpopular stand on several major issues. His Texas speeches were much like those he had made in the Richmond area during the fall of 1863. Speaking mostly in the larger cities of East and South Texas, Wigfall defended conscription, exemption, impressment, and taxation legislation but said nothing about the administration. His message was least appreciated in the western sections where paper money was less popular and Union sentiment stronger. The San Antonio *News* said that the senator's explanation of congressional measures was generally satisfactory, except perhaps in regard to revenue acts. Still, the *News*'s editor believed, Wigfall's speeches would have been beneficial in promoting patriotism in that section of the state had he not slandered Texans by deriding their unwillingness to send troops east. Wigfall spoke for two hours and fifteen minutes and, according to the San Antonio reporter, was listened to with marked attention, but "on the whole . . . left a very unfavorable impression." [33]

Wigfall's most popular speech was evidently the one he made in Houston on September 19. It was quoted in some papers east of the Mississippi, and those Halsey heard speak of it were "very much pleased" with it. Judge Ballinger heard it and noted in his diary that it was an able and interesting speech on the past legislation of Congress and the affairs of the day. Perhaps Wigfall was inspired to scale oratorical heights by a six-thousand dollar donation to him by those whom Ballinger identified only as "some gentlemen in town." [34]

J. H. Parsons, a friend of Wigfall, considered the senator's Texas tour a success. Parsons said he could tell that Wigfall had done much good because the Texas legislators who had opposed

[33] Dallas *Herald*, September 24, 1864; San Antonio *News*, undated, quoted in *Texas Republican*, October 21, 1864. Senator Oldham was more western in his outlook; his and Wigfall's speeches in Austin during the week before October 25 caused the Dallas *Herald*, November 5, 1864, to comment on their quite different views on public policy.
[34] Halsey to Wigfall, January 16, 1864, Wigfall Papers; see also Dallas *Herald*, September 24, 1864; Ballinger Diary, 190.

everything that the Confederate government did were, after Wigfall's visit, considerably relaxed in their opposition. The senator
also received Parson's commendation for the state legislature's
passage of a resolution saying that only the Confederate government, not states, had the authority to conclude the war and another resolution declaring Texas' determination to fight until
the Confederacy's independence was acknowledged. When these
were forwarded to the Confederate Congress, Wigfall pointed
out to his colleagues that the resolutions had been submitted to
him for his opinion before they were introduced in the Texas
legislature, and he had approved them.[35]

Since Sherman had already reached the sea and was turning
north in December, the Wigfalls' trip back to Richmond was
even longer and more hazardous than the one to Texas.[36] The
last session of the Confederate Congress began November 7,
1864, but Wigfall was not in his seat until January 4, 1865.

Displaying their new wealth, the Wigfalls moved into the
Spotswood Hotel when they returned to Richmond. They had
not only the donations from Texans, but also a thousand dollars
in gold which Wigfall's mother-in-law had smuggled to them
from Rhode Island. The senator promptly converted it into Confederate bank notes, a move which some of his southern friends
thought rather foolish. But, as Louly explained later, she was
sure that her father would have felt recreant to his country if he
admitted to himself that Confederate money was not as good as
gold.[37]

Thirty years later, Louly said she remembered that her father
had found the spirit of the people undaunted. Some who met
him and made more immediate diary entries, noted a different

35 J. H. Parsons to Wigfall, November 8, 1864, Wigfall Papers; "Proceedings of
Confederate Congress," 2nd Cong., 2nd Sess., LII, 257–58.

36 Wigfall went north of Sherman's army through Columbia, South Carolina.
Floride Clemson, *A Rebel Came Home: Diary of Floride Clemson*, edited by
Charles M. McGee, Jr. and Ernest M. Lander, Jr. (Columbia, South Carolina,
1961), 73.

37 Wright, *Southern Girl*, 215, 221; exchange certificate in Staff Officer's File,
dated November 18, 1864, marked "Redeemed Jan'y 27, 1865"; Chesnut, *Diary*,
485.

impression. The War Bureau chief, Kean, agreed with Judge John A. Campbell of Alabama that Wigfall represented "the masses of the Gulf States as utterly discouraged." Because of this, Campbell said, the senator had come like "Saul on his journey to Damascus breathing out threatenings and slaughter." [38] The senatorial fulminations were directed at Davis, and this time Wigfall found himself among the Senate majority. Criticism of the administration for its military policies had grown so much that the last session of the Confederate legislature amounted to a showdown between Congress and the President. Wigfall found increasing support for his efforts to discredit Davis and "win the war." The drawback to the efforts by Wigfall and other disaffected congressmen lay in the fact that their methods in achieving the first objective subverted the second.

A more constructive approach was urged by Wade Hampton. "I wish my dear Wigfall," Hampton wrote, "that you would forget the differences of the past & try to reestablish the intimate relations that once existed between Mr. Davis & yourself. You can aid him greatly, & can serve the country by giving him counsel . . . this is no time for desentions [*sic*] amongst the patriots of our land." This was not the fiery Texan's way. Had it been, there is little to indicate that Davis would have reciprocated. Each seemed determined to pursue his chosen course: Davis to ignore Congress as much as possible; Wigfall to establish a senatorial hegemony with himself in the lead. Confidence in the President was already so depreciated that even as Hampton wrote, the Virginia delegation to Congress was threatening to initiate a legislative resolution of "no confidence" in Davis' administration.[39]

With such encouragement Wigfall continued from where he had left off at the last session. On the Senate floor he called for

[38] Wright, *Southern Girl*, 215; Kean, *Diary*, 186. John Archibald Campbell of Alabama was one of the "southern" members of the U.S. Supreme Court when it rendered the Dred Scott decision. Campbell resigned from the Court after serving as a liason between Confederate agents and President-elect Lincoln and deciding that Lincoln was not conferring in good faith.

[39] Hampton to Wigfall, January 20, 1865, Wigfall Papers; Thomas S. Bocock (Speaker of the Virginia House of Representatives) to Davis, January 21, 1865, *Official Records*, XLVI, Pt. 2, p. 1118.

Davis to explain why the staff law passed by Congress in June, 1864, had not been executed.[40] On the grounds that generals knew more about such things than the President, Wigfall opposed the administration's plan to reorganize and consolidate the pieces of whatever armies were left in 1865. In accordance with his plan to curtail the President's appointive power, Wigfall helped to secure enough votes in the Senate to override the veto of a bill to provide more naval officers. Davis' principal objection was that the bill gave Congress too much of a role in the selection. Antiadministration representatives in the House, however, could not muster a large enough majority, and the veto was sustained. A few days later the opposition had more success on a minor matter. With Wigfall leading the way, both houses voted to enact over Davis' veto a bill conferring the franking privilege for newspapers sent to soldiers. It was the *only* Davis veto that was overridden by both houses.[41] It was for Wigfall a moral victory at the most, and undoubtedly the prestige of the President *and* the Congress suffered from the wrangling.

Consequently, Wigfall's efforts to achieve his second objective—Confederate military victory—were even less rewarding. In discussing a bill to compensate Confederate farmers for loss of their cotton burned to prevent its falling into the hands of the enemy, the Texan spoke passionately for a scorched-earth policy. When Senator William Graham of North Carolina voiced his opinion that it might be better if some property should fall into the hand of the enemy than for the people to be stripped of all subsistence, Wigfall vociferously condemned such a policy. Speaking vividly of the horrors of the subjugation with which the South was threatened, he pleaded with Congress not to hesitate to take any measure which would prevent it. He warned the Senate, and all southerners, that they had to be filled with the spirit which inspired the Dutch when they inundated and destroyed

40 "Proceedings of Confederate Congress," 2nd Cong., 2nd Sess., LII, 229–30. Intermittently through the remainder of the session Wigfall brought up the matter and tried to strengthen the army staffs, *ibid.*, 189–91, 386, 451.

41 *Ibid.*, 168–73, 178–83, 199–204, 218–22, 246–51, 261–63; Yearns, *Confederate Congress*, 234.

their country to prevent its subjugation. Only then would they win their independence. He would rather that Savannah were a smoldering heap of ruins than that thirty-thousand bales of cotton should have been saved for Abraham Lincoln and that Sherman should have been feted there. If *he* had commanded there, Wigfall declaimed, he would have burnt the cotton whatever the consequences. It was no time to talk of the rights of man; it was war to the finish! The Senate voted the way Wigfall wanted, but it is doubtful that his impassioned oratory inspired southerners the way it had before they had endured years of suffering and quarreling.[42]

Nevertheless, Wigfall said he had no doubt that the hearts of the people were in the contest. There was some discontent because impressment laws were being applied unequally—all of a man's property being taken because he happened to live near a railroad while another man's in the interior was left untouched. But even when the indomitable senator started out talking about correcting unjust taxation, he advocated peremptory ways of achieving it and ended by professing authoritarian disregard for individual liberties. He proposed a resolution that military officers pay full market price for the impressed goods. This would result in "redundant currency" which should be taken from the people as fast as it was issued by a new and higher tax bill, said Wigfall. He reasoned that this would cause the impressments to fall equally upon all. Perhaps *all* of a man's property would be taken, but, as he was paid market price, he could go straightway to his neighbor whose property had not been taken and buy what was needed. Further, through the tax law, the price would be borne by the whole country. It was sometime later that he figured out how the man who had lost all of his property could pay the tax and also buy what he needed. For the time being he switched abruptly to individual liberties.[43]

If Wigfall related his tax proposal to habeas corpus and individual liberties, the reporter for the "Proceedings" did not cap-

42 "Proceedings of Confederate Congress," 2nd Cong., 2nd Sess., LII, 127–28.
43 *Ibid.*, 235–38.

ture the transition. The maxim that it was better that one-hundred guilty men escape than that one innocent man should be punished, the senator said, would not do in wartime. Rather, in their situation, it would be better that one-hundred *innocent* persons should be arrested than that one *suspected* man should escape. With another incongruous but extremely significant corollary Wigfall concluded with the warning that all cabals should be broken up in order to make Congress a power in the government. The Texan's resolution was adopted, but only after it was modified so as to be sent to the judiciary committee which would look into the advisability of recommending such legislation.[44] The recommendation never came.

The next day Wigfall proposed a supplement to his tax plan. This second bill would allow the individual whose property had been impressed to satisfy his taxes with receipts given by the impressing officer. This one was referred to the finance committee. Neither part of his plan was passed. Wigfall was more knowledgeable when he was speaking for sequestration of property belonging to persons liable to military service who departed from the Confederacy without permission. That bill passed.[45]

Absenteeism and desertion from the army were becoming more and more serious problems for the Confederacy during its last days. Wigfall gave a favorable report from the military committee on a bill "to provide more effectively for the prevention and punishment" of those offenses. He made an effort to do more. In February he asked Lee if he would allow the Texas Brigade to go back to Texas to recruit. Lee said at that point he could not spare four hundred of his best men even though they might bring back others. Two weeks before Lee surrendered at Appomattox Wigfall was still trying to devise some way to force the return of deserters.[46]

44 *Ibid.*, 237. The reference to a "cabal" was probably an illusion to Davis' cabinet which Wigfall hoped to "reorganize" with the bill he introduced two weeks later.

45 *Ibid.*, 245–46, 263; *Journal of Congress*, 2nd Cong., 2nd Sess., 509.

46 "Proceedings of Confederate Congress," 2nd Cong., 2nd Sess., LII, 383; Lee to Wigfall, February 8, 1865, in Wright, *Southern Girl*, 226–27; Wigfall to Chesnut, March 26, 1865, in Williams-Chesnut-Manning Collection.

Wigfall was also perturbed at the "desertion" of senators during February, 1865. He opposed granting a request for a leave of absence for Senator Haynes, who had left to find a home for his wife and daughters in a safer part of the state. A week later when Wigfall was temporarily absent along with five other senators, they were declared "absent without leave" and the sergeant-at-arms was sent to require their attendance. Later that same day Wigfall was the only one of the six present.[47]

One obvious solution to the shortage of soldiers in the army—but one the Confederacy avoided facing for some time—was the military use of Negroes. A fascinating document in the papers of South Carolina's Governor Francis W. Pickens indicates that some Negroes not only faced the issue before the whites, but that they volunteered to fight for the Confederacy! A "Memorial of Free Negroes" dated January 10, 1861, was an eloquent avowal by twenty-three Negroes of their loyalty to their native state: "We are by birth citizens of South Carolina ... in her defense we are willing to offer up our lives and all that is dear to us. ... We are willing to be assigned to any service where we can be made useful." [48] But in 1863, due to opposition from Wigfall and others, they were still not being used for fighting. In June of that year, a British army officer visiting in the South expressed his belief that Negroes would make good soldiers for the Confederacy and that they should be used.[49]

Generally the South was not willing to bestow that honor upon a black man. The army almost from the outset used free and slave Negroes for nonmilitary, menial tasks, sometimes hiring them and in emergencies impressing them. But the planters were reluctant. Wigfall and Mary Chesnut both noted that the South Carolina planters cheerfully sent their sons off to war, but that when the slaves were impressed to construct coastal defenses, a

---

[47] "Proceedings of Confederate Congress," 2nd Cong., 2nd Sess., LII, 392–93, 434; *Journal of Congress*, 2nd Cong., 2nd Sess., 646.

[48] Pickens and Bonham Papers, 1860–61, Library of Congress.

[49] Fremantle, *Diary*, 225. Ironically, prior to 1863 a majority of northern whites doubted the Negroes' ability to soldier. Small scale experiments in late 1862 and early 1863 proved their worth.

howl arose from the owners. Wigfall concluded that the planter thought a great deal more of his Negroes than of his sons. A great change had come over the planters in two years, he lamented; they had lost their patriotism.[50]

Many Confederate leaders, arguing military necessity, were anxious to resort to a *levée en masse* of slaves, but they were afraid of the planters. Wigfall favored the use of Negroes for nonmilitary labor but was unequivocally opposed to arming or emancipating them. Among those who agreed with him were General Howell Cobb, Senator R. M. T. Hunter, Congressmen H. S. Foote and H. C. Chambers, and Governor Brown of Georgia. The crux of their argument was similar to that of Wigfall's: Admission that the Negro was fit to be a soldier was tantamount to admission that he should not be a slave, that he was not radically inferior as the southern whites had been arguing for almost 250 years.[51] To Wigfall, the Negro was unfit for the army or for freedom, and that was that.

Not even persistent pleading by his friend Johnston could persuade Wigfall to change his mind. Johnston, greatly outnumbered by Sherman in Georgia, could see vast merit in promising freedom for long-term Negro conscripts who would perform menial tasks, freeing soldiers for the front. He devised a plan which he said would give him the equivalent of ten thousand more troops. Pleaded the general, "Is it not worth trying?" Repeatedly he asked Wigfall to attend to the "Negro Scheme." Wigfall remained unalterably opposed. Nevertheless, in February, 1864, a law was enacted which provided for the impressment of twenty thousand slaves.[52]

Encouraged by the results, the generals asked for more. Davis responded, urging Congress to provide forty thousand slaves for long-term service, encouraging their loyalty by promising them

50 Chesnut, *Diary*, 222–23, 259; Fremantle, *Diary*, 225; Yearns, *Confederate Congress*, Chap. 3; "Proceedings of Confederate Congress," 2nd Cong., 2nd Sess., LII, 154.

51 Yearns, *Confederate Congress*, 111–12; Moore, *Conscription and Conflict*, 345.

52 Johnston to Wigfall, January 4, 9, February 3, 12, 1864, Wigfall Papers; *Journal of Congress*, 2nd Cong., 2nd Sess., 719, 769, 774.

emancipation at the end of the war. Although the President stated that the Negroes would not be armed, Wigfall and several other leaders felt that he favored this step. The Texan was adamant, but the tide began to turn in 1865. General Lee, whose opinions by then were virtually omnipotent, announced that he favored enlistment and eventual emancipation of slaves. Most southerners had come to the conclusion that it was their only hope and that it was worth a try.[53]

Wigfall frantically declared that the time had come when it was to be settled "whether this was to be a free negro country, or a free white man's country." For himself, he had "no choice between subjugation and universal emancipation." He would never consent to make a "Santo Domingo of his country." In some of the states, Wigfall pointed out, the slave population was greater than the white—"What was to become of the whites if the negroes should be emancipated?" It would be better to get the deserted troops back in the army than put Negroes in it, said Wigfall. That could be done, he said, if they had leaders who inspired confidence.[54]

As if in reply, Johnston wrote the next day that he had learned of no efforts by the administration to bring back soldiers to the ranks, and again he implored Wigfall to pass the Negro bill. The senator remained obdurate, but other legislators were finally persuaded. In the House, Barksdale of Mississippi, and in the Senate, Oldham of Texas, submitted virtually identical bills on

[53] "Proceedings of Confederate Congress," 2nd Cong., 2nd Sess., LI, 364, 384, 423–25. Yearns, *Confederate Congress*, 112. Professor Nathaniel W. Stephenson, "The Question of Arming the Slaves," *American Historical Review*, XVIII (January, 1913), 297, says that Davis did hope to arm the impressed Negroes; see also Benjamin Quarles, *The Negro in the Civil War* (Boston, 1953), 279; Yearns, *Confederate Congress*, 96; Moore, *Conscription and Conflict*, 345. Two weeks earlier Mary Chesnut foresaw defeat for the Confederacy, saying: "The handwriting is on the wall." Chesnut, *Diary*, 472.
[54] "Proceedings of Confederate Congress," 2nd Cong., 2nd Sess., LII, 281–83. There was little correspondence between Wigfall and Vice-President Alexander H. Stephens, another Davis critic. But this last statement seems to have elicited a comment from Stephens, who wrote shortly after: "I find spirit and vitality enough in the mass of the people . . . . All that is wanting is the proper . . . statesmanship to guide it." Stephens to Wigfall, February 13, 1865, Wigfall Papers.

February 10. Oldham would provide for 200,000 Negroes to be impressed, while Barksdale would leave the number to the discretion of the President. Both provided for emancipation with the consent of the respective states.[55] Possibly because it was an unpopular subject and possibly because of national interest, most senators preferred to discuss the bill in secret session which Wigfall opposed. He said he believed that if discussion on the subject were made known to the public, they could arrive at a decision satisfactory to the people. Again Wigfall was convinced that public opinion was with him when it was not. This time, however, he evidently reflected the opinion of most of the Texas delegation in Congress. They and a majority of representatives from North Carolina, Arkansas, and Missouri opposed the Oldham-Barksdale bills. Nevertheless, a compromise version of the two bills passed the house on February 20. All Wigfall and the other opposing senators could do was to slow the process. On February 17, the same day that the Senate Military Committee reported favorably on Oldham's bill, Wigfall secured passage of his own bill authorizing the Secretary of War to negotiate with the governors of each state for slaves for use in nonmilitary labor. But by March 13, the Senate and House had worked out their differences and passed the "200,000 Negro Bill." [56]

It was impossible, it seems, for Wigfall to reconcile himself to emancipation of slaves for any reason, even for the salvation of the Confederacy. He came up with the amazing assertion that "the whole thing was gotten up to divert attention from the movement to bring about a change in the cabinet." The change Wigfall referred to was his attempt to force Secretary of State Judah P. Benjamin out of the cabinet. If there was any connection between Benjamin and the Negro Bill, it was prob-

---

55 Johnston to Wigfall, February 3, 1865, Wigfall Papers; "Proceedings of Confederate Congress," 2nd Cong., 2nd Sess., LII, 289–93, 325–26, 309–10, 338–39; W. S. Oldham, "Memoirs of a Confederate Senator, 1861–1865" (MS in Oldham Collection, University of Texas Archives) , 55 ff.
56 *Journal of Congress*, 2nd Cong., 2nd Sess., 528, 542, 569, 585; "Proceedings of Confederate Congress," 2nd Cong., 2nd Sess., LII, 362–63, 387, 444, 452–57, 464–65; Yearns, *Confederate Congress*, 97.

ably that the secretary's plan to arm and emancipate the slaves had prompted Wigfall to attempt his removal. It was reputedly at Benjamin's suggestion that Davis had made the recommendation in the fall of 1864 which ultimately led to passage of the 200,000 Negro Bill. Evidently it was the plan to emancipate the slaves that led Wigfall to call for the "cabinet reorganization." [57]

Opposition to Benjamin, a Davis stalwart, had been growing over the years. Perhaps Wigfall was trying to capitalize on this sentiment and strike a blow at Davis. At any rate, the Texan certainly caused a furor in the Senate by introducing an exceedingly blunt resolution that stated: "Benjamin . . . having in the opinion of the Senate, lost the confidence of the country as a wise and discreet cabinet minister, will subserve the public interest by retiring from the State Department." In secret session Wigfall tamed his denunciation considerably, resolving that Davis be advised of the Senate's lack of confidence in Benjamin and requesting the President to take whatever action he deemed proper. The resolution failed by the narrowest—a tie vote of 11–11.[58]

Another of Davis' appointments—that of Hood to replace Johnston at Atlanta—made the President more vulnerable to Wigfall's attacks. Hood may have been a great *division* commander, but his tactics as the commander of an *entire army* would prove to be disastrous. Though more notable for its savagery than its sagacity, Wigfall's observation that Hood "had a fine career before him until Davis undertook to make of him what the good Lord had not" contained a good bit of truth in it. As with Davis, Wigfall had been friends with Hood at one time. Two years earlier Hood had initiated the friendship; an admiring letter congratulating Wigfall for his military legislation was immediately followed by a request to see and talk with the senator. After Hood was wounded in the arm at Gettysburg and lost a leg at Chickamauga, the Wigfalls, especially Louly, seemed

[57] Kean, *Diary*, 204–205; Robert Douthat Meade, *Judah P. Benjamin: Confederate Statesman* (New York, 1943), 306; Jones, *Rebel War Clerk*, 417.

[58] Rembrant W. Patrick, *Jefferson Davis and His Cabinet* (Baton Rouge, 1944), 199–200; *Journal of Congress*, 2nd Cong., 2nd Sess., 550, 552.

quite anxious about his welfare and were happy to have him spend part of his convalescent periods in their home.[59]

Wigfall's good relations with Hood did not end abruptly when the general replaced Johnston. The senator seemed genuinely protective of Hood's interests when he asked Mary Chesnut to get the young general to decline command of the Army of Tennessee. According to the diarist, Wigfall was concerned because Hood would "have to fight under Jeff Davis's orders." Soon, however, the senator came to the same conclusion as had Johnston—that Hood had been deceitful in his dealings. Hood's part in the removal of Johnston is not clear, but there are indications that it was not altogether honorable. While pretending to agree with Johnston, Hood was writing to Richmond condemning his superior's strategy and denying the accuracy of his reports.[60]

Davis had lost considerable support by replacing Johnston with Hood. Even friends of Hood and Davis predicted that the President would continue to lose popularity until he reappointed Johnston. Wigfall scarcely needed this encouragement to attack Davis and defend Johnston. He did both so avidly that Mary Chesnut misread his intentions, concluding that he wanted to replace Davis with Johnston, making him dictator.[61]

During a Senate debate on a resolution to request that Davis reappoint Johnston to command the Army of Tennessee, Wigfall

---

[59] T. Harry Williams, "The Military Leadership ot the North and South," uses the analysis of Hood's ability as an example of Wigfall's savage humor, in David Donald (ed.), *Why the North Won the Civil War* (Baton Rouge, 1960), 23; Hood to Wigfall, February 5, 6, 1865; Hampton to Wigfall, July 15, 1863; Charlotte Wigfall to Halsey, July 16, August 6, October 8, 1863; Wigfall to Halsey, November 21, 1863; and Longstreet to Wigfall, September 12, 1863, all in Wigfall Papers.

[60] Chesnut, *Diary*, 430; Hood to Bragg, July 14, 1864; Bragg to Davis, July 15, 1864, *Official Records*, XXXVIII, Pt. 5, pp. 879–80; XXXIX, Pt. 2, pp. 712–14. Bragg's role in Johnston's removal was questionable also. He "visited informally" with Johnston but was actually gathering detail to justify Davis' decision to remove the Virginian. Bragg to Davis, July 15, 1864, *Official Records*, XXXVIII, Pt. 5, p. 881; XXXIX, Pt. 2, pp. 712–14. See also Govan and Livingood, *Johnston*, 248–317; and King, "The Relationship Between Johnston and Davis," 128–31.

[61] Virginia Clay-Clopton (Mrs. Clement C. Clay), *A Belle of the Fifties* (New York 1904), 236–37; Ballinger *Diary*, 189; DeLeon, *Rebel Capitals*, 343; Hampton to Wigfall, January 20, 1865, and Halsey to Louly, July 31, 1864, both in Wigfall Papers; Chesnut, *Diary*, 467.

read a letter from an officer of that army stating that its troops had no confidence in Hood and were clamoring for Johnston. Two days later Wigfall brought still more of his extensive anti-Davis files into play, using them for a lengthy excoriation of the President and a defense of Johnston. Senator Thomas Semmes of Louisiana was the only one who spoke against restoring Johnston to command, pointing out that the general had been reluctant to take the offensive. Wigfall then brought forth his and Beauregard's anti-Davis letters. In 1861, Wigfall said, this "falling back general" had offered to take the initiative with sixty thousand men, cross the Potomac, take Washington, and liberate Maryland. It was time that this fact was made public, said the senator; Johnston, whose patriotism kept him quiet, had been unjustly blamed for too long. Taunting Semmes to call for the pertinent correspondence, Wigfall blamed Davis for not taking Maryland, for losing Vicksburg by giving Pemberton orders which conflicted with Johnston's, and for losing vast stores of supplies by unwisely ordering Johnston to fall back from Manassas in 1861. Perhaps the frequent applause from fellow senators and the galleries inspired Wigfall to a particularly vituperative though incongruous conclusion. There had to be "a revival of confidence in the Executive, or all was lost," said Wigfall, but so far as he could see, the President had been "an amalgam of malice and mediocrity." On this note, the resolution requesting Davis to reappoint Johnston passed.[62]

The pro-Johnston resolution was coupled with an even more serious indication of a lack of congressional confidence in Davis. On January 9, Senator Edward Sparrow, the moderate chairman of the Committee on Military Affairs, introduced a bill to provide for a general-in-chief of all Confederate armies. A week later Senator G. A. Henry introduced a resolution advising Davis to name Lee to that position and to appoint Johnston and Beauregard to command armies. Henry's resolution passed 14–2, and

[62] "Proceedings of Confederate Congress," 2nd Cong., 2nd Sess., LII, 283, 296–98, 300–306; a month earlier Wigfall had predicted that Hood's men would desert him. See Chesnut, *Diary*, 467.

the general-in-chief bill passed 20–2, Wigfall voting in the affirmative upon both. This was all in accordance with Wigfall's plan to curb the President's powers, and the senator played a major role in the passage of the general-in-chief bill. Probably, as the Galveston *News* said later, Wigfall had instigated the bill. As usual, dissension was increased without anything constructive being accomplished. Davis vetoed the bill on the ground that it violated his constitutional authority as commander-in-chief. At the same time, he put Lee in charge of Confederate military operations but under the direction of the President.[63]

Wigfall had either changed his mind about Lee's lack of ability or at least preferred him to Davis at the head of the armies. Four days before Davis made the actual appointment, Wigfall spoke of it as an accomplished fact, thanking God that they had Lee, a man of ability, at the head of their military affairs. One more change, said Wigfall fancifully, and "all would go as merry as a marriage bell." That change, of course, was to reinstate Johnston at the head of the Army of Tennessee, and Wigfall expected Lee to bring it about immediately. On February 4, still two days before Lee's official appointment, Wigfall wrote a letter to the general "earnestly but respectfully" recommending Johnston's assignment. After securing the endorsement of sixteen other senators and that of Vice President Stephens, Wigfall sent the letter to Lee.[64]

Johnston warned Wigfall that he would be disappointed in the results of the establishment of the office of commander-in-chief, that Lee would not have as much influence as the senators hoped. Indeed, Lee's reply must have set Wigfall aback. In effect Lee said that he should not, and did not, have the authority to appoint Johnston to that position.[65] Eleven days later, however,

[63] "Proceedings of Confederate Congress," 2nd Cong., 2nd Sess., LII, 111, 120, 190–91, 204; *Journal of Congress*, 2nd Cong., 2nd Sess., 432, 453–54, 457–58; Yearns, *Confederate Congress*, 227; Galveston *News*, February 19, 1874; Wiley, *Road to Appomattox*, 83–84.
[64] "Proceedings of Confederate Congress," 2nd Cong., 2nd Sess., LII, 283; Wigfall and others to Lee, February 4, 1865, copy in Wigfall Papers.
[65] Johnston to Wigfall, February 12, 1865; and Lee to Confederate States Senators, February 13, 1865, both in Wigfall Papers.

Lee, working in his own way, secured the appointment for Johnston. Because of this, Wigfall jubilantly reported to Johnston, Lee was hated by Davis as much as they were. The Texan did not exaggerate greatly, for Lee was being drawn into the conflict on Johnston's side. For one thing, Lee did not hesitate to tell anyone who asked that he had been consulted about Johnston's removal before Atlanta and had advised against it. Davis had given the impression that Lee had concurred.[66]

Wigfall was convinced that Davis was incompetent and that his influence should be diminished, giving a larger voice to the Senate and to the generals in the affairs of the Confederacy. On the last day of 1864 Johnston wrote to a fellow general that Wigfall was the only one who appeared to be disposed "to take such measures as are necessary to redeem our affairs." Unfortunately for the Confederacy, Wigfall's measures were ruinous to it. Not only did he help greatly to undermine confidence in the President when it was needed most, but he helped as well to delay arming the Negroes until it was too late to prolong the Confederacy. The extreme irony of the Civil War lay in the fact that the South was fighting for its freedom to maintain slavery, and by the end of 1864 it seemed that the only way it could achieve any freedom from the United States was to free and arm the slaves. Wigfall was the most determined of the relatively few southerners in 1864–65 who would not admit that Negroes were capable of soldiering, a profession which he revered.[67] His opposition to freeing the slaves to have them protect the Confederate

66 Wigfall to Johnston, February 27, 29, 1865, Johnston Papers; Johnston to Wigfall, March 14, 1865, Wigfall Papers; *cf.* Yearns, *Confederate Congress,* 227–28; Davis to Lee, July 12, 1864, *Official Records,* LII, Pt. 2, p. 692; Lee to Davis, July 12, 1864, Douglas Southall Freeman (ed.), *Lee's Dispatches: Unpublished Letters of General Robert E. Lee, C.S.A.* (New York, 1957), 284. Even as late as 1879, Reagan still believed, erroneously, that Lee and Beauregard had advised Davis to replace Johnston with Hood. See also John H. Reagan's Address at Memorial Services for General Hood at Houston, Texas, September 12, 1879, in Reagan Papers, III, Texas State Archives.
67 Johnston to Mackall, December 31, 1864, quoted in Govan and Livingood, *Johnston,* 337; *cf.* Albert Bushnell Hart, "Why the South was Defeated in the Civil War," in his *Practical Essays on American Government* (New York, 1893), 293–98; and Allan Nevins, *The Statesmanship of the Civil War* (New York, 1953), 50–56.

States is a good example of Wigfall's shortsightedness. Either he never realized that by 1864 or 1865 the only possible way to preserve the Confederacy was to arm the Negroes, or he would destroy the Confederacy and its citizens rather than free the slaves voluntarily.

Wigfall *was* correct when he characterized Davis as an ineffective revolutionary leader. Both men demonstrated a distinct lack of statesmanship. When the Confederacy needed unity and leadership, both men failed their "country." Although Davis lacked executive ability and diplomacy, he did at first have the confidence of most of his people and some influence over them. He could have been more effective as a leader, if only in the role of a unifying figurehead, had not Wigfall been so effective in destroying confidence in these two major assets that Davis possessed.

Mary Chesnut, in comments written on two days separated by the costly year of 1864, depicted the disappointment that many Confederates must have felt in Wigfall's "leadership" that year. In December, 1863, the diarist was still convinced that Wigfall had "strong common sense," but a year later she despaired, "Wigfall . . . , from whom we hoped so much, has only been destructive." [68]

[68] Chesnut, *Diary*, 329, 467.

Chapter IX

The Uncertainty
of the Times

THE DESTRUCTION was not yet complete. As March, 1865, began, about one more month remained for the Confederacy. For some time the Confederate States of America had been disintegrating, "dying at the extremities." [1] In the last few weeks of its existence the Confederate Congress alternated between petty wrangling and heroic, if pathetic, attempts to hold the southern states together in the face of onrushing enemies—Grant from the north and Sherman from the south. Deteriorating civilian and military morale reflected the failure of efforts at constructive legislation as well as the success of the efforts of Wigfall and other critics to destroy the influence of the President.

In March the Senate debates began with heated discussions of when the Congress should adjourn. Sherman was pushing into North Carolina with little resistance after having brought havoc to South Carolina. Lee's lines defending Richmond were stretched dangerously thin. Many Confederate congressmen were understandably eager to quit the capital. In response to calls for a quick adjournment Wigfall led a movement to keep his colleagues in session, to "stand by the ship, and let its fate be theirs." Adjournment, he declared, would be a misfortune only a little less serious than the loss of a battle. Nevertheless, a date was set.

1 Foreword to "Proceedings of Confederate Congress," 2nd Cong., 2nd Sess., LI, p. xi.

Wigfall and other proponents of an enduring session were able to keep the Congress in existence only until March 18. Even the persistent urging of Davis to hold the legislators together was ineffective.[2]

Wigfall was even more convinced than ever that all of Davis' efforts were ineffective. The troublesome senator introduced and secured Senate passage of a resolution to appoint a Senate committee to confer with the President "confidentially in reference to the present condition of the country, and ascertain, if possible, his plans and purposes." As Wigfall no doubt expected, the meeting was unproductive. Just as ineffective was the attempt by Congress to stir civilian morale by a public message which the Texan helped write.[3] The time for exhortation had passed for the Confederacy.

Congress and the President were poisoning civilian morale by persisting in their pettifogging constitutional squabbles as their country fell to pieces around them. Even as Sherman reached Fayetteville, North Carolina, on March 10, a presidential veto message claimed that a bill infringed upon executive prerogative by granting to commanding generals in the field a power of appointment not warranted by the constitution and the authority to make emergency promotions when vacancies occurred by virtue of death or capture of other officers. In the Senate, Wigfall successfully argued the constitutionality of the bill which was narrowly repassed by a vote of 11–5. But the House of Representatives sustained the veto. It was a similar story with a bill pertaining to quartermaster officers. A last ditch attempt by the administration supporters to renew authorization for the President to suspend the writ of habeas corpus passed the House but failed in the Senate, where Wigfall was this time strongly opposed—not in the interest of individual liberties but to keep

2 "Proceedings of Confederate Congress," 2nd Cong., 2nd Sess., LII, 412–13, 463–64, 472, 473, 484–85.

3 *Journal of Congress*, 2nd Cong., 2nd Sess., 633, 641, 652; "Proceedings of Confederate Congress," 2nd Cong., 2nd Sess., LI, p. xix. On March 4, Lincoln, who had been reelected on a platform which promised to quell the rebellion and extirpate slavery, was inaugurated for his second term.

Davis from having that power.[4] The habeas corpus issue was of considerable interest to Confederates even though they received the news about it at about the same time they got the news that Richmond had been evacuated and that Lee had surrendered.[5]

On its last day, March 18, the Senate had no quorum; it was as if the dying Congress and country were in a coma. But Wigfall was present, voting to override yet another veto, this one the bill to pay the army and navy the arrears owed them. He was with the 11–1 majority to override, but the vote was unofficial since there was no quorum. Even though there were so few present, Wigfall introduced bills to have printed for the use of the Senate the reports of Generals Johnston and Hood. After he gave an oral report to fasten the blame for the loss of Atlanta and other Confederate areas upon Davis, both bills were declared passed despite the lack of a quorum. If Wigfall was anything, he was a tenacious opponent. Significantly, the last Senate opposition was his successful motion to reconsider confirmation of a Davis appointee to the rank of brigadier general.[6]

The end of the Confederacy was near, but Wigfall could not admit it, probably not even to himself. To him it was a life or death struggle. On the last day of Congress, War Clerk Jones noted in his diary that Judge John A. Campbell had told him that Wigfall had sent the judge a copy of a Confederate representative's speech which looked forward to realliance with the United States. In an accompanying comment Wigfall indicated his conviction that such reconciliation would bring his execution at the hands of the Federal authorities.[7] Undoubtedly this strengthened his resolution to continue the struggle.

Even after Johnston's futile attempt to stop Sherman in cen-

4 "Proceedings of Confederate Congress," 2nd Cong., 2nd Sess., LII, 471–72, 474, 475, 485, 490, 491. In Mrs. Clay's words, Wigfall's "antagonism to President Davis had caused a profound concern . . . in this hour of the Confederacy's downfall." Clay-Clopton, *Belle of the Fifties*, 246.

5 Dallas *Herald*, March 23, April 20, 1865.

6 "Proceedings of Confederate Congress," 2nd Cong., 2nd Sess., LII, 740, 742; Johnston to Wigfall, March 14, 1865, September 24, 1868, Wigfall Papers; *Journal of Congress*, 2nd Cong., 2nd Sess., 743.

7 Jones, *Rebel War Clerk*, 452.

tral North Carolina—the day after Congress adjourned—Wigfall could not bear to see anyone quitting. A week after writing to Campbell and after Congress adjourned (and a week before Grant marched into Richmond), Wigfall, as if to demonstrate his lack of contact with reality, was trying to stem the tide of desertions from the Confederate armies. He wrote from western North Carolina, asking Colonel Chesnut to send the congressional debates of 1813 and 1814 which had information about how deserters were dealt with in the War of 1812. Chesnut was also to send a copy of the Confederate law dealing with civilians harboring deserters. Wigfall had already asked the provost marshal in the city of Charlotte to arrest two "malignants." The night before, Wigfall had summoned a party of neighbors and captured eight deserters and two civilians who had fed and sheltered them. Desertion from the army could not be stopped, he said, while the people encouraged it. He intended to make an example of some of them. About ten days later, on his way to Charlotte, Wigfall learned from Beauregard that Richmond had been evacuated on April 2.[8]

For all of their differences, the President and Wigfall had the same idea of what to do next; they each would make their way across the Mississippi and continue the fight with the armies they heard were intact there. In a speech at Greenville, North Carolina, Davis exhorted the soldiers there to join him, but according to one of them, they realized that it was a hopeless scheme, that the war was over. And when the soldiers had no more will to fight, the war *was* over. Wigfall also had difficulty finding anyone who would go with him. After touring western North Carolina and spending a week with friends in Abbeville, South Carolina, he left for the West with his family and General Hood. By this time he may have decided that the war would have to be carried on from Mexico, for Louly told Hood that they

8 Wigfall to Chesnut, March 26, 1865, Williams-Manning-Chesnut Collection; Varina Davis to her husband, April 7, 1865, quoted in Rowland, *Varina Davis*, 398–401.

were bound for the Rio Grande, aiming to shake hands with Emperor Maximilian of Mexico.[9]

Briefly the Wigfalls stopped in Washington, a little town in the heart of Georgia which was then the last Confederate stronghold east of the Mississippi. The town was filled with troops uncertain about their future and with looters providing for theirs. It was here in late April that Wigfall's mules were stolen, forcing him to return to Atlanta to look for more. When none could be found immediately, he was frantic with rage and disappointment. At about the same time, he received the news that Lee and Johnston had surrendered their armies (April 9 and 26 respectively).[10]

Even then Wigfall would not concede defeat. At LaGrange in western Georgia, the Wigfalls met with the C. C. Clays, Secretary of the Navy Mallory and his wife, and Senator Benjamin Hill and his wife at the Hill home. Clay agreed to join Wigfall in the attempt to reach Kirby Smith's army and continue the struggle, but they were uncertain of the best means of accomplishing this. As they laid plans, disturbing reports of the fate of others reached them daily. They were all concerned about the safety of the President, and according to Virginia Clay: "The magnanimity of Senator Wigfall . . . was especially marked." [11]

Clay and Wigfall were about ready to head west when Clay received word that the United States government was offering a $100,000 reward for his capture. Although Wigfall and other of Clay's friends urged him to flee, the ex-spy and ex-senator from Alabama decided not to "fly like an assassin" but gave himself

9 Clay-Clopton, *Belle of the Fifties*, 246; A. P. Austin, *The Blue and the Gray: Sketches of a Portion of the Unwritten History of the Great American Civil War* . . . (Atlanta, 1899), 174; see also Basil W. Duke, "Last Days of the Confederacy," in Johnson and Buell (eds.), *Battles and Leaders*, IV, 764–65; Varina Davis to her husband, April 19, 1865, quoted in Rowland, *Varina Davis*, 404–406; Chesnut, *Diary*, 519.

10 Eliza Frances Andrews, *The War-Time Journal of a Georgia Girl, 1864–1865*, edited by Spencer B. King (Macon, 1960), 198; see also Oldham, "Memoirs," 15, 25.

11 Clay-Clopton, *Belle of the Fifties*, 246–47.

up to nearby Federal authorities.¹² With this development and
with news of the capture of Davis, Wigfall decided that he would
have to disguise himself. He shaved off his beard and procured
a private's uniform and a blank parole which he filled out for
himself as "Private A. J. White" of the First Regiment of Texas
Volunteers, a paroled prisoner with "permission to go to his
home, and remain there undisturbed." ¹³

About a week later, on May 29, President Andrew Johnson
issued a proclamation of amnesty to most persons—primarily to
the common citizens and soldiers of the Confederacy—if they
would take an oath to support the United States Constitution,
the Union, and laws relating to emancipation. Wigfall was not
included in this amnesty, however, because of four, or possibly
five, of its provisions relating to U. S. Senators who became Confederates and to congressmen and officers of the Confederacy.¹⁴
But Clay and almost all others who were arrested were soon released without being prosecuted.

Somehow Wigfall obtained a covered wagon to carry the few
things that the family had left, four mules to pull the load, and
an escort of paroled Texas soldiers who were heading home. Wigfall walked with the soldiers. According to Louly, the caravan
excited no curiosity at all because the countryside was full of
such travelers. Confederate money was worthless, but a friend
had given the Wigfalls a large box of tobacco which was as good
as specie. Nearing Montgomery, the Wigfall party saw the first
Federal picket on their trip. It was then, said Louly, that she
felt a "suffocating sensation," that she realized it was all over.
Deciding that it would not be safe for them if he traveled far-

¹² Actually the reward for Clay was $25,000, but in most of the first proclama-
tions the amount was printed as $100,000. Clay was taken to Macon where he
joined Davis. *Ibid.*

¹³ In Wright, *Southern Girl*, 242–43. Wigfall obtained the blank parole papers
from Reagan, who got them from Major W. H. Martin, a Texan in command of
Hood's brigade. Reagan, *Memoirs*, 209.

¹⁴ James D. Richardson (ed.), *A Compilation of the Messages and Papers of the
Presidents, 1789–1902* (20 vols., New York, 1896–1907), VI, 310ff.

ther with the family, Wigfall left them in the care of friends in Alabama while he continued with the soldiers, walking all the way from Georgia to Texas.[15]

The Wigfall women were to stay near Montgomery until arrangements could be made to carry them to more suitable quarters. They waited also for further tidings from Halsey, who was also coming through Alabama on his way across the river to join Kirby Smith. It was not until Halsey reached his mother and sisters in Montgomery that they all learned that Kirby Smith had surrendered his army on June 2, 1865. The last major force of the Confederacy was gone. Wigfall found conditions in the Trans-Mississippi Confederacy so bad that he did not ask his family to join him there. They went instead to Baltimore, staying for several weeks, perhaps with Lydia Johnston and her family, before going to Providence, Rhode Island, to stay with Charlotte Wigfall's family.[16]

Wigfall knew that the situation in the West was not good; Kirby Smith had written him about it in February. For some time the western area had been showing signs of exhaustion even though it had not felt the ravages of invasion. Military authorities had impressed food and supplies and had conscripted men until the populace was greatly dissatisfied, and some regiments of soldiers were virtually unmanagable even before the defeat of the eastern part of the Confederacy. The army had practically disappeared before Kirby Smith "surrendered" it. When responsible authorities abdicated, lawlessness increased.[17]

Despite these conditions there were some Texans who wanted to continue the fight from Mexico. It was at Wigfall's home in Marshall, which had been used as a headquarters for Kirby Smith during the latter part of the war, that a group of Confed-

---

[15] Wright, *Southern Girl*, 243–45.

[16] *Ibid.*, 245; Johnston to Wigfall, June 1, 1866, Wigfall Papers.

[17] Kirby Smith to Wigfall, February 11, 1865, *Official Records*, XLVIII, Pt. 1, p. 1384. One stagecoach was said to have been held up on an average of once every five miles on the road from the Rio Grande to San Antonio. Ramsdell, *Reconstruction in Texas*, 33–34.

erate generals met on May 13 and laid plans to continue the war from Mexico under Kirby Smith. The plan fell through when Kirby Smith wisely refused to head the expedition. Soon after, the army was disbanding and many of the military and civil leaders of Texas fled to Mexico simply to escape.[18]

A number of the Confederates who were not covered by Johnson's amnesty proclamation departed because of wild rumors of dire punishments to be inflicted upon them by the victorious Federals. Wigfall went into hiding. Davis, Reagan, Judge Campbell, and others had been arrested, including all those men who had met with Wigfall in Georgia—Clay, Hill, and Mallory. The only one who would be imprisoned for any length of time was Davis, but this was not known by Wigfall in the fearful days immediately following the conclusion of the war. He probably recalled his mid-March letter to Judge Campbell about executions, and as Wigfall reflected upon the situation, Campbell was imprisoned. Furthermore, Wigfall's venomous diatribes as a United States senator may have come back to haunt him four years after they were uttered. Perhaps he remembered such speeches as that of February 7, 1861, in which he taunted the North about the unanimity of southern white support of slavery; in the summer of 1865 it may have sounded like a prophecy about to be fulfilled: "When the day comes that four and a half million Africans are turned loose . . . the slaveholders will have the means . . . and the inclination to leave the country." Those who remained would have to "contest the palm" with the ex-slaves. And perhaps it would have been easier for Wigfall to remain had not Andrew Johnson been President of the United States. After all, Wigfall had called the Tennessean a traitor and

<hr>

18 Alexander W. Terrell, *From Texas to Mexico & the Court of Maximilian in 1865* (Dallas, 1933), 3; Carl Coke Rister, "Carlotta, A Confederate Colony in Mexico," *Journal of Southern History*, XI (February, 1945), 33–50. In Mexico the expatriates obtained from Emperor Maximilian the permission to establish the "Confederate" colony of Carlotta, but it was only a settlement, not a base from which to attack the United States. Rister, "Carlotta"; see also Andrew F. Rolle, *The Lost Cause: The Confederate Exodus to Mexico* (Norman, Oklahoma, 1965).

worse. Also, economic conditions were generally bad throughout the South. There was little that the Texan could do in response to his brother's pitiful plea from South Carolina for economic aid.[19] Louis Wigfall was undoubtedly trying to get some money himself to leave the country.

There was little communication between Wigfall and his family during the years immediately after the collapse of the Confederacy; therefore almost no record exists to indicate what he was doing. He evidently remained hidden in Texas, continually fearing capture and prison. Despite public pleas from friends such as Wade Hampton, who said that southern men who left the South when it was in such a deplorable condition were in effect deserting their comrades under fire,[20] Wigfall left the United States, probably in March, 1866. He arrived in England a month later. In July he was joined by the rest of his family.[21]

Despite his dislike for business, his first problem was to find a way to make a living; his visits with Beauregard and other expatriated Confederates were more than just social calls; they were his first contacts in seeking a remunerative position. Before he left the states, Wigfall already had a "commercial scheme" in mind, probably a plan to market southern cotton in England. As usual, however, he was not enthusiastic about business matters. In his first letter from England to General Johnston, he did not even mention any economic plans. By October he had entered into an agreement with "an English house of large capital" with offices in Mobile and New Orleans. Wigfall was to receive one-half of any profits which would accrue from the sale or shipment of produce which would be placed under their control by his influence. Halsey went back to the United States to try to

19 Ramsdell, *Reconstruction in Texas*, 39; *Congressional Globe*, 36th Cong., 2nd Sess., 788; Arthur Wigfall to Louis Wigfall, August 15, 1865, Wigfall Papers.

20 J. H. Watts to Charlotte Wigfall, March 5, 1866, Wigfall Papers; Columbia, South Carolina, *Phoenix* (no date), in *Texas-Republican*, October 6, 1865.

21 J. A. Bryant to Wigfall (in London), May 1, 1866, Wigfall Papers; Dallas *Herald*, May 26, 1866. The *Herald* was mistaken in stating that Charlotte Wigfall left with her husband. Johnston to Wigfall, June 1, July 26, 1866; Charlotte Wigfall to Halsey, July 25, 1867, Wigfall Papers.

make deals with southern planters for them to sell their cotton through him and his father. Not too subtly Wigfall appealed to his friend Clay to see what he could do to help. It all depended on his friends, said Wigfall; if that failed, he would have to see what he could do with his pen in the newspaper and journals. Three months earlier the Dallas *Herald* urged Wigfall to write his account of the war. He was constantly urging Johnston to put into book form his side of the argument with Davis. Those avenues were difficult to open, Wigfall realized, but he said he thought that one who was willing to work would not starve.[22]

The law profession was another avenue not immediately open to Wigfall. He investigated that possibility and lamented that it would take three years of study to be admitted to the English bar. This had not been the case for Judah P. Benjamin, the Texan reported bitterly to Clay. Benjamin, whom he had hated as Davis' closest adviser in the Confederacy, had come out of the war with some money. Enough, said Wigfall, to entertain the right friends at expensive clubs and win admittance to the bar after only six months. He charged that Benjamin had managed to accumulate about two-hundred bales of cotton at Liverpool during the war, drawing his money from that after he arrived, as well as taking from £300 to £400 from Confederate agents. Further, upon his arrival, Benjamin claimed to be authorized by Davis to take over the financial matters of the Confederacy. It was Wigfall's belief that Benjamin and his agents in England divided all the money among themselves. He may have come to this conclusion because of an English newspaper account of Benjamin's activity which alleged that he "was sharp enough to get three or four thousand pounds, which he claimed as unpaid salary." The same paper expressed sympathy for "Poor Wigfall" and his family; it was reported by Wigfall's friends, said the journal, that he was looking "very dejected, seedy, and disappointed

22 Dallas *Herald*, July 21, 1866; Beauregard to Wigfall, June 1, 1866; also Charlotte Wigfall to Halsey, March 17, 1868; and Johnston to Wigfall, June 1, 1866, all in Wigfall Papers. Johnston was already successful as a president of a Baltimore freight company.

. . . a little of the plunder should have been saved for these un-
fortunates, for it was known that they were coming." [23]

According to his letter to Clay, Wigfall would have nothing
of a personal nature to trouble him if he were only sure of economic support. Charlotte Wigfall worried a great deal about
that, but she had another major grievance. Although she acknowledged the probable wisdom of Halsey's counsel—after he
had returned to the South—that his family should be glad they
were not there, Charlotte thought it sad to live away from one's
own people. Frequent visits and correspondence with other Confederate expatriates helped but little. Even a pleasant visit from
Johnston, who was on his way to Scotland on business, served
only to make the homesickness more poignant after he left. It
is certain that while Johnston was there, Wigfall talked with him
about the book the general was writing to present his military
operations in their "true light." The senator was pleased that the
book was being written and to contribute to it as well, since it
would present his as well as Johnston's anti-Davis arguments.[24]

Johnston was doing well, but some of their Confederate
friends were even worse off than the Wigfalls. One was so down
and out that the old senator gave his only heavy coat to him and
was to "assist him in his money matters." It is difficult to see how
Wigfall could have given anyone else any financial help; he had
almost no income himself. Though "more dissatisfied than usual" in the autumn of 1866, the Wigfalls were nevertheless hopeful, not only for Halsey's enterprise as he left for New Orleans
in October, but also for a bond scheme that Wigfall was trying

[23] Wigfall to Clay, October 17, 1866, Clay Papers; undated clipping sent to Wigfall by a Mrs. Bristow; and Charlotte Wigfall to Halsey, November 23, 1866, both
in Wigfall Papers. Benjamin's biographer noted the charge that Wigfall made in
his letter to Clay but makes no denial or affirmation of it. See Meade, *Benjamin*,
242–43.

[24] Wigfall to Clay, October 17, 1866, Clay Papers; Charlotte Wigfall to Halsey,
June 25, 1867; J. A. Bryant to Wigfall, May 1, 1866; Beauregard to Wigfall, June
1, 1866; W. M. Gavin to Wigfall, September 4, 1866; Louly to Halsey, July 29,
1868; and Johnston to Wigfall, June 1, July 26, November 24, 1866, January 27,
September 24, 29, 30, 1868, all in Wigfall Papers. Johnstons book, *Narrative of
Military Operations* . . . , was originally published in 1874 and has been cited
previously.

to develop. At one time after the war, he entertained some hope of collecting on the Confederate bonds he held. When that fell through, he talked some of his fellow expatriates into bringing suit to collect their bonds, hoping to obtain some legal fees for preparing their cases for them. Also, there was still hope that the Wigfalls could collect on some of the stock they held for some time in a Texas railroad.[25]

Until these plans came to fruition, the family's social life was austere. Dinner out and a Rossini opera were extremely rare treats. Once the "old General" took little Fanny out to lunch and a play in style, going in an elaborate carriage and sitting in a comfortable box, but the Wigfalls' usual amusements were taking walks and reading.[26]

The Texan seemed perpetually optimistic, but his wife became less and less so. There was a hollow ring to the many reports she sent to Halsey; "If your father's expectations work out . . . "; "When our ship comes in . . ."; and "[Your father] is strongly in hopes of concluding an arrangement . . . ." In June, 1867, Wigfall was excited about prospects for "very large profits" in a Texas railroad deal which never became a reality. By spring of the next year his wife had grown cynical about money matters, reporting to Halsey, "Your father is . . . trying to complete some Spanish business which he fancies will be a great success." But she confessed that her faith was gone. Nevertheless, Wigfall still expressed confidence. Charlotte wrote her son, "Your father's schemes may end in nothing, but he is very confident of being able to carry them out." [27]

Wigfall was as out of touch with reality as ever. As did the rest of his plans, the cotton-buying deal failed. Halsey had arrived in

25 Johnston to Wigfall, October 30, 1866; Louly to Halsey, October 30, 1866; and Charlotte Wigfall to Halsey, November 23, December 12, 1866, all in Wigfall Papers; Wigfall to Clay, October 17, 1866, Clay Papers.

26 Louly to Halsey, October 30, November 23, 1866, Wigfall Papers. Wigfall subscribed to a lending library for six months with four books at a time! Fanny Wigfall to Halsey, January 11, 1867, *ibid.*

27 Charlotte Wigfall to Halsey, January 1, March 17, May 30, June 1, 1867, October 13, 1869; Wigfall to Halsey, June 18, 1867, *ibid.*

the South after most of the cotton had already been consigned. After six months in the states, he rejoined his family in London to look for employment. When the search proved fruitless, he returned to New Orleans where he took a position with an insurance company.[28]

Wigfall did not even earn enough to provide for his family and had to draw from his son Halsey and his wife's mother in the United States. By the fall of 1869, all of the Wigfall's sources had failed and they were heavily in debt. They could realize no profit or income from the little land they had in Texas; it was even difficult for them to keep the taxes paid on it so that it would not be forfeited. As Charlotte Wigfall put it, it was hard work for them to keep their heads above water.[29]

Pending culmination of one of his deals, Wigfall took odd jobs. As close as he could get to practicing his profession was doing legal legwork, looking up legislation and documents for law firms. Anxiety took its toll upon his wife who worried herself into a severe nervous condition. Perhaps that is why, in the summer of 1870, she and her daughters Louly and Fanny moved to Baltimore to stay with her mother, who had gone there from Rhode Island after the war.[30]

Wigfall did not share his family's nostalgia even though his problems were compounded by his having developed a severe case of gout in 1870. And although all exemptions from the amnesty had been removed some two years earlier and Wigfall could receive pardon without taking the oath, he continued to register only disgust and dismay over the developments in the United States. Soon after his arrival in London, he had written to Clay for his judgment of the situation. The Texan was pessimistic. He supposed, correctly, that the Radical Republicans had

---

[28] Charlotte Wigfall to Halsey, February 6, May 17, 1867, June 1, 1868; Wigfall to Halsey, January 23, 1867; Louly to Halsey, October 25, [1867]; *ibid.*

[29] Charlotte Wigfall to Halsey, January 1, November 24, 1867, October 13, 1869, *ibid.*

[30] Charlotte Wigfall to Halsey, November 24, 1867, *ibid.; cf.* Dallas *Herald*, November 16, 1867; Mrs. Cross (Wigfall's mother-in-law) to Charlotte Wigfall, November 11, 1870; and Louly to Halsey, August 27, November 6, 1871, all in Wigfall Papers.

carried the congressional elections of 1866 and that this meant harsher times for the South. Even more upsetting to him, it seemed, were reports that "the ill feeling on the part of the South [had] actually abated." He doubted that this could be true and asked Clay to write and tell him everything about their "poor, oppressed & downtrodden Country." [31]

The next year he asked Wade Hampton for the same report. The South Carolinian's reply was a dirge, as if he were informing Wigfall that a loved one were dead: "We have no country . . . ," life itself was being squeezed out of "our poor unfortunate people." The aristocratic Hampton saw nothing in the future of the South but anarchy and ruin. The recent Reconstruction Acts by the Radicals in Congress were the most atrocious outrage ever perpetrated, said Hampton; the acts disfranchised most of the whites and gave "all the Negroes the right to vote." The Carolinian could not give Wigfall even a glimmer of hope. Prospects were no better at the beginning of the next year when Johnston wrote "in the vein of the old song that began: 'Let's all be melancholy together.' " [32]

Grant's victory in the presidential election made Wigfall even more despondent. He had hoped that the Democrats would carry the northern states, that the Radicals would attempt to override Democratic victory in the North with Negro votes in the South, then the Democrats would resist the inauguration of the radical President on the grounds that they still had "a white man's government," and thus the election could be settled by the bayonet instead of the ballot. Wigfall feared, however, that even if the northern Democrats and Republicans were at one another's throats, the Negro "element" would make it almost impossible for the South to do anything. Believing in his own previous warnings, he had the impression that the southern whites were being watched over by armed Negroes and was afraid that any move-

31 Wigfall to Clay, October 17, 1866, Clay Papers.
32 Hampton to Wigfall, May 19, 1867; Johnston to Wigfall, January 27, 1868; an equally bleak analysis came from Halsey in a letter to his mother, July 25, 1867, Wigfall Papers.

ment on the part of the whites would lead to a war between the races in which the unarmed whites would be helpless. The major hope which Wigfall saw for a revival of the Confederacy was for the United States to "drift into a war" with some nation strong enough to open the South's ports and wealthy enough to supply rebels with arms and other accoutrements of war, a nation which would lend a body of troops strong enough to hold the country until the people could rise and organize another blow for independence. In Wigfall's warped judgment this would be advisable and might be successful. Even then, said Wigfall, he feared there would be divisions among southerners, especially among the leaders; Lee and Longstreet might even fight for the United States. And what would be the course of Hampton and others who had taken the oath of allegiance to the United States? (Wigfall said he would hate to have that oath on his conscience.) Impatiently he would bide his time. If an occasion came "to strike for liberty & independence," Wigfall vowed, "I shall feel it my duty to return to my own country without calculating the chances of success . . . & share the fate of the good men & true who . . . determine the day & the hour for the struggle." [33]

Great Britain was undoubtedly Wigfall's choice as to which nation he would like to have seen go to war with the United States. As he was writing, there was a serious controversy between the two countries over the Alabama claims (by the United States for damages done to shipping by commerce raiders built in England for the Confederacy), the desire of some in the United States to annex Canada, boundary and fishing disputes, and the Fenian raids. This time there seemed to be nothing that Wigfall could do to incite a war. He was investigated at least once by English authorities who suspected him of being a member of the Fenians, a society of Irish-Americans "hateful to Great Britain" and working for the independence of Ireland, but no charges were brought against him. Indignantly protesting, Wigfall convinced Benjamin Moran, the American chargé d'affaires in England, that he

[33] Wigfall to Halsey, September 20, 1868, *ibid.*

had been a Tory all of his life and was innocent of Fenianism. Altogether, said Moran of Wigfall, "I like the *man*, although he is no doubt very unscrupulous." The Texan quickly verified this assessment to Moran's satisfaction by entering into what Moran described as a conspiracy against the United States. Talking "treason . . . by the hour," working "daily in the city . . . to destroy [United States] credit," Wigfall and other rebels fostered the growth of a "very bad spirit" against the United States.[34] But his efforts to help provoke war between the United States and Great Britain were fruitless. The two countries settled their differences peaceably by the Treaty of Washington (1871).

Wigfall decided to go back to the United States anyway, to go into gold mining. The Wigfall women had already left. He had planned to join them in Baltimore soon after. But first he would finalize negotiations with some people in London about a gold mine in Colorado. These negotiations had started more than two years earlier, and Wigfall felt they were worth the time and trouble, for if they succeeded he would have "a large interest in a very valuable property." To facilitate matters, Halsey made a trip to the Rocky Mountain state and then joined his father in London. Wigfall planned to move with his family to Colorado (except Louly, who was soon to be married to a Baltimore man) as soon as the deal for the mine was closed. Charlotte Wigfall expected her husband to arrive in August, 1871, but the negotiations were drawn out and she had to borrow more money from her mother for him and Halsey to pay their expenses. This went on for over four more months, with Wigfall missing Louly's wedding and Christmas with his family. All the while, the ex-senator was evidently impatient to move his family to Colorado, but Charlotte termed this impractical. Citing the "uncertainty of the times," the getting there, and then the possibility of having the venture not come to fruition, she counseled her husband

34 Samuel Flagg Bemis, *A Diplomatic History of the United States* (4th ed., New York, 1955), 103, 223, 291, 378–79, 380, 382, 406, 407, 408, 409; "Journal of Benjamin Moran," January 31, February 5, 1868, in Sarah A. Wallace (ed.), "Confederate Exiles in London, 1865–1870: The Wigfalls," *South Carolina Historical and Genealogical Magazine* (April and July, 1951), 86–87, 148–49.

to get a final commitment first. Hers was the wiser course; typically, the gold mine deal fell through in London.[35]

Due largely to the efforts of his wife, Wigfall, who was evidently ill, had a home to come to when he arrived in Baltimore in 1872. Charlotte had sold a small portion of land for more money than they had expected to obtain for it and bought a comfortable home in Baltimore. The Wigfall family was finally back together for the first time for any lengthy period since the war had begun eleven years earlier (Louly, then Mrs. C. Giraud Wright, lived only a few blocks away). They remained in Baltimore for about two years, but in January, 1874, the senior Wigfalls moved to Texas, where he planned to open a law office. He was evidently well received there by many and was almost immediately asked to address the Southern Historical Association when it met in Dallas the next month. But Wigfall had been ill from the time of his return to Texas; he died quietly in Galveston from some undisclosed cause on February 18, 1874, at the age of fifty-seven.[36]

Wigfall had his mourners. The Johnstons had "dearly loved" their "true faithful friend." He had been the friend not only of the Johnstons but also of the Clays and a number of other generals and politicians. And among the later generations of Texans who prefer to face backwards Wigfall might still be considered a patrician hero.[37] They can point to his 1859 proposal for a pro-

[35] Louly to Halsey, June 7, 1869, August 27, 1871, Wigfall Papers. Halsey married while in London at this time. *Ibid.*, April 15, 1871; Charlotte Wigfall to her husband, September 1, 21, 27, November 6, 1871; Charlotte Wigfall to Halsey, October 6, 1871; and Louly to Halsey, October 18, November 6, December 24, 1871, all in Wigfall Papers.

[36] Charlotte Wigfall to her husband, September 1, 1871; and Louly to Halsey, October 18, 1871, both in *ibid*; Galveston *News*, February 19, 1874; Dallas *Weekly Herald*, February 7, 1874; other death notices in Dallas *Herald*, February 28, 1874, Houston *Mercury*, February 20, 1874, Austin *Daily Statesman*, March 10, 25, 1874, Charleston *News and Courier*, February 23, 1874. Wigfall was buried in Episcopal Cemetery in Galveston.

[37] Lydia Johnston to Louly, April 27, 1874, Wigfall Papers; Kittrell, *Governors Who Have Been, and Other Public Men of Texas*, 150; Joe B. Frantz, Presidential Address delivered at the 45th Annual Meeting, Southwestern Social Science Association, Dallas, Texas, March 27, 1964, in the *Southwestern Social Science Quarterly*, XLV (June, 1964), 14.

gressive university, his determined stand against nationalism and democracy, his role in the secession movement, as well as his sense of strategy and his staff and cabinet plans to improve the military and governmental efficiency of the Confederacy.

The fact of the matter is, however, that Wigfall was as ruinous to the Confederate States as he had been fractious to the United States. The significance of his actions can be appreciated only if one realizes that the defeat of the Confederacy was not inevitable. It was not simply a matter of the southerners' being overpowered by sheer numbers. The northern population outnumbered the Confederate by 2 to 1, but southerners had an offsetting advantage in being on the defensive. The Federals had to conquer the South in order to win, and the ratio was not favorable for attacking armies. Furthermore, the Confederacy was able to put as many troops into battle as the Union did until 1864.[38] It was not just a lack of transportation; it has been argued that the South had adequate transportation facilities. At any rate, the Confederacy failed to make use of what it had.[39] Defeat did not stem from the fact that the South was blockaded, or that it lacked a centralized government, money, and manufacturing; under similar conditions the United States had won its independence from Great Britain.[40] In the American Revolution, however, the Americans were able to maintain something which made up for their disadvantages. They had spirit, a will to win. The people of the Confederacy lost that essential factor.

The Civil War was so nearly a total war that it required high civilian morale as well as high soldier morale; civilian resistance was as important as military resistance. The South, however, suffered a thorough demoralization of its armies and the people,

[38] Implicit in the major interpretations of the causes of the defeat of the Confederacy is the belief that its fall was not a foregone conclusion. Wigfall's role should not be overemphasized, however, for explicit in these studies is the fact that causation is plural and complex, not singular and simple. Commager, *The Defeat of the Confederacy*, 10, 12.
[39] Black, *Railroads of the Confederacy*, 294.
[40] Commager, *The Defeat of the Confederacy*, 10.

leading to what Edward A. Pollard, a Confederate newspaper editor, described as "a general decay of public spirit."[41] This will to continue was lost for three major reasons. One was the lack of a just cause, a factor with which Wigfall had little to do except argue vehemently that it *was* just. The others were internal dissension and the government's apparent disregard for individual liberties and suffering, factors to which Wigfall contributed greatly.

The Confederacy, the only important government in Christendom which had not abolished nor was in the process of abolishing slavery, carried within itself the seeds of its own destruction. Allan Nevins has cogently argued that Confederate leaders could not, when fighting to perpetuate slavery, display the "moral earnestness" of a George Washington or of other leaders fighting for liberty. Significantly, although Wigfall liked to compare the Confederate cause to that of the United States in 1776, he often rejected the founding fathers as models worthy of imitation. In particular he belittled George Washington, speaking of him as "the mother of his country" and deprecating his sense of justice.[42]

Nevertheless, Confederate leaders could have used some of Washington's ability to inspire and *sustain* dedication to a cause. The appeals by Wigfall and other southern leaders for individual sacrifice to perpetuate states' rights and slavery were not strong enough to overcome the northern devotion to union and democracy. Neither were their exhortations strong enough to counteract the decay of southern will because of obnoxious laws and quarreling among leaders.

In his study of the failure of southern leadership, Bell I. Wiley cites the following factors—along with "the tremendous decline of public morale": the loss of confidence in leadership, the breach between Davis and Congress, and legislation deeply obnoxious to the people, such as the laws providing for conscrip-

---

41 Vandiver, *Rebel Brass*, 18; Edward A. Pollard, *The Lost Cause* (New York, 1866), 726–27.
42 Nevins, *Statesmanship of the Civil War*, 50–51; Chesnut, *Diary*, 347.

tion and the suspension of habeas corpus.[43] Wigfall's role in each factor is clear. His bills for conscription, confiscation, and impressment might be termed necessary evils; such "obnoxious" legislation is not unusual in war and was perhaps necessary to the Confederacy. But it was made unnecessarily obnoxious by its authoritarian implementation as sanctioned and urged by Wigfall. He seemed to have no concept of the necessity for explaining such laws to the people or that the administration of legislation should be tempered by mercy and justice. By urging harsh application of the impressment laws to provide goods for the armies, Wigfall helped destroy the morale of the people and of the armies. As General Johnston described their actions, the impressment officials often preyed upon the most defenseless of the citizens, especially farm women whose husbands were in the army. As those women then found it increasingly difficult to provide for themselves and their families, they sent distress notices to their husbands. The married soldiers had to choose between their military service and the strongest obligation they knew—their duty to their wives and children. Many of the soldiers deserted to go home.[44] Johnston and other generals named desertion as the chief cause of military failure. Thus Wigfall's intensive efforts to enlarge the southern armies helped instead to deplete their ranks.

Certainly a rebel government must be greatly concerned with military affairs. But Wigfall was so much so that he neglected other areas with which he should have been involved. He was a member of the Senate Foreign Affairs Committee as well as the Military Affairs Committee, but, significantly, he was so pre-

43 Wiley, *Road to Appomattox,* 121; see also Eaton, *A History of the Southern Confederacy,* 261; and Duke, "Last Days of the Confederacy," in Johnson and Buell (eds.), *Battles and Leaders,* IV, 762–67.

44 Johnston, *Narrative of Military Operations,* 423–24; see also Richard N. Current, "Why the North Won the Civil War: Economic Considerations," in Donald, *Why the North Won the Civil War; Essays . . . .* A state study which demonstrates the demoralizing effects of Wigfall's policies and other factors is Bessie Martin, *Desertion of Alabama Troops from the Confederate Army . . .* (New York, 1932), 76–97, 121–23, 147–53, 156, 257–58; Johnston, *Narrative of Military Operations,* 421–29.

occupied with military matters that he virtually ignored foreign affairs.

Wigfall's strong military views intensified internal dissension, the third factor which subverted southerners' spirit. There were several contributing controversies, such as Wigfall's drinking, the "women's war," and the way the President treated Johnston, but the basic disagreement between Davis and the Texan was over military policy and strategy. Davis was perhaps as good an executive as the South could have had, considering the men available. But he was not good enough. He was petty, inflexible, unimaginative, and he quarreled and meddled with governors, cabinet members, generals, and Congress. Wigfall was the more astute strategist, but he was just as inflexible and quarrelsome as his President.

There were other Confederate congressmen, such as Henry S. Foote, who harbored as deep and abiding a hatred for Davis as Wigfall did. But no one else was as determined, as systematic, and as effective in undermining confidence in the President. Bell Wiley has said that perhaps the most costly of the Confederacy's shortcomings was its disharmony, which became so intense that it sapped the South's vitality.[45] This valid analysis helps to put Wigfall's role into perspective. With the possible exception of Jefferson Davis himself, there was no greater contributor to this disastrous internal dissension than Louis Wigfall.

Wiley and other analysts of southern history have suggested several reasons why Confederates were so contentious. One is the exaggerated individualism which the southern way of life had nurtured. By law and custom each member of the planter class had been a petty dictator.[46] Wigfall was of this class, except from the standpoint of owning a large number of slaves. Perhaps his lack of wealth is the reason that he seized so many opportunities to insist that he was of the aristocracy. As early as the 1830's he was jealous of the elite's power and money, such as that displayed by his friend John Manning. Wigfall may have thought of him-

45 Wiley, *Road to Appomattox,* 78.
46 *Ibid.,* 99–101.

self as an outsider trying to obtain admission into the planter class by championing vehemently their mores and subscribing even more strongly than they to their outdated code of chivalry. Thus, his aristocratic ideals and his hypersensitivity to honor may have been in part a matter of overcompensation.

Another possible reason for Confederate contentiousness was habit, developed during the extensive controversy with northerners over slavery and states' rights. After secession removed the abolitionists as a direct source of contention, Confederates, "from long addiction to controversy, turned on each other." [47] Wigfall did seem always to need an object for his hostility.

But this begs the question of primary motivation. Consideration of Wigfall's psychological makeup offers an intriguing possible key to the understanding of why he acted as he did. He may have suffered from paranoia, a major psychosis characterized by suspiciousness and a well-established system of delusions which do not vary and would be perfectly logical, were the initial psychopathological concepts correct. In Wigfall's case the initial concepts would be slavery, states' rights, and the belief in a northern conspiracy to destroy the South. Paranoiacs lack the bizarre behavior, failing emotional stability, grotesque hallucinations, and aberrant ideas of other psychopathological states. But their conduct is usually ignominious and self-aggrandizing, and many are able to maintain only superficial economic and social adjustments, as Wigfall barely managed to do.[48]

Many of Wigfall's characteristics fit generally recognized symptoms of clinical paranoia, and he is certainly a "spokesman of the paranoid style" as the term is defined by Richard Hofstadter in his valuable study, *The Paranoid Style in American Politics.* Wigfall tended to be "overheated, oversuspicious, overaggressive,

47 *Ibid.*, 101–102.

48 Sigmund Freud. *A General Introduction to Psycho-Analysis* . . . (New York, 1935), 367–68; Ernest Jones, *The Life and Work of Sigmund Freud* (2 vols., New York, 1955), II, 270, 449–50; Roland Dalbiez, *Psychoanalytical Method and the Doctrine of Freud* (2 vols., New York, 1941), I, 350–51; C. G. Jung, *Freud and Psychoanalysis,* translated by R. F. C. Hull, vol. IV of C. G. Jung, *Collected Works,* edited by Michael Fordham, and others (20 vols., New York, 1961).

grandiose, and apocalyptic in expression" and felt that a hostile and conspiratorial world threatened his section and his way of life. Further, his conviction that his political passions were unselfish and patriotic went far to intensify "his feeling of righteousness and his moral indignation." [49]

The defense mechanism of projection is strongly prominent in paranoia. Wigfall often attributed to others his faults and desires. An example of this is the charge of "rule or ruin" which he leveled at Douglas Democrats in 1860. This projection may work in reverse. One paradox of paranoid behavior is "imitation of the enemy." [50] Fear of conspiracy is central in paranoia and was present in much of Wigfall's thinking, but he obviously found great enjoyment in conspiring—when he was secretly editing the Edgefield *Advertiser* and helping to overturn a ruling clique in South Carolina; when he was spying, treasonously recruiting Confederate troops, and buying guns while a United States Senator; when he was plotting to depose or at least to subjugate President Davis; and during Reconstruction when he was trying to help goad England into a war with the United States.

There is no denying that there are conspiracies in history, and there is nothing paranoid in detecting these. Nor is there any denying that Wigfall and others of his section were harmed by the protective tariff, or that abolitionism threatened millions of dollars worth of slave property, and that the Southwest lacked adequate federal protection of its frontiers. But Wigfall took that "leap into fantasy" so characteristic of paranoia, the delusion of persecution.[51] Not only abolitionism, but even the northern farmers' desire for a homestead bill was seen by Wigfall as a part of a plot to overthrow southern civilization.

In typical paranoid fashion Wigfall saw the culmination of this conspiracy in apocalyptic terms—a terrible war. Since a paranoid is a militant leader and as he is capable of perceiving the

49 Richard Hofstadter, *The Paranoid Style in American Politics and Other Essays* (New York, 1965), 3–40.
50 *Ibid.*, 32–34; see also Ernest Jones, *Life and Work of Sigmund Freud*, II, 271.
51 Hofstadter, *Paranoid Style*, 4, 11–23, 37; see also Freud, *Psycho-Analysis*, 367–69.

"conspiracy" before it is fully obvious to an unaroused public, he feels it is his duty to awaken them. For seventeen years before the war broke out, Wigfall's mission was, as he told Calhoun, to alert southerners to the impending dangers. When he had the opportunity, he also warned northern "transgressors" of the terrible consequences of their actions. It was almost a religion with him. Richard Hofstadter might have been describing Wigfall's apocalyptic warnings which aroused "passion and militancy" and were similar to themes in Christianity: "Properly expressed, such warnings serve somewhat the same function as a description of the horrible consequences of sin in a revivalist sermon: they portray that which impends but which may still be avoided." [52] Wigfall told the northern senators what must be done if they and the Union were not to be destroyed—they must abolish the abolition societies and pass constitutional amendments protecting slavery in the territories. But he was sure they would not do it; the battle of Armegeddon would come and the forces of good would triumph.

Typical of the paranoid spokesman, Wigfall would listen to no counterarguments that would weaken his sense of righteousness. He was thus protected from having "to attend to disturbing considerations" that did not fortify his ideas. Wigfall actually knew little about northern people. He had, when he married, made a brief trip to Rhode Island; otherwise he knew little about the North. And he was unwilling to learn. Characteristic of the paranoiac, Wigfall blocked incoming communication from the world outside his group—especially from those who doubted his views.[53]

A related aspect of the paranoid style is an inclination for pedantry. Some of Wigfall's rationalistic speeches on abolitionism and states' rights, as well as the fantastic conclusion that the national legislature was divided into three departments (House, Senate, and President), are representative of the specious reasoning of the paranoiac.[54]

[52] Hofstadter, *Paranoid Style*, 30–31.
[53] See *ibid.*, 37–38.
[54] *Ibid.*, 35–36, 37–39.

Wigfall's reaction to what he felt was persecution of southerners by New Englanders, especially by Massachusetts abolitionists, was thus nothing less than psychopathological. The "persecuted" paranoiac is forever dedicated to aggressiveness, to the overpowering of his enemies, and to the ultimate achievement of history-making masculinity. Thus is described the violent, self-aggrandizing Wigfall.[55] To him, sectional persecution provoked the Civil War. There was no doubt in his mind of the justness of the southern cause.

But why had the South failed in its "just cause"? Interestingly, Wigfall said little to answer that question other than his memoranda contributed to Johnston's *Narrative of Military Operations* and several articles in *Century Magazine*, which took specific issue with Davis' policies. Davis acknowledged Wigfall's contributions to Johnston's publications and denied their validity.[56] In his two-volume *The Rise and Fall of the Confederate Government*, Davis said little about Wigfall directly but blamed the administration's political opponents in general for the loss of the war, and Wigfall was the most destructive of these opponents.

Yancey, often considered one of the most obstinate of the fire-eaters, was constructive when compared to Wigfall. The Alabamian evidently had no more confidence in Davis than did Wigfall but was aware that a crew which hated its captain should not be mad enough to mutiny while a storm was raging, for then all hands and the ship were bound to go to the bottom. Despite warnings from Yancey and others, Wigfall probably never real-

55 Wigfall had reacted similarly to earlier problems. At risk of life and limb, and at considerable social and financial costs, Wigfall tried to overrun the Brooks family which he felt was persecuting him. The danger of indiscriminate usage of psychoanalysis has often been pointed out. Barbara Tuchman in "Can History Use Freud? The Case of Woodrow Wilson," *Atlantic Monthly*, CCXIX (February, 1967), 39–44, is critical of the famous doctor's use of psychoanalysis in the book, *Thomas Woodrow Wilson . . . , A Psychological Study* (New York, 1966), which Freud co-authored with former Ambassador William C. Bullitt. According to Tuchman, they analyzed the nature of Wilson's neuroses brilliantly and convincingly but were addicted to the *oversimplified single* explanation of great events. See also Jung, *Freud and Psychoanalysis*, IV, VI; and Andrew Salter, *The Case Against Psychoanalysis* (New York, 1963).

56 L. B. North to Davis, September 11, 1885, Louisiana Historical Association Collection, Jefferson Davis Collection, Tulane University Library, New Orleans, Louisiana.

ized the destructiveness of his course.[57] Purposefully, systematic-
ally, almost diabolically, he undermined confidence in Davis,
attempting to subordinate him to the Senate.

Wigfall's aristocratic militarism, his cavalier disregard for individual rights and suffering, and his shortsighted determination
to destroy Davis as a leader contributed greatly to the demoralization of the people and the armies of the Confederacy, decaying
public spirit so thoroughly that no appeal to states' rights, per-
petuation of slavery, or individual loyalty could sustain the
South's will to fight.[58]

Sam Houston had been right; the United States were strong
enough to survive such leaders as Wigfall. But the Confederate
States were not.

[57] See Chesnut, *Diary*, 207.
[58] *Cf.* Pollard, *Lost Cause*, 727.

Critical Essay on Authorities

PRIMARY SOURCES

Manuscripts

THE PRINCIPAL SOURCE for this study is the collection of Wigfall Family Papers in the Library of Congress, consisting primarily of letters to and from Louis T. Wigfall, his wife, and children during the period 1859–74. The most important source of information about Wigfall's earlier life is the Williams-Chesnut-Manning Collection in the University of South Carolina Archives, Columbia. Other collections dealing specifically with Wigfall are the Staff Officer's File of Brigadier General Louis T. Wigfall in the War Department Collection of Confederate Records and the Compiled Military Service Record of Colonel Louis T. Wigfall, both in the National Archives, Washington, D.C.

The papers of a number of Wigfall's contemporaries which shed varying degrees of light on his career include the William Pitt Ballinger Collection; the Guy M. Bryan Letters; the Sam Houston Papers; the Francis R. Lubbock Papers; the Ben and Henry McCulloch Collection; the William Simpson Oldham Collection; the Oran Milo Roberts Papers; the Thomas J. Rusk Papers; and the Ashbel Smith Papers; as well as Episcopal Diocese of Texas Records; all in the University of Texas Archives, Austin, Texas. Also of use in Austin are the John H. Reagan Papers in the Texas State Archives. The Duke University Archives in Durham, N. C., hold the Armistead Burt Papers and the C. C. Clay Papers, both useful in this study. Two additional Library of Congress collections which are helpful in describing Wigfall's life in the 1830's and early 1840's are the James H.

Hammond Papers and the Francis W. Pickens and M. L. Bonham Papers. The Samuel Wragg Ferguson Memoirs in the Louisiana State University Archives, Baton Rouge, also contain some information about Wigfall in the Confederate period.

Official Records and Documents

A fundamental source for the study of Wigfall's career in the U.S. Senate is the *Congressional Globe* for the Thirty-Sixth Congress, from which one can analyze Wigfall's debating skill and vituperative wit. The U.S. War Department *War of the Rebellion: A Compilation of Official Records of the Union and Confederate Armies* (130 vols.; Washington: U.S. Government Printing Office, 1880–1901) is indispensable for its information about Wigfall's role as a Confederate general as well as his career as a senator quite concerned with military matters. The two most important records of his Senate career in the Confederate Congress are the *Journal of the Confederate Congress*, and "Proceedings of the Confederate Congress," the latter as kept by Richmond newspaper reporters and published later in the Southern Historical Society, *Papers*, XLIV–LII (1923–59).

Newspapers

Many newspapers of Wigfall's time were interested in what he was saying and doing, thus they provide a great deal of important information. The most useful newspapers to this study are the Austin *Statesman* (1871–73); Austin *Texas Democrat* (1846–60); Charleston *Mercury* (1822–68); Charleston *News and Courier* (1844–46, 1859–65); Clarksville, Texas, *Northern Standard* (1846–61); Dallas *Herald* (1846–74); Edgefield, South Carolina, *Advertiser* (1840–46), which is especially important for the short time that Wigfall was secretly its editor; Galveston *News* (1846–74); Galveston *Tri-Weekly News* (1855–60, 1865–73); Marshall, Texas, *Harrison Flag* (1858–61, 1865–68), one of the two of Wigfall's "hometown" newspapers; Houston *Telegraph* (1857–74); Marshall *Texas Republican*, the best newspaper source of Wigfall's activity during the period 1849–69; Montgomery, Alabama, *Advertiser* (1861); New Orleans *Daily Picayune* (1859–74); New Orleans *Times Picayune* (1861–67); New York *Times* (1859–74); Richmond *Daily Dispatch*, and Richmond *Enquirer* (1859–65); Richmond *Sentinel* (1863–66); San Antonio *Express* (1868–74); San Antonio *Herald* (1858–74); Columbia, South Carolina, *Southern Chronicle* (1860–65); Austin *Southern Intelligencer* (1856–67); Austin *Texas State Gazette* (1849–60); and *Texas State Times* (1855–59).

Pamphlets

Of the several pamphlets which contributed to this study, the most significant are the *Catalogue of the Euphradian Society of South Carolina College* (Columbia: R. W. Gibbes, 1859); William J. Hutchins, *To the Senators and Representatives in Congress from the State of Texas* (Houston: News Printing Office, 1864): and a published speech of Wigfall, *On the Pending Political Issues, Delivered at Tyler . . ., Texas, September 3, 1860* (Washington: Lemuel Towers, n.d.). Other Wigfall speeches were published, but they are more conveniently located in the *Congressional Globe*.

Contemporary Accounts

There are numerous published diaries and memoirs which touch on various aspects of Wigfall's life. The two most important, for their direct observations of Wigfall's personal and public activities, are Louise Wigfall Wright (Mrs. D. Giraud Wright, Wigfall's daughter Louly), *A Southern Girl in '61* (New York: Doubleday, Page, 1905), which actually includes the period of 1860–65; and Mary Boykin Chesnut (wife of Senator James Chesnut), *A Diary from Dixie*, edited by Ben Ames Williams (Boston: Houghton Mifflin, 1961), indispensable for its observations and analysis from inside the Washington and Richmond social circles.

The Annals and Parish Register of St. Thomas and St. Denis Parish from 1680 to 1884, edited by Robert F. Clute (Charleston: Walker, Evans and Cogswell, 1884), is important in tracing Wigfall's genealogy and early life.

Some of Wigfall's activities and writings during his antebellum Texas days (1846–59) are dealt with in *Correspondence Addressed to John C. Calhoun, 1837–1849*, edited by Chauncey S. Boucher and Robert P. Brooks in *Annual Report of the American Historical Association, 1929* (Washington: U.S. Government Printing Office, 1930); *Correspondence of John C. Calhoun*, edited by J. Franklin Jameson in *Annual Report of the American Historical Association, 1899* (2 vols.; Washington: U.S. Government Printing Office, 1900) II; *Works of John C. Calhoun . . .* , edited by Richard K. Crallé (6 vols.; New York: D. Appleton, 1854–60); and *Writings of Sam Houston, 1813–1863*, edited by Amelia Williams and Eugene C. Barker (8 vols.; Austin: University of Texas Press, 1938); and A. W. Terrell, "Recollections of General Sam Houston," *Southwestern Historical Quarterly*, XVI (October, 1912), 113–36.

A number of Wigfall's contemporaries have left accounts which shed light on his brief but stormy career in the U.S. Senate during the secession crisis (1859–61). Among the most important of these are James G. Blaine, *Twenty Years of Congress . . .* (2 vols.; Norwich, Connecticut: Henry Bill, 1884); *Works of James Buchanan . . .*, edited by John B. Moore (12 vols.; Philadelphia: Lippincott, 1911); *Diary of a Public Man . . .* (New Brunswick: Rutgers University Press, 1946); Horatio King, *Turning on the Light . . .* (Philadelphia: Lippincott, 1895); Ward Hill Lamon, *Recollections of Abraham Lincoln, 1847–1865*, edited by Dorothy Lamon Teillard (Washington: D. L. Teillard, 1911); Benjamin F. Perry, *Reminiscences of Public Men* (Philadelphia: J. D. Avil, 1883); and Ben Perly Poore, *Reminiscences of Sixty Years in the National Metropolis* (2 vols.; Philadelphia: Hubbard Brothers, 1886).

Important contemporary accounts of developments in the era of the Confederacy which are useful for a study of Wigfall are *Life and Writings of Rufus Burleson . . .* , confused reminiscences edited by Georgia J. Burleson (by author, 1901); Samuel Wylie Chapman, *The Genesis of the Civil War: The Story of Sumter, 1860–1861* (New York: Charles L. Webster, 1887); Virginia Clay-Clopton (Mrs. Clement Clay), *A Belle of the Fifties*, put into narrative form by Ada Sterling (New York: Doubleday, Page, 1904); *The Diary of Floride Clemson . . .*, edited by Charles M. McGee, Jr. and Ernest M. Lander, Jr. (Columbia, South Carolina: Walker, Evans, and Cogwell, 1884); Jefferson Davis, *The Rise and Fall of the Confederate Government* (1881; reprint ed., 2 vols.; New York: Thomas Yoseloff, 1958); Thomas C. DeLeon, *Belles, Beaux, and Brains of the '60's* (New York: G. W. Dillingham, 1909) and *Four Years in Rebel Capitals* (Mobile: Gossip Printing, 1890); Abner Doubleday, *Reminiscences of Forts Sumter and Moultrie in 1860–1861* (New York: Harper and Brothers, 1876); Henry S. Foote, *Casket of Reminiscences* (Washington: Chronicle

Publishing Co., 1874) and *War of the Rebellion* . . . (New York; Harper and Brothers, 1866); Horace Greeley, *American Conflict* . . . (2 vols.; Hartford: O. D. Case, 1864); Constance Cary (Mrs. Burton) Harrison, *Recollections Grave and Gay* (New York: Charles Scribner's, 1911); *Harper's Pictorial History* (2 vols.; Chicago: McDonnell Brothers, 1866); Joseph E. Johnston, *Narrative of Military Operations* . . . (1874; reprint ed., Bloomington: Indiana University Press, 1959); J. B. Jones, *A Rebel War Clerk's Diary at the Confederate States Capital*, edited by Harold Swiggett (2 vols.; New York: Old Hickory Bookshop, 1935); *Inside the Confederate Government: The Diary of Robert Garlick Hill Kean, Head of the Bureau of War*, edited by Edward Younger (New York: Oxford University Press, 1957); Eliza Frances Andrews, *The War-time Journal of a Georgia Girl, 1864–1865*, edited by Spencer Bidwell King, Jr. (Macon: Ardivan Press, 1960); *Wartime Papers of Robert E. Lee*, edited by Clifford Dowdey and Louis Manarin (Boston: Little, Brown, 1961); James Longstreet, *From Manassas to Appomattox: Memoirs* . . . (Philadelphia: Lippincott, 1896); C. W. Raines (ed.), *Six Decades in Texas: Memoirs of Francis Richard Lubbock* (Austin, Texas: Ben C. Jones, 1900); John G. Nicolay, *The Outbreak of Rebellion* (New York: Charles Scribner, 1881); Edward A. Pollard, *The Lost Cause* (New York: E. B. Treat, 1866); Sara Agnes (Mrs. R. A.) Pryor, *Reminiscenses of Peace and War* (New York: Macmillan, 1904); Sallie A. (Brock) Putman, *In Richmond During the Confederacy* . . . (New York: R. M. McBride, 1961); *Private Journal of Henry William Ravenel, 1859–1897*, edited by Arney R. Childs (Columbia: University of South Carolina Press, 1947); John H. Reagan, *Memoirs: With Special References to Secession and Civil War*, edited by Walter Flavius McCaleb (New York: Neale, 1906); Jerome B. Robertson, *Touched With Valor: Civil War Papers and Casualty Reports of Hood's Texas Brigade*, edited by Harold B. Simpson (Hillsboro, Texas: Hillsboro Junior College Press, 1964); Gustavus W. Smith, *Confederate War Papers* . . . (New York: Atlantic, 1884); Richard Taylor, *Destruction and Reconstruction*, edited by Richard B. Harwell (1879; reprint ed., New York: Longmans, Green, 1955); Alexander W. Terrell, *From Texas to Mexico . . . in 1865* (Dallas: Book Club of Texas, 1933); George T. Todd, *Sketch of the History of the First Texas Regiment, Hood's Brigade* . . . (n.p., n.d.); John S. Wise, *End of an Era* (Boston: Houghton Mifflin, 1902).

Several Confederate contemporaries' accounts bearing upon this study have been published as articles. These include Mary S. Estill, editor, "Diary of a Confederate Congressman . . .," *Southwestern Historical Quarterly*, XXVIII (April, 1935), 270–301; XXXIX (July, 1935), 33–65; F. L. Parker, "The Battle of Fort Sumter as Seen from Morris Island by Francis Le Jan Parker," *South Carolina Historical Magazine*, LXII (April, 1961), 70. Clarence Clough Buell and Robert Underwood Johnson have contributed greatly to Civil War studies with their edited work *Battles and Leaders of the Civil War* (4 vols.; New York: Thomas Yoseloff, 1956) which is composed of articles originally written for *Century Magazine* by participants in the war. Nine of these articles, written by Joseph E. Johnston, William T. Sherman, and others, include information important to this study. Extremely valuable for information about the Wigfalls' exile in England is Sarah A. Wallace, editor, "Confederate Exiles in London, 1865–1870: The Wigfalls," *South Carolina Historical and Genealogical Magazine*, LII (April, 1951), 74–87.

Two contemporary British travelers' accounts have been helpful in this study, James A. L. Fremantle, *Diary* . . . , edited by Walter Lord (Boston: Little, Brown, 1954); and William H. Russell, *My Diary North and South: The Civil War in America* (1863; reprint ed., New York: Harper and Brothers, 1954).

SECONDARY SOURCES

Special Studies

There is not space here to mention all the monographs which bear upon facets of Wigfall's life or illuminate the backdrops of it; only a few of those most helpful are included here: Jesse T. Carpenter, *The South as a Conscious Minority* . . . (New York: New York University Press, 1930); W. J. Cash, *Mind of the South* (Garden City: Doubleday, 1956); *Antislavery Vanguard: New Essays on the Abolitionists* (Princeton: Princeton University Press, 1965), edited by Martin Duberman, is a sympathetic reexamination of the abolitionists; John A. Chapman, *History of Edgefield County* (Newberry, South Carolina: Elbert H. Aull, 1897); Clement Eaton, *Freedom of Thought in the Old South* (New York: P. Smith, 1951), and *Mind of the Old South* (Baton Rouge: Louisiana State University Press, 1964); William W. Freehling, *Prelude to Civil War: The Nullification Con-*

troversy in South Carolina, 1816–1836 (New York: Harper and Row, 1966); Eugene D. Genovese, *The Political Economy of Slavery* . . . (New York: Pantheon Books, 1966); Edwin L. Green, *A History of the University of South Carolina* (Columbia, South Carolina: State Co., 1916); Robert Gray Gunderson, *Old Gentlemen's Convention: The Washington Peace Conference of 1861* (Madison: University of Wisconsin Press, 1961); Richard Hofstadter's provocative *Paranoid Style in American Politics* (New York: Alfred A. Knopf, 1965); Daniel Walker Hollis, *South Carolina College* (proposed 2 vols., Columbia: University of South Carolina Press, 1951) I, an excellent study; Allan Nevins, *Emergence of Lincoln* (2 vols.; New York: Charles Scribner, 1950); J. B. O'Neall, *Biographical Sketches of Bench and Bar of South Carolina* (2 vols.; Charleston: S. G. Courtenay, 1859); Rollin Osterweiss, *Romanticism and Nationalism in the Old South* (New Haven: Yale University Press, 1949); Louis Ruchames, editor, *A John Brown Reader: The Story of John Brown, in his Own Words, in the Words of Those who Knew Him, and in the Poetry and Prose of the Literary Heritage* (New York: Abelard-Schuman, 1959), a favorable reinterpretation of Brown; Harold S. Schultz, *Nationalism and Sectionalism in South Carolina, 1852–1860* (Durham: Duke University Press, 1950); John Timotheé Trezevant, *The Trezevant Family in the United States* . . . (Columbia, South Carolina: State, 1914), quite useful for information about Wigfall's family, 1685–1914; T. Harry Williams, *Military Leadership of the North and South* (Colorado Springs: United States Air Force Academy Press, 1960), an important analysis; Ralph A. Wooster, *The Secession Conventions of the South* (Princeton: Princeton University Press, 1962); Dudley G. Wooten, editor, *Comprehensive History of Texas* . . . (2 vols.; Dallas: William G. Scarff, 1898); and Wilfred Buck Yearns, *Confederate Congress* (Athens: University of Georgia Press, 1960).

Articles and Unpublished Sources

Many articles have information relevant to this study, the following are only those which bore most directly upon it: Alvy L. King, "Emergence of a Fire-eater: Louis T. Wigfall," *Louisiana Studies*, VII (Spring, 1968), 73–82; Clyde W. Lord, "Young Louis Wigfall: South Carolina Politician and Duelist," *South Carolina Historical Magazine*, LIX (April, 1958), 96–112; two helpful articles by Anna Irene

Sandbo are in the *Southwestern Historical Quarterly,* "Beginnings
of the Secession Movement in Texas," XVIII (July, 1914), 41–73, and
"First Session of the Secession Convention of Texas," XVIII (Oc-
tober, 1914), 162–94; Nathaniel W. Stephenson, "The Question of
Arming the Slaves," *American Historical Review*, XVIII (January,
1913), 295–308; and Jack Kenny Williams, "Code of Honor in Ante-
Bellum South Carolina," *South Carolina Historical Magazine*, LIV
(July, 1953), 122–23.

Several unpublished studies of Wigfall exist, but only two were
found to contain any information worth noting. They are: Clyde W.
Lord, "Louis T. Wigfall" (M. A. Thesis, University of Texas, 1925),
which makes much use of the Marshall *Texas Republican* and does
not go beyond Wigfall's election to the U.S. Senate; and Alvy L. King,
"Relationship Between Joseph E. Johnston and Jefferson Davis . . ."
(M. A. Thesis, West Texas State University, 1960), dealing with a
controversy in which Wigfall was much involved.

Index

Abney, J., 45
Adams, John Quincy, 19
Addison, Allen B., 11
Alabama: secession of, 108
Alabama Claims, 229
"Alabama Platform," 93, 94
"American Democracy," 65. *See also* Democratic Party
American Party, 59. *See also* Know-Nothings
American Revolution: compared to Civil War, 232, 233
Anderson, Robert, 119, 120, 121
Association for Relief of Maimed Soldiers, 155, 155n

Bacon, Sam, 21
Ballinger, William Pitt: on Wigfall, 50, 143; on reaction to Wigfall speech, 199
Baltimore Convention, 94, 97
Barnwell, Robert Woodward, 13
Beauregard, P. G. T.: CSA commander at Charleston, 118; on strategy, 175; misused by Davis, 184; on Wigfall-Davis quarrel, 193–94; visited by Wigfall in England, 223
"Beecher's Bibles," 97
Bell, John, 94
Benjamin, Judah P.: and Wigfall attack on Douglas, 95; on Davis' military ambitions, 170; opposed by Wigfall and others, 208–209; and postwar CSA funds, 224

Bingham, Kingsley S., 96
Bird, Thomas: killed by Wigfall, 32, 33; ghost of, 34; mentioned, 36
Blaine, James G., 113
Bluffton Movement, 43
Bonham, Milledge, 7
Bragg, Braxton: criticized by congressmen, 154; defended by Wigfall, 154; in Tennessee, 163; on Vicksburg, 163; criticized by Wigfall, 165, 191; replaced by Johnston, 166, 188
Breckinridge, John C.: on Homestead Bill, 88; nominated for presidency, 97
Brewster, H.P., 130
Brooks, Preston: controversy with Wigfall, 25–35 *passim*; allegations against Wigfall, 29; duel with Wigfall, 33; canes Charles Sumner, 34
Brooks, Whitfield: controversy with Wigfall, 25–35 *passim*; allegations against Wigfall, 29; called coward by Wigfall, 32
Brown, Albert G., 82, 84–85
Brown, Joseph E., 197, 206
Brown, John: and Wigfall, 4, 70–78 *passim*; and Reagan, 70–72; mentioned by Wigfall, 99. *See also* Harper's Ferry
Bryan, Guy M., 139
Buchanan, James: supported by Wigfall, 61; and Homestead Bill, 91; denies right of secession, 101; and Wigfall's rumored plan to kidnap, 106

of, 15, 21–22; in Seminole War, 16; reputation as a duelist, 18; intellect of, 19; as orator, 19; as fire-eater, 20; on law profession, 20–24 *passim*; problems as young man, 20–25 *passim*; as hedonist, 21; on sense of honor, 21; reputation as marksman, 21; efforts to reform, 21–24 *passim*; on wine and women, 21–24 *passim*; and Manning, 22; fatuousness of, 22; quest for respectability, 23; on reputation, 23; on moral character, 23; as militia colonel, 23; public speeches, 23; on money, 24; on love, 24; "distaste" for politics, 25; as editor of *Advertiser*, 27; on morality in politics, 28; lack of caution and tact, 28; faith in *Code Duello*, 30, 32, 35; challenges Whitfield Brooks to duel, 32; duel with J. P. Carroll 32–33; kills Thomas Bird, 33; duel with Preston Brooks, 33; wounded, 33; ruin of reputation and finances, 34; appointed to Governor Richardson's staff, 34; reputation for violence, 35; marriage, 36; debts, 36, 38–39, 66–67, 107, 168, 174; supports Polk and opposes Clay in 1844, p. 39; interest in politics, 39; opposes Protective Tariff, 39–40, 64; creed of, 39–40; on R. B. Rhett, 40; loses faith in Polk, 40; as early secessionist 40–41, 42–44; on northerners, 42, 52, 89, 101, 239; on slavery, 42, 42n, 52; prefers secession over nullification, 43; on Union, 43; fears war with Great Britain, 44; on Oregon, 44–45; defends Calhoun, 45, 46; spirit and temper of, 45; love of for South Carolina, 46; seeks Calhoun's council, 46; —In Texas: arrival of, 46–47; death of son, 47; alerts Texans to "dangers," 48, 59; law partners of, 47, 49; moves to Marshall, Texas, 49; law practice in Texas, 49–50; helps organize Texas Democracy, 50–51, 52, 57; on Wilmot Proviso, 51–52; on Constitution, 51–52, 53; on slavery in territories, 52; on California and New Mexico, 53–54; clashes with Houston, 54–56, 57, 58–59, 60, 63; fails to attend Nashville Convention, 55; on squatter sovereignty, 56; on Compromise of 1850,

pp. 56–57; leads fight against Texas Know-Nothings, 59–61; role in 1856 campaign, 60–61; role in 1857 Texas election, 61–64; at 1858 Texas Democratic convention, 64; on majority rule and democracy, 64–65; on Kansas controversy, 64–66 *passim*, 68, 96–97; on abolitionists, 65; leadership in state politics, 66–67; on revival of foreign slave trade, 67–69, 69–70; candidate for U.S. Senate, 67–76, 77; on Missouri Compromise and Kansas; 68; in 1859 gubernatorial campaign, 69–70; proposes State University for Texas, 70; elected Senator, 70–78; and John Brown, 70–78 *passim*; criticizes Texas legislators, 75; on Republicans, 77, 86, 89, 95, 100–101; supports Buchanan, 77; on states' rights, 78, 137–38, 144, 146, 147–50, 152–53; —In Washington: as fire-eater, 79; freshman senator from Texas, 79–80; Congressional committees, 80; on Mexican War, 80; on Compromise of 1850, pp. 80, 83–85; on Massachusetts congressmen, 80–81; and Henry Wilson, 80, 82; on separation of powers, 81–82, 99; on Daniel Webster, 81, 82, 111; in 1860 campaign, 82, 94–100 *passim*, opposes Brown Resolutions, 82, 84–85; supports Davis Resolutions, 83; and David Collamer, 83; on Union, 83–85, 89, 97; on federal aid for Texas frontiers, 85–87; and transcontinental railroad, 87, 89–90; opposed to homestead bill, 87–91; on African slave trade, 88; war coming, 89; on King Cotton, 89; on "capitalists," 90–91; and C. C. Clay, 91; on territories, 91; quotes poem about Arnold Winklereid, 91; and 1860 Democratic Convention, 93–94; and split with Northern Democrats, 94–95, 96; on slavery, 95, 116; on popular sovereignty, 96; on Constitutional Unionists, 98; on terrorism of "Mystic Red," 99; on John Brown, 99; criticizes Buchanan, 101, 107; debates John P. Hales, 102; on threat of war, 102–103, 109, 112, 115, 118; on conditions for compromise and re-union, 102–10 *passim*, 115–17; on Crittenden